PRESS, POLITICS AND SOCIETY

PRESS, POLITICS AND SOCIETY

David Winterson

CENTRUM PRESS
NEW DELHI-110002 (INDIA)

CENTRUM PRESS
H.O.: 4360/4, Ansari Road, Daryaganj,
New Delhi-110002 (India)
Tel: 23278000, 23261597, 23255577, 23286875
B.O.: No. 1015, Ist Main Road, BSK IIIrd Stage,
IIIrd Phase, IIIrd Block, Bangalore-560085 (INDIA)
Tel: 080-41723429
Email: centrumpress@gmail.com
Visit us at: www.centrumpress.com

Press, Politics and Society

First Edition, 2010

ISBN 978-93-80836-32-4

PRINTED IN INDIA

Printed at Mehra Offset Press, Delhi

Contents

Preface

Communication as a means of transmission of information and as a process of development underwent a sea-change with the invention of the printing press. It was, however, expedited, strengthened and stabilized with the publication of newspapers. Over the years the press has played a dominant role in the dissemination of news and information. A magnificent gift to the mankind and highly indispensable, it does a splendid job, performs a crucial role as a communicator. Because of its importance and significance, it has been highly acclaimed, admired and appreciated. And it won't be unpalatable to say that what air is to the living beings, the press is to the society.

Politics is a process by which groups of people make collective decisions. The term is generally applied to behavior within civil governments, but politics has been observed in other group interactions, including corporate, academic, and religious institutions. It consists of "social relations involving authority or power" and refers to the regulation of a political unit, and to the methods and tactics used to formulate and apply policy.

Chapter 1

Freedom of Wise Society

This chapter in vokes something that is not generally appealed to in contemporary philosophy: the idea of a wise society. One of its aims is to stimulate exploration of this idea, which is pertinent to several branches of the subject. These include both political philosophy and epistemology, in particular social epistemology. The idea of wisdom, in general, is a longstanding part of the philosophical repertoire. The very word "philosophy," as is well known, comes from the Greek for "love of wisdom."

That is not to say that there is general agreement on what wisdom is. Nor is it to say that latter day philosophical discourse is peppered with references to "wisdom," Paradoxically perhaps, it isn't. It is even less common to find references in this discourse to the wisdom of a society as opposed to that of an individual person. The same is true of the frequent contemporary philosophical references to knowledge, belief, and other close cousins of wisdom. There are incomparably more discussions of the knowledge and beliefs of individuals than of the knowledge and beliefs of societies.

Outside the circle of professional philosophers-and, indeed, within it-discussion of the latter topic may recently have been stimulated by a popular work in which James Surowiecki argues that the wisdom of a crowd-"loosely defined"-may be superior to that of an expert on a given subject. As will emerge, a society, as I understand it, is a subtype of "crowd" in Surowiecki's sense. I take it that if a society can be wise, it will be better for being so, all else being equal. It is therefore important to consider both whether a society can be wise, and, if so, what that wisdom entails. For instance, given what it is, does a society's wisdom militate against its having some other valuable feature or features?

This paper addresses one aspect of the question just mooted: can a wise society be a free one? One's first response to this question is likely to be "Of course!" or at least "Why on earth not?" My main aim in this paper is to show how one can argue for a negative answer.

More precisely, it is to show how one can argue that, in plausible senses of the pertinent terms, the wiser a society is, the less free it is.

For the sake of a label, I call the argument I present the negative argument. It is essentially conceptual. It raises various evaluative questions but does not itself proceed at the level of evaluation. Given its focus, the paper might be categorized as an essay in political philosophy. Given that a good deal of time is spent elaborating an account of a wise society, however, it might also be categorized as an essay in social epistemology.

Before setting out the negative argument I must explain how I am interpreting its key terms. They are all open to, and have received, a variety of interpretations. Thus some degree of clarification is necessary. It is possible that the negative argument works for interpretations other than those I offer here. It is also possible that it fails to work for one or more plausible construals. For present purposes I set these possibilities aside.

I take a society to be a kind of social group, where paradigmatic social groups include informal discussion groups, army units, sports teams, and labour unions. To give a rough and partial characterization of such a group one might say, echoing Rousseau, that its members are unified in such a way that they constitute more than a mere aggregate of persons.

Typically a society, in particular, includes many smaller social groups. Thus within a given society there may be many families, labour unions, sports teams, and so on. A society is therefore relatively large, in contrast with a family, say, or a sports team. For now, this brief characterization of societies will suffice.

PERSONAL FREEDOM AND A FREE SOCIETY

The freedom of a society, as I shall construe that, is closely tied to the personal freedom of the individual members of that society, understood in a certain way. A concern for personal freedom in some sense of the phrase is central to a number of evaluative stances in political philosophy.

Thus, on one account of it, anarchism involves "a concern for preserving individual freedom and a distaste for the coercive measures of governments...." A government coerces by "threatening to use force or impose punishments if a person does not follow its laws". Now, in what I take to be the central sense of the term, punishment requires a special standing or authority. As I understand it, to have the authority to punish is not necessarily to be justified in doing so, but it does away with a possible objection to its use by a given agent. It cannot be objected "It is not for you to do that."

Indeed, anarchism is often characterized in terms of distaste, not so much for the coercive measures governments take but rather for government itself. Here government is construed as a matter of the authority to command, to demand or insist on compliance when noncompliance is threatened, and, where appropriate, to punish. The problem of government is posed in terms of the loss of personal autonomy inherent in the authority of one person over another, whether they command, demand conformity, or punish. That is the tenor of the well-known brand of philosophical anarchism that was advocated by Robert Paul Wolff, for instance.

The anarchist's concern is often couched in terms of the authority of one person, or of a body of persons smaller than the society that is in question. I take it, meanwhile, that there can be whole societies-even societies reasonably thought of as political societies or polities-without such a ruling person or body. Even in such "acephalous" societies, there are issues of personal autonomy. Such societies are likely to have a variety of rules. Each member will then have the authority to insist on any other's conformity to a given rule and to rebuke any other for not conforming to it.

Evidently, I take it that one cannot rebuke someone without a special standing or authority. One can, of course, speak in a rebuking manner without such authority, just as one can speak in a demanding manner, without the authority actually to demand.

Rebukes and demands may be unaccompanied by physical force or by threats that such force will be applied unless what is demanded is done. There is, nonetheless, something forceful about any rebuke, just as there is something forceful about demanding. Indeed, in The Concept of Law, Hart suggests that rebukes lie at the informal end of a spectrum at the formal end of which lie punishments imposed through due process of law.

Penal sanctions may sound-and may be-worse than informal demands and rebukes, but most people do not relish such forceful interventions from others. Most would prefer not to incur the reproofs of strangers, the rebukes of colleagues, or the reprimands of friends and intimates. Mill, the great philosophical champion of liberty, saw this clearly. And verbal chastisement can be the precursor of physical violence.

Suppose, now, that there is a rule in my society that women are not to contradict men. I know that if I, a woman, contradict a man on some point, the other members of my society have the authority to rebuke me for doing so. Accordingly, I may regularly decide not to make some point though I desire to do so. In other terms, my freedom is limited in an important way: there is something I want to do, but I risk an authoritative forceful negative response should I do it. The account of a society's freedom that I shall make use of in developing the negative argument reflects the idea that the standing threat of such a response is an important limitation on personal freedom. In speaking of a "threat" here I do not mean to imply that the response is imminent, or even probable, but rather that it is "in the cards." If someone has the standing to rebuke me for doing something, I know that, should he speak to me in a rebuking manner, I cannot dodge the issue by saying "It's none of your business." If he has the standing to rebuke me, it is his business.

I shall say that a given member, M1, of a society S, is personally free to perform a given action, A, in face of another member, M2, if and only if M1 is under no threat of an authoritative forceful negative reaction from M2 should M1 perform A or, indeed, should M1 propose to perform A. For the sake of brevity, I shall generally refer in what follows to being under no threat of a rebuke. It should be understood that all forms of authoritative forceful negative reaction are included under this heading.

Now, a given member, M1, of a society S, may be under a threat of rebuke from another member, M2, where these rebukes are not grounded in his membership in S as such. For instance, M1 promised M2, and no one else, that he would not do A. I am not concerned with such grounds here. The definition of personal freedom just given should be interpreted accordingly. What is at issue is rebukes whose ground is some aspect of the membership of M1 and M2 in society S.

I take it that a society itself can be "personally free" in the defined sense, insofar as it can be a member of a society of societies. Meanwhile, the type of societal freedom with which this essay is concerned relates to the personal freedom of a society's members as just defined. This might be referred to as the society's internal freedom. My focal case continues to be a society whose members are individual human beings as opposed to other societies.

I shall assume that, as a matter of definition, a society becomes less free as particular personal freedoms are subtracted from those its various members already have. This is clearly only a partial account of societal freedom. It concerns only a single condition under which a society can be said to become less free than it was. Nonetheless it is of interest to ask whether a society's relative freedom in the respect at issue is altered by one or another factor.

I shall not attempt to offer a full account of a free society. Given the notion of personal freedom with which I am operating, however, a plausible account will not allow that a society is free when its members have little personal freedom. Nor will it demand that a free society be maximally free, where a maximally free society is one in which, for any action whatever, each member of the society is personally free to perform that action in face of any other member. It may reasonably be questioned whether a maximally free society, as just defined, is possible. As will emerge, it can be argued that it is not, given what a society is.

A WISE SOCIETY

Some may be inclined to deny that there is such a thing as a society that is wise to any degree. They may point to the fact that wisdom involves or is closely connected to knowledge or, at least, good judgment and argue that a society is not the kind of thing that can be wise. Individual human beings can be wise but societies are not sufficiently like them for a wise society to be possible.

When it is presented, this argument may look plausible. Yet people regularly talk about a society's beliefs, judgments, decisions, and knowledge. Thus a particular society may be said to have made a wise (or unwise) decision, wrongly to consider itself superior to other societies, and so on.

When people talk about the belief of a society or other social group, they think of themselves as speaking literally rather than metaphorically. Rather than assuming that they are misguided, one might do well to consider what phenomenon on the ground, so to speak, they have in mind.

Perhaps because they think along the skeptical lines mentioned above, contemporary political philosophers have not paid attention to the idea of a wise society. Following John Rawls, they have considered the key quality of a good society to be its justice and focused on that.

In the Republic, Plato also focused on a society's justice. This did not lead him to neglect the idea of a wise society. Indeed, he thought of a society's wisdom as necessary to its justice. Notoriously, he did not think this way about its freedom. Plato does talk about freedom. His picture of what he called "democracy" in Book of the Republic is perhaps the closest to true anarchy-and maximal personal freedom-that one can imagine. It is not clear, indeed, how consistent a picture this is. There is some talk of "laws" and "courts" of law, yet-he says-one can do anything one pleases. Those condemned to death or exile walk about as if they are heroes and nobody cares.

This is not Plato's favored scenario. In the type of political society he favors, the laws are taken seriously. Most important for present purposes, the rulers are few in number and carefully selected and trained. Those with the right natural aptitudes go through the rigorous training necessary for one who loves wisdom-a philosopher-to reach his goal, knowledge of the Good.

Before the details of this training have been developed Plato considers what it is for a political society to be wise. What he says is open to different interpretations, and I shall not attempt carefully to probe it here. At a minimum, it seems fair to characterize his opinion as follows. The judgments of the rulers, in making rules and decisions for the society, must, in a phrase, track the Good.

I shall work with an account of a wise society that has something of the same spirit. I shall not require that such a society is ruled by a particular person or body of persons, however-let alone a body of persons trained from birth for the purpose. Thus I shall allow that in principle an acephalous society can be wise. I shall not attempt carefully to explore either the idea of wisdom in general or the idea of a wise society in particular. The account of the latter that I shall work with has something to be said for it, but it may well be that an alternative account is more plausible. I hope that my discussion will help to stimulate consideration of precisely this issue. In the meantime, it is important to see that on the account of a wise society proposed, the negative argument is sound. A wise society, on this account, is a society possessed of features that, whatever their relation to wisdom in particular, would appear to be desirable, all else being equal.

The working account I shall adopt appeals, simply, to a

society's true value judgments, in particular those relating to the goodness and badness of human and societal features and actions. Such judgments may be very general-as in the judgment that wantonly destroying a human life is a very bad thing-or quite specific-as in the judgment that Hitler was an evil man. They may not lead to specific decisions or actions or they may. If one judges that wantonly destroying another's life is a very bad thing to do, for instance, one is likely to avoid such destruction.

A true value judgment evidently tracks the Good at least to some extent. It may be plausible to argue that if a value judgment fully tracks the Good it must not only be true but it must also have been made on good grounds. It is not, then, "fortuitously" true. That said, I focus here on the simpler condition. I shall assume that, by definition, the true value judgments of one who is wise will be relatively numerous.

This, along with the following points, is intended to apply both to individual human beings and to human societies. I shall assume one who is wise, as a matter of definition, does not make false judgments. If the truth on some matter of value is hard to discern, one who is wise will if necessary act on working assumptions understood to be such. These are relatively stringent conditions. They are not, however, as stringent as they might be. At the upper limit of wisdom, one would get everything right. I shall take the stated conditions to be both necessary and sufficient for one to be wise. I shall make the following comparative judgment about one who is wise on the above account. Any new true value judgment one makes in addition to those one has already made amounts, by definition, to an increase in one's wisdom. This is only intended to be a partial account of what makes for an increase in wisdom, but it suffices for presentation of the negative argument. It is now time to turn to the core of the negative argument. This is the pertinent account of what it is for a society to endorse a particular value judgment.

A SOCIETY'S VALUE JUDGMENTS

I have elsewhere developed an account of what it is for a

group to believe that such-and-such. I have also proposed a related account of what it is for a group to make a particular value judgment. Here I shall do little more than sketch the account, saying only what I take to be needed to make the negative argument. I proceed in terms of an illustrative value judgment, which may or may not be true: marriage is a valuable social institution. I shall refer to this judgment as V. Obviously any other particular judgment might stand in its stead.

According to my account of such matters, in terms that will be explained, a society judges that V if and only if its members are jointly committed to judge as a body that V. I have argued at length elsewhere that the concept of a joint commitment is a fundamental part of human life, embedded in many of those central concepts with which human beings approach their interactions with one another. I must now say something about what a joint commitment amounts to.

A joint commitment, as I understand it, is a commitment of two or more parties. It is not a combination of commitments, one of one party, one of another, and so on. Given their joint commitment, each party has sufficient reason to act accordingly, just as one has sufficient reason to act according to a personal decision one has made. As I understand the phrase, if one has sufficient reason to do something, then one is rationally required to do it, all else being equal.

Any joint commitment is a joint commitment to "do" something as a body, in a broad sense of "do" that includes judging that V. To say that certain people are jointly committed to judge that V as a body means something like this. They are jointly committed as far as is possible together to constitute a single body-or person-that judges that V. I say more about this shortly.

How do people become jointly committed? Failing special background understandings-in the basic case-a given joint commitment can only be created by all of the parties together. The same is true of its rescission. Here is a rough account of the conditions under which such a commitment is created in the basic case.

Each of the would-be parties must express his readiness to be jointly committed with the others in a particular way, and the fact that these expressions have taken place must be open to all or, in something like David Lewis's sense, common knowledge. Though I shall not attempt to elaborate on this point here, this account does not rule out joint commitments on a large scale. I take it that people can enter joint commitments in situations of strong pressure. Just as you can make a decision under pressure to do so, you can enter a joint commitment in such circumstances. To say that is not, of course, to contest the desirability of one's making decisions and entering joint commitments in the absence of such pressures.

Special background understandings allow for nonbasic cases. Thus all of the members of a given population, large or small, may create an open-ended joint commitment such that one person or a smaller population of persons is in a position to create new joint commitments for the population as a whole. For example, the members of a labour union may jointly commit to conform as a body to any fiats issued by Jones under certain conditions. In that case when Jones issues a fiat under the relevant conditions, the union members are jointly committed to conform, as one, to that fiat. To keep things simple here, I am going to focus on societies where no such special background understandings prevail.

For the purposes of the negative argument the most important feature of a joint commitment is this. If I am jointly committed in some way with another person, I am answerable to him with respect to my proposed or actual nonconformity to the commitment. Not only do I owe him an explanation of any proposed or actual nonconformity, I also owe him actions that conform to the commitment. I owe these to him insofar as he participates in the joint commitment.

I have said that the negative argument is essentially conceptual rather than evaluative. The point just made may seem to refute that. However, it relates to what a joint commitment is, as opposed to its value or the value of any related actions.

One way of amplifying the point is as follows. There is a sense in which, by committing each party to act in certain ways, a joint commitment in and of itself creates in each party ownership of the actions in question. Being in the future, the actions are owned but not currently possessed: in that sense they are owed.

Evidently this puts each of the other parties in a special position in relation to me. If I propose not to perform an action the commitment requires, he has the standing or authority required in order that he demand it.

He can say, in effect, "Give me that! It's mine-qua party to the joint commitment!" He also has the standing to rebuke me. After the fact, he can say, in effect, "How could you not have given me that! It was mine!" Thus those who either propose to violate a standing joint commitment or who do violate one lay themselves open to the authoritative forceful negative reactions of the other parties.

So much, then, for the nature and implications of joint commitment. I turn now to the relationship of joint commitments to social groups. I have argued elsewhere that those who are jointly committed in some way constitute a social group in a central sense of the phrase. This accords with the rough characterization of a social group offered earlier in this chapter: its members are unified in such a way that they constitute more than a mere aggregate of persons.

Given this amplification, if certain persons are jointly committed to judge that V as a body then they constitute a social group. Indeed, they constitute a social group that judges that V. As I have argued elsewhere, to say that under these conditions people constitute a social group that judges that V answers to a standard everyday concept of a social group that judges that V.

In sum, the present account of a society's value judgment is not merely stipulative. It accords with entrenched, everyday understandings of the component ideas. On the account proposed, then, a society judges that V if and only if the members are jointly committed to judge that V as a body. That is, they are jointly committed as far as possible to constitute a single body that judges that V. How might this commitment be fulfilled?

When people are acting in conformity with the commitment, they might confidently state that V when talking to one another. They would refrain from calling V or obvious corollaries into question without preamble. In short, they would suggest by their actions and emotional expressions that V. They would refrain, therefore, from acting contrary to V and from reporting contrary actions with bravado.

Thus one would not say out loud, with an air of bravado "I've managed to avoid getting married again!" or, critically, "Marriage? That's for the birds!" I do not say that in order to act in conformity with the commitment people must personally judge that V. There are several reasons for this, but for now I simply state my understanding that a joint commitment to judge that V as a body does not require the parties personally to judge V. Should one judge that not-V, however, he is committed not to say this without preamble. Rather, he must say, for instance, "Personally, I don't think marriage is such a wonderful thing." This indicates that he is speaking not from the perspective of the group as a whole but from his personal perspective.

So much for the definitions and assumptions in terms of which I shall present the negative argument. They all have some plausibility, and it is worth considering what follows from them for the question: can a wise society be a free one? I am supposing that, by definition, a wise society endorses a fair number of true value judgments and eschews false ones, and that a new true value judgment added to its current stock of such judgments increases its wisdom. The negative argument can be put as follows.

Suppose that society S is wise. Suppose now that it adds a new true value judgment J to its current stock of true value judgments. By definition, it becomes wiser. Given the nature of societal value judgments in general, J provides the members of S, as such, with a ground for rebuking one another for a new range of possible actions, R. R includes speech acts as well as actions that do not involve speech. Thus S becomes less free.

A query may arise as to this conclusion. What if there was already a joint commitment in S-one distinct from that underlying S's new value judgment J-such that members of S have a ground for rebuking one another for the very same range of actions R covered in the case of J? Assuming for the sake of argument that this is possible, it is still fair to say that S becomes less free on making J, for now there is a new ground for rebukes in relation to R.

People can certainly have the standing to rebuke one another for performing a given action on more than one ground. Perhaps, for instance, several of us agreed not to do something, and I made a special promise to you that I would not do it. Then you can upbraid me both on the ground that we agreed not to do it and on the ground that you promised me not to do it. It seems fair to say, generally, that the more grounds for rebuke there are for one's performing a given action, the less free one is.

Now it is true, of course, that if S were to add a false value judgment to its current stock of value judgments, it would also become less free. The striking thing about the negative argument, however, is this: something that on the face of it is a bonus-S's increasing wisdom-turns out to have a specifiable cost-a corresponding loss in S's freedom. That assumes, of course, that a lessening of societal freedom, in and of itself, is a bad thing, while an increase in societal wisdom is a good thing. As said, at least on the face of it, this is so.

I should emphasize that the negative argument does not render problematic the idea that, all else being equal, it is better for a society to replace a false value judgment with a true one, if these are the alternatives. It implies, however, that it would make for more freedom in a society with a false value judgment if that judgment were simply abandoned-if the society were left with no view on the matter-rather than replaced by the corresponding true judgment. True judgments, just like false ones, reduce the freedom of society.

The negative argument raises or highlights several important questions. Before concluding I note and discuss a number of these without attempting fully to answer any.

It may be proposed that the loss of personal freedom entailed by a wise society's increasing wisdom will make no practical difference if each member was happy to enter the relevant joint commitment. It may be added that it will matter even less if at the time they happily entered the joint commitment they personally endorsed the society's value judgment.

This seems not to be so. Suppose Qiong was happy to enter the joint commitment at issue in my focal example, personally believing that marriage was an excellent social institution. Suppose that through personal or vicarious experience she later changes her mind. Her change of mind is one thing; her society's change of mind is another. The joint commitment may still stand. She is then still subject to it.

At this point Qiong may well find none of her choices attractive. She can baldly make concordant statements she believes to be false and act in ways she takes to express a false value. She can cause herself to stand out from the crowd by saying, as the joint commitment permits," Personally, I think marriage as an institution is problematic." She can publicly violate the commitment and lay herself open to authoritative forceful responses. One may well shrink from any of these options, and from others that might be available-such as giving up one's membership in the society in question.

Knowing all this, one who is simply contemplating a personal change of mind may turn away from that option. Or the very movement toward such contemplation may itself be suppressed.

Note that Qiong's option of prefacing her antimarriage statement with" Personally" may do more than make her stand out from the crowd. (Some people might find that outcome relatively attractive.) Another possible outcome is likely to be less attractive. Though the joint commitment does not require her personally to endorse the value judgment in question, when she says or implies that she personally doesn't endorse it, she puts herself in a problematic position. People have reason to wonder if she can be relied upon to fulfill the commitment in the future. Might her contrary opinion not soon break out untrammeled? Might she be a spoiler? She may find herself shunned, though she did not violate the commitment.

In sum, even if each one of a number of people is happy to enter a given joint commitment, and each one's personal judgment at that point accords with the societal value judgment thus created, its providing a basis for rebuke makes a practical difference. It allows, in general terms, for a tension to arise between a given member's joint commitment, on the one hand, and his personal judgment on the other.

Some are inclined to think that if any human being violates a moral rule, any other human being has the standing to rebuke him for this. Moral rules, in turn, may be conceived of as existing independently of all actual societies, and as corresponding to the subset of true value judgments at issue in the present discussion.

It may then be argued that the standing to rebuke another member of one's society that one gains from a new, true value judgment of that society does not make much practical difference to anyone's situation.

Irrespective of our status as members of one or another society, we are all always open to rebukes from others for the violation of any moral rule. The fact that with an increase in a society's wisdom some people have a new ground for some such rebukes is of interest, to be sure.

However, it would not seem to make much difference from a practical point of view. I have argued elsewhere against the idea that human beings as such have the standing to rebuke one another for violations of moral rules. If they do not then the argument in the previous paragraph must be rejected: its central premise is false.

At the least, the truth of its central premise is not immediately obvious. Given that this is so, people who attempt to rebuke others" because what you are doing is morally wrong" may be given short shrift by those to whom they speak. These latter may simply, and sincerely, respond that" It's none of your business."

Thus even if rebukes were automatically in order by reason of the existence of moral rules as such, the practical impact of an increase in societal wisdom could be considerable." This runs counter to our values" may well be received as a more pertinent explanation of rebuke than" What you are doing is morally wrong."

Rather than attempting to curtail a society's wisdom-perhaps by making sure it does not address particular issues-is there a way of keeping its wisdom intact, and, indeed, increasing it, while reducing its impact on the society's members? The full spectrum of true value judgments may, indeed, include some that will lead a society that makes them to minimize the impact of its own value judgments.

I have in mind here value judgments associated with when and how to tell people off for violating a given joint commitment. It may be that it is best to start in a kind and nonforceful manner.

A maximally wise society, at least, will take this value judgment on board. It will then be incumbent upon its members to act appropriately if someone baldly says something contrary to a value judgment of the society. For instance, he might mildly observe "That's not a very democratic sentiment!" or "I'm surprised to hear someone from these parts saying that!" or "I take it that you are simply expressing your personal opinion?" If the person addressed answers the last question affirmatively, the joint commitments to which he and his interlocutor are parties will offer little basis for rebuke.

A society's embracing the value judgments currently under consideration-those advocating an initially kindly approachwill most likely reduce the frequency of rebukes. If a rebuke is considered acceptable in face of a recalcitrant interlocutor, however-one who will not say the expressed opinion is his personal one, or take it back in the light of gentle suggestion-they may well sometimes occur.

Moreover, as all will understand, the members of the society will at all times have the standing to rebuke provided by the joint commitment that underlies any of that society's value judgments. Thus should one forego an initially kindly approach and immediately offer a rebuke, the person rebuked will not be able to respond, "It's none of your business." The parties, then, are still threatened with rebuke, in the sense in question here. What if forceful responses, though authoritative, never occurred? What might the effects of this be? How necessary to the very existence of a society's wisdom is the imposition, at least after gentler responses, of rebuke?

This question recalls Patrick Devlin's argument for the very strong thesis that a society risks disintegration if at least its core value judgments are not supported with the weight of the criminal law.

His idea was, roughly, that the very existence of the society depends on the persistence of those core judgments as its judgments.

If action contrary to those judgments was permitted by law, this would be liable to increase such action and would lead, eventually, to the demise of the society's value judgment as such.

The general question is: what is necessary to ensure that a given true societal value judgment will persist? I shall not attempt to answer this question here.

That it can be raised suggests, at least, that there may be a cost to mitigating the effects of a society's wisdom to the point that even informal rebukes are disallowed. The cost in question is the loss of the society's wisdom.

EVALUATIVE QUESTIONS

Many evaluative questions arise. How good a thing is it that a society makes true value judgments as these have been understood here? Is it better, all things considered, that a society minimize its evaluative judgments or sticks only to certain areas of value judgment? Is a society that is good overall one that looks the other way as far as values, or some kinds of value, are concerned-irrespective of its capacity to get things right? If so, why is that? Personal freedom is likely to be invoked at this point. Invocation alone, however, is not enough.

Given that a diminution in personal freedom is always a loss, how is it to be weighed against an increase in the wisdom of a given society? All else being equal, is it indeed better for a society to make a true value judgment rather than no judgment on the topic or a false one? These questions are important and timely. They press us to think further about the wisdom of a society, its implications and its value.

Chapter 2

The Indian Movement and Political Democracy

This work investigates the implications of the Ecuadorian Indian movement for democratic politics. While its empirical questions focus on Ecuador's political processes, a key purpose is to offer a Latin American perspective on the broader debate on the "civil society argument"; namely, the proposition that civil association has intrinsically positive effects on democracy.

The assumption herein is that particularization is essential for appraising this wide-ranging claim. Civil society and democracy are knotty concepts because they refer to complex realities that can be approached from different points of view. To cut through the complexity, this study follows a strategy of double specification, concentrating on social movements as a distinct type of civil association and demarcating discrete functional terrains to observe their bearing on democracy. Applied to the case at hand, this strategy provides a basis for a contextualized assessment of the putative democratic benefits of civil association and offers insights on the conditions of political engagement that social movements share with other kinds of civil society groups.

The pivotal claim of this study is that civil society actors may or may not contribute to democracy and that, in the particular case of social movements, the underlying tension between the participatory and insti- tutional dimensions of democracy may be expressed through a mixed bag of favorable and unfavorable effects on the different components of political democracy. The analysis of the Ecuadorian Indian movement demonstrates that to understand the varying impact of civil activism on democracy, scholars must adopt a nuanced, context-specific approach that does not lose sight of the particularistic orientations of civil associations and that pays close attention to their definition of means and ends, the institutional responses evoked by their initiatives, and the unintended consequences of their actions.

The relevance of the case cannot be overstated. The Ecuadorian Indian movement is often cited as the best-organized and most influential indigenous movement in Latin America. Its origins date back to the rise of local and regional organizations that, in the 1980s, came together in CONAIE, the Confederation of Indigenous Nationalities of Ecuador.

The spectacular battles of the 1990s transformed the movement into a powerful force that, in addition to pressing indigenous demands, took up a leadership role in the wider resistance to the imposition of neoliberal reforms.

By 1997 CONAIE had launched the party Pachakutik to take part in elections, and its political clout had been boosted by its role in the developments that led to the fall of president Abdalá Bucaram and the convening of a constitutional assembly. In January 2000, amid an economic and political crisis of unprecedented proportions, CONAIE joined a group of military officers led by Colonel Lucio Gutiérrez in a nonviolent coup that toppled President Jamil Mahuad but failed to hold on to power.

Three years later, the same actors made another bid for power as an electoral coalition, which succeeded in winning the presidential elections. The presence of Indian leaders in the government was a high point for the movement, but it did not last long. After six months of conflicts over President Gutierrez's neoliberal turn, CONAIE withdrew its support and Pachakutik's ministers abandoned the cabinet.

Clearly, this is a movement that has reached well beyond the bounds of a bid for indigenous rights. Much more has been at stake, including matters of national economic and social policy and issues that are directly related to the struggle for political power and the fate of Ecuadorian democracy. In the context of contemporary Latin America, then, this case is highly relevant to the discussion of the various types of impact that social movements can have on democracy.

This chapter lays the groundwork for the analysis with a conceptual discussion elucidating the notion of civil society, the specificity of social movements as a variant of civil association, and the paradoxical relationship between social movements and democracy. The factors behind the rise of Ecuador's Indian movement, the broadening of its struggles, and the saliency of its political protagonism are then reviewed. The inquiry is framed as a scrutiny of the movement's consequences for the participatory and institutional dimensions of democracy. After exploring the bases of CONAIE's support, the study examines the movement's two main modalities of political engagement: its efforts to influence government policies and its struggles to conquer positions of power.

The appraisal of the effects on the democratic regime covers four areas: interest representation, control of state power, legitimacy, and political socialization. The conclusions assess the significance of the Indian movement for democracy, briefly rejoining the debate on the "civil society argument" and commenting on the present challenges for Ecuadorian indigenous activists.

CIVIL SOCIETY, SOCIAL MOVEMENTS, AND DEMOCRACY

This work adopts a modified version of Michael Walzer's definition of civil society, taking it to refer to the ensemble of social practices that generate a space of voluntary association and the sets of relational networks, or social actors, that occupy that space. Within this scope, the cast of civil society actors includes all voluntary groups formed for the sake of the common aspirations and concerns of its members. This formula is useful because it grasps civil society on its own terms, avoiding the pitfalls of definitions that imply assumptions about its relationships with the political institutions, such as the idea that civil society is necessarily autonomous from the state, necessarily opposed to the state, or necessarily good for democracy.

A good antidote to the mystifying sway of prescriptive definitions of civil society is to keep in mind that the realm of voluntary association is thoroughly marked by pluralism, particularism, and inequality.

Civil society is pluralistic because its practices are based on multiple forms of participation, express many social identities, and pursue a wide variety of goals.

Civil society is particularistic because its groups have their own norms and because, with rare exceptions, they restrict benefits to members and pursue goals that reflect their own priorities-even when, as often is the case, they claim to represent the public interest.

Moreover, civil society is tied up with inequality not only because different groups have different levels of opportunity to associate and further their ends, but also because a great deal of what associations do has consequences in terms of widening, maintaining, or narrowing existing social gaps.

Social movements are a particular form of civil association. They can be defined as organized drives to promote or resist change through collective practices that are embedded in a structure of conflict, involve episodes of mass participation, and challenge existing institutions.

The reference to conflict implies that social movements confront opponents in struggles over values and claims to resources, status, or power, a feature that sets them apart from civil associations that are not involved in such confrontations (e.g., social clubs, churches, and charitable foundations). On the other hand, the emphasis on events in which large numbers of people engage in noninstitutional forms of action foregrounds popular participation and defiance of prescribed rules, two elements that are absent in the case of associations whose activities are carried out by small circles of activists or professionals who follow" the proper institutional channels" (e.g., interest groups and advocacy organizations). To understand movements, one must ascertain what is at stake in the conflicts in which they are involved. In empirical studies, the stakes can be inferred from their goals, their actions, and the context of their struggles.

The conceptual distinction between civil and political engagement is a useful tool for initiating that inquiry. In civil engagement, the conflict is located in civil society itself. There are two variants of this kind of engagement: construction of collective identity, in which movements seek to alter the self-consciousness of actual or potential followers; and cultural crusades, in which movements act on the general public to change dominant values or attitudes.

In political engagement, the conflict is played out through interactions with state actors or other agents from political society; that is, the arena of competition for control over the state apparatus and public policy. Here, the actions of movements are usually aimed at inducing policy changes. Sometimes, however, their struggles may turn into attempts to control the positions of power themselves.

Social movements are a modern form of participation that emerged with the changes related to the consolidation of capitalism, the national state, and liberal democracy. As a rule, movements have served as a medium for the participation of excluded groups and for the politicization of issues that the institutions are unwilling or unable to address.

By engaging in confrontational practices like marches, boycotts, and demonstrations, movements have shown that ordinary people can capitalize on numbers, unity, and determination to achieve goals against the will of the most adamant opponents or rulers. Movement practices, then, must be seen as practices of noninstitutional power. Lacking other resources, excluded and powerless people use disruption. They generate might by withdrawing the tacit support that power holders derive from" business as usual," thus creating a political market in which they can trade the lifting of their sanctions for the changes they seek.

Some authors have argued that movements and revolutions are variants of contentious politics; namely, a particular kind of political activity in which challengers use noninstitutional means in their interactions with elites and the state. By itself, though, the opposition of institutional and noninstitutional means cannot capture the diversity that exists in civil society's political practices. In the view of this study, it should be combined with another distinction that, considering the actors' ends, marks the contrast between the politics of influence, which focus on swaying public policy decisions; and the politics of power, which are played as attempts to seize the positions from which the decisions are made. On the basis of the combinations of means and ends, identifies four alternative forms of civil society's political engagement.

As a static categorization, this matrix marks out the specificity of movements in regard to other forms of civil political involvement. But the framework can also serve as a dynamic referent for variants and transformations. Variants are relevant because movements often combine the use of noninstitutional means with conventional modalities of action.

Transformations are also relevant because movements develop over time in a sequence of events that at some point is completed. At the peak of its cycle, a movement that initially focused on reforms may blend into a revolution, a sweeping challenge to the structure of power, which is usually violent and, if successful, involves dramatic changes in the organization and policies of the state.

Far more frequent, however, is institutionalization, which takes partial forms when movements spawn lobbying agencies or political arms and final forms when they abandon the unconventional forms of action and reorganize themselves as interest groups or political parties.

What is the relationship between movements and democracy? To elucidate this, we must first dispel the myth that civil society activities are always beneficial to democracy. It is true that civil associations can assist democracy by disseminating its values, representing social interests, resisting state arbitrariness, and educating people for democratic participation. But although associations can fulfill these positive functions, they may not always do so.

Indeed, they may also harm democracy in various ways, such as upholding antidemocratic ideologies, using corruption to get privileges, and seeking co-optation as state clienteles. The key point is that civil society actors may or may not contribute to democracy; and in both cases, what they actually do may vary greatly.

The groups that are not helpful run the gamut from associations whose activities are devoid of political consequence to organizations that may be conspiring to subvert a democratic regime. When associations contribute to democracy, by contrast, they rarely do it by design, but as a byproduct or contingent result of their efforts to attain their own particularistic goals.

All the foregoing holds true for social movements, but with a special twist: their status in democratic polities is haunted by an intrinsic ambivalence.

Definitions of democracy can be broadly divided into procedural definitions, which view democracy as a regime based on electoral representation and guaranteed civil and political rights; and substantive definitions, which see it as a principle of participation that guides all political practices.

This counterpoint highlights a fundamental tension between two ingredients of democracy: the principle that" the people rule" and the institutional procedures that, at any given time, embody that principle. Generally speaking, institutions produce social order by imparting stability and meaning to behaviour.· In their domain, democratic institutions contribute to that order by protecting citizens' rights and providing means for their participation in politics.

But institutions have a downside, aptly captured in Jean-Paul Sartre's assertion that they amount to" the systematic self-domestication of man by man". In dictating the acceptable ways of doing things, institutions foreclose alternatives, generating an effect of suppression that is magnified by their tendency to get entrenched in their own inertia.

The case of representative democracy is especially poignant because, for most citizens, the same institutions that enable them to choose their rulers also imply their exclusion from further participation. This tension underlies the paradox of social movements in democracies. As a form of political engagement that involves large numbers of normally excluded people, movements fulfill the principle of citizen participation. But their reliance on noninstitutional means implies that they are often in breach of the rules that define how the polity works. What turns the inconsistency into a paradox is that it has not prevented the emergence of movements as a regular feature of political life.

To the contrary, viewed from the side of democracy, the key element in the relationship is that political democracy is an open invitation to social movements. Democracy offers fertile ground because it guarantees the rights of expression and assembly and, perhaps more important, because its own claim to legitimacy, grounded as it is in a discourse of popular sovereignty, citizenship rights, and inclusion, lends legitimacy to the claims of those who do not feel represented and want changes in public policies, in the definition of rights, or in the democratic institutions themselves.

Viewed from the side of movements, however, the relationship cuts both ways. In positive outcomes, the paradox is resolved in the deepening of democracy; that is, in situations in which a movement helps make a polity more democratic by winning reforms that broaden citizenship rights and provide for greater citizen participation in politics. Europe and the United States offer many examples of movements that advanced democracy through struggles against slavery, for labor's freedom of association, for the enfranchisement of women and the poor, and for the civil rights of racial, ethnic, and religious minorities.

But there have been negative outcomes, too, including the Nazi and Fascist movements, which ushered in a catastrophic period when democratic institutions were wiped out, the political and civil rights of entire populations were revoked, slavery was reinstated, and genocide became state policy. Finally, there may also be cases in which a movement's impact is a mixed bag of favorable and unfavorable effects on different components of political democracy.

The paradox of social movements should give us pause. We cannot assume that movements always contribute to political democracy just because they involve popular participation.

But it is also a mistake to think that movements automatically detract from democracy because they infringe on institutional rules. Mindful of the complexities, political philosophers have long been engaged in discussing the circumstances in which civil disobedience may be justified in democratic polities. For social analysts, the challenge is different. We must use the complications as pointers for trying to provide more nuanced answers to empirical questions about the origins of social movements, the sources of their power, and their consequences for democracy. These are the questions addressed in this work on the Ecuadorian Indian movement.

The Contentious Cycle of the 1990s

In 1979, Ecuador turned from military to civilian rule. By way of background, it is worth calling attention to three aspects of that transition. First, the Ecuadorian generals did not display the repressive and probusiness zeal that typified military rule elsewhere in Latin America. Instead, they pursued a nationalistic agenda focused on the development of oil exports, agrarian reform, and "inward-oriented" industrialization.

During the 1970s, the economy expanded, and there were ostensible improvements in the living standards of the popular sectors. This, and the absence of severe repression, fostered attitudes of support for the military regime.

Second, the democratic transition was initiated and tightly controlled by the armed forces. The "handed down" democracy did not inspire the sense of commitment that could have existed if the political parties and civil society had played a greater role in wresting it from the military.

Because they had not been crafted through political compromises, moreover, the new institutions proved ill-suited for the resolution of conflict, which set the stage for relentless strife between the executive and congress, constitutional tampering in all branches of government, and a chronic exacerbation of party fragmentation, regionalism, and personalistic politics.

Third, the transition to democracy offered opportunities for the political involvement of the indigenous population. The 1979 Constitution eliminated the literacy requirement, which had excluded most Indians from the vote.

The process was boosted by the first civilian president, populist politician Jaime Roldós, who promoted the participation of Indian organizations in rural development and literacy programs.

The downsizing of these initiatives under president Osvaldo Hurtado (from the centrist Christian Democratic party, 1981-84) and their elimination altogether by León Febres Cordero (from the conservative Social Christian party, 1984-88) provided an early rallying point for criticism and contentiousness among the Indian activists.

These elements must be kept in mind to understand the developments of the 1990s. On the one hand, they draw a connection between the tumultuous nature of Ecuadorian politics and the reality that after a decade of civilian rule, Ecuador was still plagued by the flaws of its democratic institutions, the dubiousness of its politicians' allegiance to the rules of democracy, and the shallowness of its citizens' democratic political culture.

On the other hand they indicate that, by the late 1980s, favorable conditions for an Indian movement had appeared. The extension of political rights and the openings in government policy had stimulated indigenous organization. The subsequent withdrawal of state support, the policies of adjustment, and the downturn of the economy would provide strong motives for the Indian insurgency of the 1990s.

RISE OF THE INDIAN MOVEMENT

In the 2001 census, only 6.6 per cent of all Ecuadorians identified themselves as Indians. Including those who declared that they or their parents spoke indigenous languages, the proportion rises to 14.3 per cent, which is the best available approximation of the size of the indigenous population. The Quichuas of the Sierra account for about three-quarters of that population, with most of the rest distributed among smaller groups in the Amazon. Throughout Ecuador, the basic unit of Indian settlement is the community, which, despite variations, presents generic characteristics that will be discussed later.

The process of Indian organization was a classic example of bottomup networking based on local and regional associations of communities. In the Amazon, it came in response to the arrival of peasant colonists, oil companies, and state agencies. In the Sierra, the stimulus was the fight for the land, which peaked with the military's agrarian reform of the 1970s. With the return to democracy, the indigenous organizations continued to work for development and the defence of their culture and lands, coming together under umbrella federations in the Sierra and the Amazon and eventually under CONAIE, the Confederation of Indian Nationalities, in 1986.

Since its inception, CONAIE has combined livelihood goals and citizenship aspirations. The former have focused on economic improvements, education, health, and the protection of Indian lands; the latter on the redefinition of Ecuador as a plurinational state, the end of discrimination, territorial autonomy, representation in state institutions, control over education and development programs, and official recognition and funding for the indigenous organizations.

CONAIE's first achievement came in 1988, when it negotiated with President Rodrigo Borja (the creation of a national programme of bilingual education, funded by the state and run by indigenous personnel connected with the Indian organizations. But the presentation of CONAIE's contentious credentials was the 1990 levantamiento (uprising), a huge mobilization that vented the frustrations of a rural population that had been severely punished by the adjustment policies and the long recession of the 1980s.

The uprising was a peaceful civic strike in which tens of thousands of highland Indians blocked highways and marched into cities to seize public offices. The protest continued for several days, until the government agreed to discuss the demands. There were measures to alleviate the situation in the rural areas and settle some pending land conflicts, but an issue that remained unsolved was the status of the ancestral lands in the lowlands. Two years later, CONAIE sponsored a large march from the Amazon. Once again, President Borja was forced to negotiate with the Indians, who stayed put in the capital until he agreed to demarcate and title their lands.

The Sierra uprising and the Amazon march revealed the depth of the Indians' discontent and opened the eyes of all Ecuadorians to their return as actors who could exert influence in national politics. The uprising, in particular, was a real shake-up. As a rural protest on a national scale, it had no precedent in the country's history. In most respects, it was a feat of collective creativity, the spontaneous invention of a new form of contention that turned into a blueprint for the string of mobilizations that would follow in the 1990s.

The Indian-Peasant Front

The 1992 election gave the presidency to Sixto Duran, a conservative independent candidate. His economic plan focused on deregulating trade and capital flows, reducing social spending, eliminating subsidies, and privatizing state enterprises and social security. But Durán lacked reliable support in the legislature, and his privatization initiative was also opposed by the military, which saw the state enterprises as an important legacy of the military regime. In addition, Durán encountered resistance in civil society. The main challenges came from the Indian movement, which, buoyed by its initial successes, was displacing the labour federations as the beacon of popular opposition.

The first confrontation took place in 1993, over the plan to cut the social security budget and liquidate the health service for rural areas. CONAIE and other peasant organizations supported the strike of the social security employees and a massive protest of the beneficiaries of the rural health service. After two days of blockades and demonstrations, Durán was compelled to restore the budget and reaffirm the continuity of the health service.

The success of this struggle proved that well-organized protests could thwart an antipopular policy. In addition, it was an important precedent of collaboration between the Indian movement, other peasant organizations, and the unions from the public sector.

Next came the battle over the government's Law of Agrarian Modernization. The bill sought to abolish the legal basis for land expropriation, concentrate state support on capitalist agriculture, eliminate communal property, and privatize irrigation water. CONAIE sponsored the formation of the Coordinadora Agraria Nacional (CAN), a coalition that included smaller Indian and peasant organizations, such as FEINE (Indigenous Evangelical Federation) and FENOCIN (Federation of Peasant and Indigenous Organizations, influenced by the Socialist Party). CAN proposed its own bill and staged public debates on the issue.

In June 1994, the Coordinadora Agraria called an uprising that, once again, paralyzed the country for several days. Eventually, President Durán was forced to negotiate the bill. In its final version, the law defined peasant agriculture as deserving full state support, reaffirmed that water was a public resource, and recognized the legality of communal and cooperative forms of ownership.

The Popular Front

By 1995, CONAIE and its allies had participated in the formation of the Coordinadora de Movimientos Sociales, a broad coalition that included Indian and peasant organizations, unions from the public sector, and a large number of neighborhood associations, feminist groups, and human rights activists.

Meanwhile, President Duran had called for a referendum that proposed constitutional reforms to strengthen the executive, weaken the unions, and allow the privatization of the state enterprises and social security.

While the business sector generously financed the "yes" advertising campaign, the Coordinadora de Movimientos Sociales and the labour federations mounted an intense grassroots effort to bring out the "no" vote. On the day of the referendum, the voters rejected all the reforms. The defeat closed the books on Durán's initiatives, leaving in place an empowered popular coalition.

The success of the "no" campaign reinforced the position of the activists who had been calling for electoral participation. In its December 1995 assembly, CONAIE launched a political party that was intended to be based on the Indian movement and its allies. The Pachakutik Movement of Plurinational Unity (Pachakutik means "time of resurgence" in Quichua) entered the scene in the elections of 1996, in alliance with an independent group led by television commentator Freddy Ehlers. Ehlers did not qualify for the second presidential round, but Pachakutik won 10 per cent of the congressional seats and significant representation in provincial legislatures, local councils, and mayoralties.

The victory of Abdalá Bucaram in the 1996 election opened a period of enhanced turbulence in Ecuador. This clownish politician led the Roldocista Party, a populist force with its main base of support in the suburbs of Guayaquil. As mayor of that city, Bucaram had earned a reputation for corruption, but he had also extended his clientelist networks. During the campaign he attacked "the oligarchy" and Durán's aborted reforms.

As president, however, he focused on dividing the Indian movement, creating a Ministry of Indigenous Affairs and trying to buy the support of some Indian leaders. At the same time, Bucaram stuffed the government with relatives and friends, and it soon became evident that the country was sinking to new depths of corruption.

Bucaram's discourse had also changed. Now he spoke about promarket reforms, trying to ingratiate himself with the International Monetary Fund and inviting Domingo Cavallo, the architect of Argentina's neoliberal programme, to be the consultant for his economic plan.

Bucaram announced that plan at the beginning of 1997, when the labour unions and CONAIE were preparing a rally opposing neoliberal policies, corruption, and the Ministry of Indigenous Affairs. The measures included stiff budget cuts, higher electricity and gas rates, labour reforms, and a timetable to tie the currency to the dollar. The rally turned into a mobilization for the president's removal, and was supported by the main political parties.

As Quito swarmed with Indian demonstrators, Congress removed Bucaram on grounds of mental incompetence and named its speaker, Fabian Alarcón, as acting president. In the process, CONAIE and the other organizations extracted the promise that an assembly would be convened to reform the constitution. The 1997 elections for that assembly gave Pachakutik 10 per cent of the seats. Its delegates pushed through several reforms, including sections that defined Ecuador as a multicultural state and recognized social, cultural, and political rights for the indigenous peoples.

The next presidential election was won by Jamil Mahuad, from the Christian Democratic Party. The new president faced strong pressure from the IMF, which was vexed by the stagnation of Ecuador's reforms. At the same time, he confronted a popular coalition that rejected those reforms and had proven its oppositional power. To top it off, the economy sank into its worst recession since the 1930s.

The economic collapse of 1998-99 was triggered by the fall of oil prices and the devastation of the coast by the climatic phenomenon of El Niño. When the banana and shrimp exporters stopped repaying their loans, the banks plunged into crisis and, despite Mahuad's billion-dollar bailout programme, the financial system collapsed. A massive flight of capital ensued, the gross domestic product shrank by 7.1 per cent, and it became obvious that the country would not be able to pay its external debt.

Mahuad devalued the currency, froze bank accounts, and focused on securing the support of the Social Christian Party, traditional advocate of the coastal exporters and banks. But the IMF's conditions for a stabilization loan were tough: eliminate all subsidies, privatize public enterprises, raise taxes on income and rent, and refrain from saving the banks. Mahuad's situation became untenable. On the one hand, the popular opposition fought back against the cuts and privatization. In 1998 and 1999, Mahuad had to deal with three large mobilizations in which the popular front led by CONAIE broadened to include middle-class sectors, such as truckers, bus operators, and small and medium-sized entrepreneurs. On the other hand, the IMF's insistence on tax reform and forsaking the banks alienated the business sectors. When the Social Christian Party pulled out of the negotiations, it became clear that Mahuad's presidency would not last long.

In the last days of 1999, Mahuad announced a plan to dollarize the economy and implement the IMF measures. Assisted by soldiers, Indian crowds flocked to Quito demanding his dismissal and occupying Congress and the Supreme Court. On January 21, 2000, indigenous activists and young military officers cheered in Congress as Colonel Lucio Gutiérrez and CONAIE's president, Antonio Vargas, proclaimed a "government of national salvation." After frantic consultations among generals, politicians, and U.S. diplomats, however, the armed forces announced that they were restoring constitutional order by installing Vice President Gustavo Noboa as the new president.

Gutiérrez and the other officers involved in the coup were arrested, and the Indian leaders were forced to order the protestors to retreat.3 In the ensuing months, the detainees were granted amnesty and discharged from the army. While dollarization was maintained, the IMF negotiations were eventually abandoned without an agreement.

Much speculation has been offered about who manipulated whom in the military-Indian coup. In some versions, the conspirators appear as victims of a plot to get rid of a weakened president and proceed with dollarization. But the truth is that the colonels had been pressing their superiors for decisive action against Mahuad and that their contacts with the Indian leaders intensified after the Parlamento Popular, an assembly in which more that three hundred delegates of CONAIE and other groups called for Mahuad's removal and the formation of a popular government.

Thus it is unquestionable that the coup's organizers were acting on their own initiative. Their inability to hold on to power, however, proved that the whole enterprise had been utterly misguided.

Disillusionment and Demobilization

In preparation for the 2002 elections, Colonel Gutiérrez founded the Patriotic Society Party, PSP, which put forward his candidacy for president. After failed attempts to forge a centre-left coalition, CONAIE and Pachakutik decided to form an alliance with the PSP. Benefiting from the Indian vote and a fragmented field of 11 candidates, Gutiérrez won the first round with 20.4 per cent of the total. In the second round he defeated banana tycoon Alvaro Noboa, an independent conservative, by 9.6 per cent. Like previous presidents, Gutiérrez lacked majority support in Congress, where the PSP-Pachakutik alliance had won only 17 of the 100 seats.

After the coup, Gutiérrez had cultivated the image of a progressive populist. As the elections approached, however, he toned down his discourse and included business leaders among his advisers.

He visited Washington to meet with IMF and U.S. officials and, immediately after his election, started to talk about austerity measures.

The new attitude was reflected by the make-up of his cabinet. Although Gutiérrez appointed some Pachakutik ministers, the posts responsible for economic policy were assigned to the advisers who had been functioning as links with the business sectors and the IMF.

Gutierrez's priority task was a deal with the IMF, which wanted the fiscal deficit elminated. Knowing that an agreement would open the door to loans for social investment and development, Pachakutik's cabinet ministers went along with the austerity measures, doing their best to moderate them. The result was a salary freeze in the public sector and higher prices for fuel, transportation, and electricity. Many activists saw this as a betrayal. The Indian federation of the Sierra, Ecuarunari, demanded the resignation of the responsible ministers. CONAIE echoed Ecuarunari's reproofs, calling for a rectification of the government's economic policies.

By mid-2003, disagreements over several issues, including the government's handling of strikes by teachers and oil workers, had aggravated the tensions in the coalition. Gutierrez's intense proselytizing in rural areas irritated the indigenous activists, who decried it as a scheme to bypass CONAIE and form clientelist networks. While the cabinet was torn by mutual accusations, the "allies" maneuvered in opposite directions in Congress, where Pachakutik tried to form a centre-left block and the PSP courted the Social Christian Party. The alliance collapsed in August 2003, when Pachakutik refused to support a bill that modified labour contracts in the public sector and Gutiérrez dismissed its ministers.

With the end of the alliance, CONAIE's internal divisions rose to the surface. Amazon groups criticized the leaders for leaving the government, and radical sectors of the Sierra reproached their delay in breaking with Gutiérrez. Meanwhile, Gutiérrez went on the offensive to weaken CONAIE further, issuing a decree that allowed him unilaterally to appoint the personnel of the state agencies that dealt with indigenous issues. This ended the practice by which the officials were nominated by CONAIE and ratified by the president. The next step was the replacement of the agencies' staff with activists who had signed up with the PSP and leaders from FEINE and FENOCIN.

By the end of his first year in office, Gutiérrez was facing accusations of nepotism and corruption. He had not succeeded in winning support from the Social Christian Party (Notisur 2003d). CONAIE proposed a rally to demand his dismissal, but the Amazon groups opposed it, and the other organizations ignored the call. FEINE had chosen to back Gutiérrez in exchange for programs for the Protestant indigenous communities, and some of CONAIE's own groups, particularly in the Amazon, were involved in similar dealings. Despite the warning signs, CONAIE staged a protest in February 2004. The Indian federation of the Amazon and the other organizations refused to participate; the grassroots response was decidedly weak; and by the end of the first day, the mobilization was called off. Four months later, CONAIE organized another protest. The outcome was the same, aggravated by the Amazon groups' public support of Gutiérrez, who had just appointed his former fellow coup leader, Antonio Vargas, minister of social welfare. Vargas, himself a Quichua from the Amazon, had left CONAIE in 2002, eventually joining FEINE and becoming a staunch supporter of Gutiérrez.

The failure of the 2004 protests exposed CONAIE's crisis. But Gutierrez's success in neutralizing the movement did not solve his problems in Congress. In November he barely survived an impeachment vote amid charges that he had bribed legislators and had secured the Roldocistas' support by promising the return of their exiled leader, Bucaram. Then Gutiérrez dismissed 27 of the 31 Supreme Court justices, installing docile judges who overturned Bucaram's corruption convictions. On April 15, 2005, after three months of constitutional upheaval, Gutiérrez declared a state of emergency and ordered the police to repress protesters in Quito. The move backfired when the radio stations opened their microphones to an outpouring of indignation against his attempts to assume dictatorial powers. Following a week of demonstrations, the military withdrew its support, Gutiérrez abandoned the presidential palace, and Congress replaced him with Vice President Alfredo Palacio.

Once again, an Ecuadorian president had been ousted on the crest of street protests. This time, however, the main protagonists had been the urban crowds of Quito. CONAIE's leaders were slow in deciding to join in the protests, and when they finally did, their calls brought few Indians to the capital. Ironically, the fall of Gutiérrez offered further evidence of the prostration of the indigenous movement.

The Indian Movement and Democracy

This section elucidates the implications of the Indian struggles from the point of view df democracy. First, it looks at participation as a source of power for the Indian movement. Next, it assesses the consequences, through separate inquiries into the politics of influence and the politics of power. The last part examines the various impacts on Ecuador's democratic institutions.

The Secret of the Indians' Power

The Indian movement became a significant force because it was able to compel governments to pay heed to its demands. It was a classicexpression of the power that grows out of the effective use of disruption. To determine the sources of that power would entail exploring many factors, including the geopolitical assets of the Indian groups (strategic location in places where they could block the main national highways), the functional capabilities of their activists and organizations, and the financial and logistical assistance of external allies, such as progressive sectors of the Catholic Church and a variety of domestic and foreign NGOs. Some of these elements were addressed in a previous study; therefore the focus here is on what can be considered the main source of the effectiveness of the mobilizations: at the grassroots level, people were willing and ready to participate in them.

Throughout Ecuador, the decisions to respond to CONAIE's mobilization calls were taken by the Indian communities. Legally recognized as rural neighborhood associations, these communities have roots that go back to the colonial system of resguardos, or reservations. Their revitalization was boosted by the land struggles of the 1960s and 1970s, which, insofar as they involved appeals to primordial loyalties of extended kinship and reciprocity, reinforced the old community as the natural framework for these relationships. At the same time, the agrarian reforms diluted the landowners' power, creating spaces in which the communities, by taking up the representation of the Indian peasants, gained prominence as relevant actors in local and regional politics.

Today, Ecuador has about 2,100 Indian communities, functioning as self-regulated entities based on the authority of their asambleas (in which everybody participates) and cabildos (executive committees of five members). All important issues are discussed in the asambleas, where agreement is usually reached by consensus rather than by voting. The decisions are binding for all members, with formal and informal mechanisms to ensure compliance. Thus, joining in a mobilization is always the result of a decision of the community, which exerts its influence to make sure that the members join in the roadblocks and rallies.

The secret of CONAIE's power, then, lies in its ability to harness the resources for collective action that exist in the Indian communities. Pierre Bourdieu's concept of social capital helps elucidate this process. Bourdieu sees social capital as the aggregate of resources linked to the possession of a network of relationships of mutual acquaintance or recognition. Members of a group that, like the Indian community, is based on reciprocity and solidarity can claim access to the resources of their peers by virtue of belonging to the group. But the group as such can also use the resources embedded in the network. Indeed, the accumulation and use of social capital are always guided by contextual norms and institutions. This is particularly visible in communal groups, whose formal and informal rules define the available resources, the ways they can be claimed, and the sanctions that enforce delivery. The rules circumscribe and aggregate social capital, ensuring that its use is restricted to members and taking advantage of the effect of concentration to maximize benefits. In such circumstances, social capital is an asset that belongs to the group, which can institute itself as collective beneficiary in activities that benefit the group as a whole.

In practical terms, this means that a community that joins a mobilization is making a claim on its social capital, and that the members' readiness to participate is a resource that they owe to the community. As Alejandro Portes has shown, different motives may be at play when members contribute resources, including feelings of obligation (internalized norms), expectations of future repayment (norm of reciprocity), identification with the group (bounded solidarity), and fear of sanctions (enforceable trust). The same motives can explain the behaviour of each individual community within the networks of communities that make up the Indian movement. The general point is that the Ecuadorian Indian movement operates as a network of networks, whose activities can be analysed as a process of accumulation, concentration, and deployment of the social capital embedded in its grassroots community structures. By bringing that social capital to bear on the political system, CONAIE has been effecting its conversion into political capital; that is, into leverage that can be used to wrest concessions from governments or to compete for direct access to power.

The Politics of Influence

In the politics of influence, social movements seek changes in public policy decisions. We are interested, then, in these questions: On which issues did the Indian movement try to influence government policy? What was at stake in those issues? and How effective were the mobilizations in achieving their goals? Here, we should keep in mind that the issues changed with the evolution of the struggles. Initially, when the Indians were fighting alone, they focused on their own demands. Later on, CONAIE's coalition-building initiatives broadened the confrontation, incorporating issues that were relevant to the other rural groups and, eventually, to the popular sectors at large.

Through the issues we can discern the stakes. The Indians' demands focused on achieving the status of recognized ethnic groups with terri- torial rights and some degree of autonomy. This challenged the existing notions of nationhood and citizenship; the former by defying the assumption that white-mestizo identity was the foundation of Ecuadorian identity, and the latter by questioning the liberal axiom that citizen rights could only be individual, not collective rights. The Indian claims, then, sought changes in the existing conditions. By contrast, the struggles over agrarian and national economic policy matters were attempts to resist changes. The fights over the Seguro Campesino and the Agrarian Modernization Law focused on thwarting initiatives that would have worsened the situation of the rural population. Similarly, the national protests against neoliberalism were defensive responses to attempts to unload the burdens of reform onto the shoulders of the popular sectors. The stakes, then, had to do with the distribution of the costs of adjusting the economy to the new conditions of global capitalist development.

Did the struggles achieve their goals? We may start with the opposition to the neoliberal agenda, the results of which are trickier to appraise. Studies have shown that Ecuador ranks among the least effective reformers in Latin America. Clearly, the popular struggles played a role in this outcome, but their influence cannot be disentangled from the effects of the lack of political support and the hostility of the business sector to some reforms. Besides, we should not forget that neoliberalism was never really defeated in Ecuador, as its setbacks were always followed by renewed attempts to enact its reforms. We can conclude, then, that in this area the struggles had limited success. Interacting with other factors, they delayed the reforms and, in some cases, mitigated their impact on the popular sectors; but they were unable decisively to vanquish the neoliberal agenda.

On the rural-agrarian front, CONAIE and its peasant allies were much more effective. After soundly defeating the attempt to scrap the rural health service, they succeeded in influencing the new agrarian legislation to keep water in the public domain, secure the status of communal property, and restore the state's support to the peasant economy. Eventually, the 1998 constitutional reform enshrined all these attainments in the Ecuadorian charter.

Concerning Indian ethnic demands, the initial fights established CONAIE's contentious credentials and led to significant gains on the land rights front, particularly in the Amazon. Later, the confrontations over broader national policy issues became an effective means for attaining the particularistic goals of the Indian movement. In the give and take after the fall of Bucaram, for example, CONAIE won one of its most important achievements: the creation of CODENPE (Ecuadorian Council of Indian Nations and Peoples), the agency that now coordinates all support programs for indigenous groups with participation of their own organizations. Further concessions were wrested from Mahuad in the battles of the late 1990s, including an investment fund for Indian areas, the legalization of traditional medicine, and budget increases for the state's indigenous agencies.

On the whole, the movement was able to accumulate an uneven but substantial record of success in influencing government policies. One upshot was that CONAIE could reinvest political capital earned through the mobilizations in other forms of action and more ambitious goals. On the one hand, its lobbying drives yielded significant gains without having to resort to protests, including the creation of PRODEPINE (Development Programme for Indian and Black Populations, initiated in 1997 with World Bank funding), the establishment of a health programme for Indian communities, and the launching of CODENPE projects of infrastructural works, water and irrigation, soil improvement, rural housing, and organizational capacity building. On the other hand, the Indian movement took steps to establish itself as a contender in the struggle for political power.

The Politics of Power

In the politics of power, agents participate in contests to occupy the positions that control and direct public policymaking. The three main manifestations of the Indian movement's struggles for power were the fight for control over the state's agencies of indigenous affairs, Pachakutik' engagement in electoral politics, and CONAIE's involvement in the coup against Jamil Mahuad.

For the Indian movement, the agencies in charge of bilingual education and indigenous health; the council of indigenous peoples, CODENPE; the development programme PRODEPINE; and the indigenous investment fund constituted a first major arena of power contestation. Steered by the movement, the agencies of indigenous affairs could serve as a means to attain objectives while fulfilling the programmatic ambition of exercising autonomy. Controlled by governments, they could be turned into tools of clientelistic domination. In the heat of the struggles, CONAIE wrested from the government an informal deal whereby the officials were appointed on the basis of its nominations. Later, however, President Gutierrez's actions showed that, in a less favorable climate, CONAIE's grip could be easily broken. The situation was complicated by the rivalry among indigenous-peasant organizations. Under the initial arrangement, CONAIE monopolized the representation of the Indians; this had always been resented by smaller groups like FEINE and FENOCIN. Thus, Gutierrez's repeal of CONAIE's privileges was more than a step to exclude it from the agencies' resources. It was also a gambit aimed at luring the other organizations into a network of patronage and using their example to entice CONAIE's local and regional chapters onto the clientelistic bandwagon.

The second front in the struggle for power was electoral competition. Pachakutik was launched in 1996 as a party based on CONAIE and its closest allies. In practice, however, it has been the political arm of the Indian movement, which provides most of its candidates for office. The best indicator of Pachakutik's overall strength are the congressional elections, in which its candidates have won, on average, 7.5 per cent of the seats. While this falls short of the estimated size of the indigenous population, it can still be seen as a fair result for a new party. Moreover, the 2002 presidential election proved that Pachakutik's vote can be decisive, since Gutiérrez qualified for the second round by a margin of less than 5 per cent. But it is at local and regional levels where Pachakutik's results have been especially significant. In the 2000 elections it won 4 governorships, 17 mayorships, and substantial representation in the provincial, municipal, and parish councils of the Highlands and the Amazon. The party's performance was similar in 2004, with 3 governors and 20 majors elected. Thus, while Pachakutik has not yet fulfilled its potential, it is clear that it is serving as a vehicle for self-government in the main indigenous areas.

We do not have enough studies to draw a panoptic picture of Pachakutik's performance at the different levels of government. One area in which the outcome can be readily recognized is the country's charter. In the 1997 constitutional assembly, Pachakutik negotiated important provisions, including the definition of Ecuador as a multicultural state, the designation of the indigenous groups as peoples, and the recognition of their rights to preserve their culture and their forms of political organization and administration of justice. Together with other clauses about the creation of indigenous territorial entities, these rights offer a framework for some degree of autonomy. But implementation depends on further legislation by Congress, where Pachakutik's moves have been conditioned by its minority status and its role as an opposition party focused on undercutting initiatives coming from the executive.

In contrast to its adversarial role in Congress, Pachakutik's gains in local elections created real opportunities for exercising power. The initial research on these experiences has focused on counties with dense Indian populations or visibility as touristic or artisanal centers, including Guamote, Otavalo, Cotacachi, Saquisili, and Bolívar.

The studies cast light on innovative efforts to encourage grassroots participation, establish practices that are free of corruption and clientelism, foster fairness in the distribution of resources, and promote multiculturalism by adapting traditional indigenous institutions. But they also show that the progress has been uneven and that, in some cases, Pachakutik's local authorities have been disappointing.

The third and by far the most dramatic incursion of the Indian movement into the politics of power was the January 2000 coup against Mahuad. In that episode, CONAIE conspired with military officers to overthrow the government and assume the powers of the state.

One way of coming to terms with the outcome is to look into the reasons for the coup's failure. In retrospective accounts, the Indian leaders have mentioned the generals' betrayal, the machinations of the elites and the U.S. embassy, the hostility of the press, the lack of popular response in the cities, and their own unpreparedness to take power. From this, one can conclude that the coup failed because it was marked by improvisation and, ultimately, because it reflected a gross misreading of the political scene.

Another way of assessing the coup's significance is to consider its repercussions for the Indian movement itself. The evidence indicates that there was public support for the removal of Mahuad but not for a military-Indian takeover. In the polls taken on the day of the coup, only 6 per cent believed that Mahuad could continue, 71 per cent approved the protests, and 79 per cent thought that Mahuad had to be replaced without breaking the constitutional order.

Two days later, the polls showed that 80 per cent were pleased that democracy had been maintained, 77 per cent supported the investiture of Vice President Noboa, and only 13 per cent would have preferred to keep the military-Indian junta. The overall pattern is clear.

While CONAIE fulfilled a well-regarded role in expressing public discontent, its attempt to take power by force was rejected. The payoff for the Indian movement was also ambivalent. At the time, its image as a powerful player may have been boosted and its undemocratic behaviour may have been glossed over amid the general complacency with Mahuad's removal. But in the long run, CONAIE's collusion with the colonels put it on track for further blunders whose consequences would be far more damaging.

Recapitulating, what can we make of the Indian movement's involvement in these diverse forms of the politics of power? As we saw in the conceptual section, it is not rare for a movement to launch a party and combine protest with electoral participation. The juxtaposition of CONAIE's struggles over the indigenous agencies and Pachakutik's electoral ventures, then, are an example of what a movement undergoing institutionalization typically does.

The coup, though, was a very different matter. If we were dealing with a revolutionary group, we might think about the use of force as part of the strategy of" combining all forms of struggle." But CONAIE and Pachakutik have never claimed to be revolutionary organizations.

We are left, then, with the sense that the coup was an

anomalous deviation from the path that the movement had been following.

To account for it, one could make allowances for the magnitude of the crisis, the intensity of the public's outrage, and the leaders' rashness and lack of vision. What is difficult to fathom is why, to this day, the activists have not conducted a real evaluation of those events and their fallout.

In the absence of soul searching, the naive opportunism that transpired in the coup kept haunting the Indian movement. Indeed, the leaders' decision to support Gutiérrez in the 2002 elections can only be seen as an attempt to cash in on whatever political capital they believed they had gained from the January 2000 adventure. Gutiérrez won the election, but the quick unraveling of the alliance showed that the move had been another serious mistake. The Indian movement could not stop Gutiérrez's neoliberal turn, Pachakutik was forced to leave the government, and CONAIE was weakened by divisions. But the worst damage came from the disappointment at the grassroots, where Pachakutik's presence in the government had been hailed as an opportunity to access the resources that had been always denied to the Indians. Combined with the effects of Gutierrez's clientelist strategy, the loss of trust at base level became a major factor in the failure of CONAIE's latest mobilizations.

Impact on Democracy as a Political Regime

This assessment of the Indian movement's impact on the regime is grounded on elaborations of four ways that civil associations may impinge on democratic institutions. The first of these is interest representation. In democratic regimes, political parties are the prescribed medium for representing citizen interests. Very often, however, party systems cannot express the diversity that exists in society. Civil associations can compensate for this deficit by conveying the interests of specific sectors to the political system. The Ecuadorian Indian movement exemplifies this function.

It gave voice to excluded groups, projected their concerns into the public agenda, and opened new areas for policymaking. Furthermore, its strategy of alliances was instrumental in aggregating and expressing the demands of all the rural groups and, eventually, the popular sectors at large.

To this we can add the creation of a party that incorporated marginalized interests into the system and spurred indigenous participation in elections.

Interest representation by civil associations can help fulfill three principles of democratic governance: responsiveness (serving all sectors), consensus orientation (mediating among different interests), and equity (treating everyone equally). Realizing this potential, however, does not depend on the civil groups alone.

It also depends on the institutional actors' willingness to consider their views and adhere to democratic principles. In Ecuador, incumbent governments had many opportunities to hear what the indigenous and popular sectors wanted and to fulfill their side of the democratic governance bargain.

But those governments chose to ignore the input that came from below. Insisting on the imposition of unpopular reforms, they wasted the opportunities for building the kind of consensus that would have strengthened democratic governance.

This calls attention to a second function of civil associations: the control of state power. Liberal formulations emphasize the notion that citizens should protect themselves from state intrusion in private affairs and from violations of civil and political rights. Broader interpretations, however, include additional issues related to transparency and accountability. Once again, we find a connection with the principles of democratic governance, since the contribution of civil associations consists in holding governments responsible for fulfilling those principles.

In Ecuador, the popular opposition to neoliberal governments repudiated the governments' insensitivity to the concerns of the majority, unwillingness to compromise, and unilateral commitment to the priorities of the business elites and the IMF. Thus, in the process of defending the interests of the popular sectors, the Indian movement and its allies were also fulfilling the watchdog role of trying to counterbalance what was widely seen as an unfair use of authority.

The foregoing interpretation leads to a third function: legitimation. In democratic polities, governments are acutely dependent on legitimacy because it is the people's support that justifies the right to exercise authority. Citizen groups can reaffirm legitimacy in two ways: explicitly, through actions that convey support; or tacitly, by doing nothing that might be construed as opposition.

The denial of support, however, must take the form of explicit oppositional action if it is to be understood as such. It is also worth noting that, in democracies, legitimation is rarely an all-or-nothing matter. The reason is that civil associations can legitimate or delegitimate authority at different levels.

Opposition to a policy does not necessarily imply disaffection with a government, and disaffection with a government does not necessarily entail rejection of the regime. Indeed, a common result of challenges at lower levels is the reinforcement of legitimacy at higher levels, as illustrated by cases in which a negotiated solution of a policy conflict boosts the image of a government, and situations in which the constitutional replacement of an unpopular government reaffirms the credibility of a democratic regime.

The legitimacy issue is particularly sensitive in the case of social movements because their motives are oppositional and their activities assume noninstitutional forms. Still, taking into account the nuances of legitimation, there is much room for their fulfillment of this function.

The Ecuadorian Indian movement was certainly shoring up the political institutions when it created a party and urged its base to go to the polls. Beyond that, the routine challenges of the movement focused on policy matters that did not question the legitimacy of the governments or the regime as such. Through a different route we return to the point that, if the Ecuadorian governments had been more open to negotiation, the results could have enhanced their standing. Instead, their inflexibility became a factor in the escalation of conflict that led to their delegitimation. It was against this background that the Indian movement played an active role in the demise of two presidents. In the fall of Bucaram, the legitimacy of the regime was not at stake. The ousting of Mahuad was different because it involved a conspiracy to usurp power, which, had it succeeded, would have implied the breakdown of democracy. But the coup failed, and as a result, its actual impact on regime legitimacy is difficult to assess.

Intuitively, one would think that, by exposing the frailty of the institutions, the affair may have eroded their credibility. This inference, though, is not supported by the evidence. Over the last decade, the Latinobarómetro polls have shown a general softening of support for democracy, but the trend has been much less pronounced in Ecuador than in the rest of the Latin America.

Comparing the periods 1996-99 and 2000-2004 (before and after Ecuador's January 2000 coup), support for democracy declined by 12 per cent in the region as a whole but only by 6 per cent in Ecuador. One can speculate that, to some extent, Ecuadorians felt reassured that their democracy had survived the crisis.

Speculations aside, the movement's attempt to subvert the regime raises questions about a fourth function attributed to civil society: political socialization. In one of the most prominent formulations of the "civil society argument," associations are presented as frameworks in which citizens acquire the values and dispositions that are needed for a workable democratic polity. This claim relies on two basic assumptions about political socialization: that it is a matter of the formation of individuals, and that its results can somehow "free-float" into the public sphere as a resource that can be readily harnessed for the benefit of democracy.

What these assumptions miss is the significance of the mediation of the group, which becomes a collective subject of its own socialization process, inculcates its particularistic norms along with the more general dispositions, and regulates the use of the resources that make up the network's social capital. In so doing, civil society groups invariably condition the impact their socialization may have on the political system.

Taking this into account, we can tackle what appears to be one of the most puzzling questions about the Ecuadorian Indian movement. This study has demonstrated that the movement's struggles have induced vast changes in the behaviour of the indigenous groups. Because those changes would not have been possible without processes of socialization, it is clear that the movement has been doing a massive job teaching people to work together, cultivating interest in policy issues, and providing knowledge and skills for participating in public activities, such as mobilizations and elections.

The seemingly puzzling question is how these contributions to political socialization, which, according to the celebrated claim, should be functional to democracy, square with the attempt to take power by force. The matter is less baffling if we keep in mind that movements do not socialize people to help the workings of democratic regimes; they do it to attain their goals. The real question, then, concerns the movement's lack of commitment to Ecuadorian democracy.

This lack of commitment can be traced to three sources. One is the conviction that Ecuador's democracy is a fraud. Time and again the Indian militants have decried what they view as a corrupt democracy, with institutions that are discriminatory and governments that benefit the elites at the expense of the common people. Another source is the disrespect of all the political players for the rules of democracy. Willy-nilly, the indigenous activists have "learned the ropes" of practical politics within a system of interactions in which the prevailing attitudes are not distinguished by reverence for constitutional conventions.

The third source is the tension between the principles that inspire the indigenous internal practices and the liberal notions of democracy. At one level, it is a matter of the contrast between direct and indirect democracy; the former embodied in the participation of all in communal decisionmaking, and the latter in the elected officials who decide for all citizens in the broader Ecuadorian polity. At another level, it is a contrast between two canons of representation.

When the communities elect representatives to the associations, and when the associations elect representatives to the next-level federations, the elected persons function as delegates, whose powers are limited to specific mandates and whose authority can be revoked at will by those who elected them. In a liberal democracy, by contrast, elected officials operate as fiduciaries who use their discretion to interpret the interests of the represented and act on their behalf.

This raises the question of what the Indian movement's democratic ideals are, and whether these ideals and the standards of Ecuador's democracy are so incompatible as to justify the repudiation of the latter by the activists. In a political declaration approved in 1993, CONAIE called for a "plurinational communitarian democracy" based on equality, liberty, fraternity, and social peace. This goal would be achieved through a political reorganization aimed at guaranteeing the full participation of the Indian peoples and the other social sectors.

The platform adopted by the first congress of Pachakutik in 1999 was more specific, proposing a "radical democracy" based on a semiparliamentary system, decentralization, civil society representation in some state agencies, and direct participation through citizen initiatives, referenda, and recall of elected officials. These proposals could be easily integrated into an agenda to "deepen" the democratic character of existing institutions. The activists' lack of commitment, then, is not rooted in an unbridgeable programmatic rift.

Rather, it seems to result from a double ideological distortion: a view of Ecuadorian democracy that chooses to dwell on its deficiencies (ignoring that the conquest of indigenous rights and the Indian movement itself would hardly have been possible without it), and an exaggerated sense of the contradiction between the indigenous principles and those of the existing institutions.

This work has investigated the consequences of the Ecuadorian Indian movement for democracy. Its inquiry was based on conceptualizations that defined the specificity of movements as a form of civil society's political engagement and offered guidelines for studying their effects on the participatory and institutional dimensions of democracy. The analysis showed that the Indian movement had roots in communal mechanisms of direct democracy, that its multilayered structure had been built through bottom-up networking based on delegative representation, and that its protagonism in the contentious cycle of the 1990s marked a historic milestone for the involvement of the indigenous groups in Ecuador's public life.

The participatory breakthrough came on two fronts. Practicing the politics of influence, the movement forced new issues onto the public agenda, wrested concessions from governments, and led alliances that repeatedly hindered the imposition of neoliberal reforms. Engaging in the politics of power, it contested the control of the state's indigenous agencies and spawned a party that made strides in the electoral representation of the Indian groups, the procurement of their collective rights, and their progress toward self-government. These initiatives fulfilled important functions for Ecuador's democratic institutions. In the areas of interest representation and control of state power, the demands and protests provided ideas and contributions for improving the quality of democratic governance and imposed restraints on policies that were widely rejected by civil society. The launching of a new party was also significant as a development that upheld the legitimacy of the democratic regime.

It is unquestionable, then, that the Indian movement has made remarkable contributions to Ecuadorian democracy. Yet we have also seen that the swell of activism was not an unmitigated blessing for democratic politics. The critical drawback was the January 2000 attempt to subvert the constitutional order. At that point, CONAIE transgressed the threshold beyond which, in a democracy, an opposition becomes disloyal. The analysis here showed that the coup was inconsistent with the behavioural pattern of the Indian movement and that its negative impact was mitigated by its own failure and by the special conditions under which it happened. But the extenuating circumstances cannot absolve the movement of responsibility for threatening the democratic regime. Further scrutiny emphasized the reality that political socialization within the Indian movement had not fostered a sense of commitment to Ecuadorian democracy.

This evidence of contradictory consequences is consistent with the critique that the "civil society argument" plays up beneficial effects and ignores the possible downside. It also underscores that in Latin America, the study of the impact of civil associations on democracy cannot overlook three crucial points. The first is that the realization of the democratic potential of any civil society initiative depends on how the political institutions process it. Democratic governance is enhanced when decisionmakers take the concerns of civil associations into account. Conversely, democracy suffers when governments ignore citizen feedback, treat it perfunctorily, or demonstrate biases in their reactions to the bidding of different sectors.

The second point is that when civil associations mobilize broad support, the institutional responses to their functions of interest representation and control of state power can be highly consequential for regime legitimation. The legitimacy of democratic politics is strengthened when governments take notice of popular sentiment; but democratic regimes may fall into a tailspin of delegitimation when the inputs from below are repeatedly rebuffed.

The third point is that it is a mistake to view civil society groups as neutral purveyors of citizens trained for democracy. Like other social capital resources, the results of political socialization remain embedded in the networks of interaction that produce them. As collective structures that constitute the primordial source of social capital, regulate its uses, and mediate between individuals and society, civil associations impart their particularistic slant to socialization and influence its fallout in the political system.

For Ecuador's indigenous activists, the stark contrast between the successes of the 1990s and the more recent frustrations underscores the urgency of rethinking their bearings.

To a large extent, their present predicament is a result of their own inability to respond to the complexities of the movement's institutionalization process. Two tasks in particular were sorely neglected. One was in the area of strategic development. To maintain coherence in situations of partial institutionalization, social movements must define a roadmap for combining protest with the use of prescribed means, and they must do it in such a manner that the two forms of action reinforce rather than interfere with each other.

The other neglected task was ideological elaboration. In the politics of influence, social movements can afford to condemn unstintingly the poverty of democracy. But in a democratic system, whatever its shortcomings, a movement that acts in the name of democracy cannot make the transition to the politics of power without taking a more constructive stance toward the existing institutions.

Essentially, it is a matter of reframing the movement's ideology by shifting the emphasis from antisystem representations to imageries of democratic renovation from within. In Ecuador, the lack of strategic guidelines and the shortsighted attitude toward the democratic institutions jumbled the responsibilities of CONAIE and Pachakutik, muddled their priorities, and paved the way for the missteps that weakened the Indian movement.

It may be a commonplace to say that a crisis can be turned into an opportunity, but that is precisely the challenge that the Ecuadorian indigenous activists face today. Whether or not they succeed will depend on their willingness to recognize that the time for reckoning and self-criticism is long overdue.

Chapter 3

Critique of the Role of the Public Defender

It is a recurring image on our television screens: a young man - frequently Black: and poor - is hustled from police car to courthouse door. As two burly police officers grip him tightly by the arms, he tries to hide his face with his hands. His efforts are futile. He succeeds only in exposing his handcuffs to the bright television lights. In the background, a reporter's urgent voice describes the despicable act which led to the young man's capture. His anguished face, framed by gleaming handcuffs, is the garish image we remember.

When I was a public defender, I would watch episodes like this with dread. "What if," I would wonder, "that young man was to become my client at the next day's arraignment call? Could I be of any help to him? Or would I be essentially useless, since he had already been tried and convicted on television and in the hearts and minds of any potential jurors?" Certainly, I could do something. I could ameliorate the onslaught of state power by holding the government to its promises and making sure no shortcuts were taken.

Occasionally, in an exceptional case, I might even win an acquittal. But, by and large, in case after case, my presence has had little bearing on the outcome. In the vast majority of cases, the conclusion was foregone, the conviction assured, the case open and shut.

I was a necessary, but irrelevant. Player in a game with a predetermined outcome. We Americans often speak of our criminal procedure as if it were one of the main bulwarks of democracy. We like to consider the criminal trial, with its adversarial process, as one of the great institutions of abstract justice. But the American criminal justice system is a sham. The centerpiece of the criminal justice system - the trial - is itself a sham. It is not, in the main, a mechanism for determining the truth.

In the majority of criminal cases, the truth is already assumed from the start. While belief in the presumption of innocence is professed, the defendant is treated as if his guilt were assured. In reality, it is up to the defendant to prove, if possible, his innocence and to somehow show that he is an exception to the rule.

More concretely, the criminal trial is flawed because it is not adversarial (or at least not as adversarial as it should be). Instead of two evenly matched adversaries, the advantages are decidedly weighted in the prosecution's favour. The prosecution has tremendous resources at its disposal that are ordinarily not available to the defence: police investigators, government laboratories, a professional legal staff, an endless supply of expert witnesses and, most importantly, a far greater reserve of credibility.

This imbalance is even greater when the defendant is represented by a public defender. This is doubly cruel because the defendants who are at greatest risk in the criminal justice process - those with the least personal resources - are the ones most likely to be represented by public defenders.

Of course, the defendant has the protections of the Fifth and Sixth Amendments - including the right to a fair trial, the right to effective assistance of counsel, the right against self-incrimination, the right to compulsory process, the right of confrontation, and the requirement of proof beyond a reasonable doubt - but these are, by and large, merely formal protections.

How defendants are treated in fact is what is important, not simply abstract theory. To have any relevance, the formal protections afforded to defendants must be appraised in the cultural context which gives them meaning.

Trials take place within a culture, a culture which gives us certain ideas about the prosecution and certain opinions about the defendant. Every culture produces its own belief system. This belief system is transmitted to each member of society through such means as formal educational systems, media, authoritative pronouncements and word of mouth. A cultural belief system allows us to attach meaning to symbolic representations that appear in culturally determined contexts.

Thus, the imagery of the courtroom - the "dignity" of the proceedings, the "impartiality" of the judge, the adversarial posture of the litigants - and the juxtaposition of symbols of authority - the flag, the judge's black robe, the police officer's badge - all communicate culturally determined meaning to prospective jurors.

There should be no mystery as to what meaning it is that the criminal justice system communicates to the American public. Our society is one where jurors are taught repeatedly, through both obvious and subtle means, that the preferred outcome of any trial is the conviction of the accused. In an environment such as this, a requirement of proof beyond a reasonable doubt is of little value.

The image of the accused presented in criminal procedure books - that of an average citizen, who is merely "suspected" of crime, and who consequently retains his rights and social status until the state meets a heavy burden of proof - is a widespread fraud. Instead, the defendant plays the mythical role of "Criminal" in a broader morality play, the well-known script of which allows the audience to boo and hiss as soon as the villain enters the scene. The defendant in a criminal case is supposed to lose, just as a villain in a Hollywood movie is also supposed to lose. More often than not, a criminal trial consists merely of two groups of actors playing their appointed parts - the prosecution in white hats, the defence in black.

The criminal trial, then, is an allegorical tale disclosing the way that society would like to discover, expose and exorcise crime. As allegory, the trial does more than merely determine the fate of the defendant standing trial, although it does that too. The trial represents something deeper. The trial expresses fundamental notions about justice and injustice, right and wrong, law-abiding and crime, good and evil. Within the confines of this allegory, the public defender's role is essentially symbolic. The public defender demonstrates that justice is being done and that the trial is fair. Symbolically, it matters little whether the public defender can actually assist the defendant because, as a mythical "criminal," the defendant is always guilty.

The allegorical nature of the trial is not apparent on the surface. It becomes visible only when one is aware of underlying notions of justice and attitudes about crime. Then one can trace the relationship of these notions and attitudes to the adversarial process. In this chapter, I use semiotic theory to explain how the adversarial criminal trial is given substance and meaning that belies its formal description. I situate the criminal justice system in its broader societal context, and then employ critical media analysis to "read" the trial and disclose its allegorical form. Semiotic analysis reveals how our perceptions of guilt and innocence, of criminals and victims, of prosecutors and defenders, are ordered to fit a profound and pre-existing structure.

I begin by describing what I call "the myth of criminal justice." In Part I, I disclose the parameters of this myth by presenting the formal protections that the right to counsel, along with the defendant's other trial rights, afford to those accused of crime. In Part II, I explain semiotic theory and how it can be used to determine the social construction of meaning. I point out that by placing the defendant's trial rights in their cultural context, semiotics can reveal the functional meaning of the adversarial process. Next, in Part III, I employ semiotics to disclose how the criminal justice system is structured by a broader discourse about crime and criminals. I show how ideas about crime work to limit our conceptions of justice, so that defendants' rights may be articulated, but not taken seriously. In Part IV, I view popular culture through the medium of television. I employ the window of television to illustrate how crime is represented in ways that separate criminals from society and define them as "bad" and undeserving of rights.

I also examine how the cultural images represented on television play out in the context of a criminal trial. In Part V, I point out how these latent cultural images, privilege the prosecution and disfavor the defence. I argue that the discourse on crime skews the adversarial process and makes it difficult for defendants to receive a fair trial. In Part VI, I demonstrate how public defenders are especially handicapped in their ability to convince jurors of the innocence of their clients, since they too lack credibility in the eyes of the public. Finally, in Part VII, I suggest a way that the federal government could use its persuasive power to make the adversarial process more meaningful. I propose the establishment of a Federal Defender General in order to improve the image and effectiveness of public defenders.

Formal Rights and the Persistence of Myth

The adversary system is a carry over from the English common law. The system is not mentioned in the Constitution. Nor is it preserved, by and large, by statute. Yet, the adversary process is the linchpin of our criminal justice system. A person charged with a crime is not just the accused, but the defendant - someone who retains the capacity to combat and contest the government's accusations.

The adversary system receives praise from many quarters because, it is argued, the self-interest of the parties will motivate them to more thoroughly prepare their submissions to the fact finder than if a more dispassionate investigator were charged with the responsibility. Also, it is assumed that a disinterested fact finder is less likely to show bias because he or she has no vested interest in the way that the investigation is conducted or how trial preparations are made. The adversarial system works on the assumption that truth will prevail from the conflict between two opposing forces. Within the adversary system, the criminal defendant is entitled to an impressive array of rights. The most important of these, from an adversarial standpoint, is the right to counsel, for it is through counsel that the defendant is best able to exploit the adversarial process and champion his cause. The right to counsel originates in the Constitution. In Gideon v. Wainwright the Supreme Court read the Sixth Amendment to require that counsel be provided to indigent criminal defendants in felony cases at state expense.

Later, the Supreme Court interpreted the indigent's right to appointed counsel to be applicable in all cases in which actual imprisonment was imposed, as well as to appeals as of right.

In other cases the Court broadened the right to counsel to require state provision of expert witnesses, trial transcripts, and other "basic tools of an adequate defence." Finally, courts have made some effort to address the quality of legal services provided to criminal defendants. On the surface, then, the obligation of the state to provide legal assistance to those who are too poor to secure their own defence seems quite extensive.

There are other rights that a defendant may claim to help bolster his or her defence. A defendant has a right to be present at trial, the right to confront the witnesses against him or her, and the right to cross-examine those witnesses. The defendant also has the right to present a defence and the right to compulsory process in order to obtain witnesses or evidence. Furthermore, the defendant has a right to testify and a right to remain silent. Finally, the defendant has a general right to fairness in the prosecution of his or her case - i.e., the right to due process of law.

Many of the aforementioned rights would only make sense within an adversarial process. For example, in a non-adversarial process a defendant would need no right to present a defence, and a right to remain silent would seem incongruous. The purpose of the defendant's trial rights is to place the defendant on an even footing with the prosecution so that he or she might be a more effective adversary to the prosecution. The presumption of innocence and the requirement of proof beyond a reasonable doubt are also central to the notion of an adversarial system of justice and are considered to provide additional protection for the criminal defendant. The presumption of innocence is implied by the accusatorial structure of the criminal justice system. It holds that the burden of proof is on the government and absent sufficient proof, the defendant must go free. In the adversarial framework, the defendant has no obligation to produce evidence of his or her innocence.

Proof beyond a reasonable doubt is the burden the government is required to meet in order to obtain a conviction. It is a "heavy" burden of proof, the highest such standard in the criminal justice system. The burden of proof beyond a reasonable doubt is intended to provide protection against erroneous convictions. In principle, a burden of proof beyond a reasonable doubt moderates the adversary system and makes it more responsive to individual rights.

Taken together, the formal rights extended to criminal defendants, along with the presumption of innocence and the requirement of proof beyond a reasonable doubt, constitute a "myth" that permeates the criminal justice system and defines how the system is envisioned. In short, the myth proceeds along these lines: A defendant who is presumed innocent must be proven guilty beyond a reasonable doubt at an adversarial trial that is fair and at which he or she has counsel.

The basic assumptions behind the myth (that is, the points that the myth seeks to validate) are:

- The existence of formal rights adequately protects the individual from the state.
- Because these formal rights make it difficult for the state to secure convictions in an adversarial context, those convictions that do occur are "hard won" and thus more legitimate. The function of the myth, then, is to bestow peace of mind by encouraging the belief that justice is being done in the criminal justice system.

Of course, the "myth" that I have described here presumes that the parties are more or less evenly matched, that no external values or interests influence the fact-finder, and that the rules are enforced.

It should go without question that these are pretty broad assumptions to make. And yet, most analyses of criminal procedure in general, and the right to counsel in particular, accept the formalistic posture represented by the myth. In their formalistic approach, typical criminal procedure analyses reveal their commitment to positivist assumptions. Under positivism, rules are viewed abstractly as concrete principles with a definite meaning and effect.

Thus, like numerical values, they may be ordered and reordered "scientifically." This type of formalism has been powerfully criticized by adherents to the legal realist school. The realist critique argues that formal rules cannot be accepted blindly and taken for granted, hut rather that rules must first be situated in their appropriate context and then examined critically to determine whether they actually function as purported.

Semiotic theory provides a useful tool to determine the actual functioning of rules in context. Semiotics furthers the realist critique not only by helping to disclose whether rules "say what they mean" (do the rules function as claimed), but also by helping to discover whether rules "mean what they say" (are there hidden meanings). Semiotics does this by disclosing the framework-through which law takes its meaning. I am particularly interested in observing how the adversary process functions when a criminal defendant is represented by a public defender. In the following sections of this chapter, I employ semiotics to accomplish this task.

Semiotics and the Criminal Justice Process

Semiotics is the study of signs and symbols. Semiotics arose from the study of language problems and attempts to determine the structure of language. These early structuralist attempts sought to expose the internal relationships that governed how language developed and how it was used. Later, semiotics was broadened to include not only languages but any signifying system. Semiotics assumes that "all communication is a process of exchange of meaningful signs." Thus, it may be stated that semiotics involves the study of systems of rules underlying messages, whether those messages be contained in speech, film, literature, or the like. Semiotics makes a distinction between the signifier, or the form that the sign takes, and the signified, that is, the meaning associated with the sign.

The meaning of any sign is always relational. It is contingent upon the values agreed to by those who read the sign, which are in turn dependent on the relationship of the sign to other signs.

A sign is communicated and read within a social matrix that changes and evolves, thus the meaning of a sign changes and evolves as well.

Many scholars have recognized that law is itself a semiotic process, since it involves the communication of a value system through its rules, precepts, and principles. For example, the doctrine of caveat emptor may be used to demonstrate the semiotic essence of legal concepts.

This textual phrase, caveat emptor, is a sign - a representation of an idea or concept - recognized and understood within the legal community. This sign can be studied historically to discover the nature and circumstances of its emergence or creation as a legal sign.... In studying the creation, evolution, and slow demise of caveat emptor, one undertakes a study of the dynamic and creative dimensions of semiotics.

One is called upon to evaluate the process by which new ideas (signs) are created and validated in legal discourse and practice.... In this sense, law is a fluid and spontaneous system for the creation of new relationships and new ideas. It is a system of evolving sign exchanges; thus, the law is a semiotic process.

Kevelson argues that law and semiotics involves the study of both legal discourse and legal practice. This would suggest a broader interpretation of the parameters of semiotic inquiry than that of those who would only, or predominantly, apply semiology to investigate law's internal structure.

It should be obvious that semiotics is not only relevant to the investigation of law's internal structure, but also is crucial to a critical understanding of law's external context - i.e., its relationship to society. Others have also suggested that legal semiotics could be used to connect juridical statements to their place in the broader society, for example, the connection of laws to political theory or ideology.

In my view, this connection has not been fully developed - at least, not within that legal scholarship that self-consciously identifies itself as semiotic. The majority of these efforts have stopped short of exploring law as part of a larger structure which includes ideology as one of its components - that is, viewing the law as a sign in a larger system of signification, whose texts would contain both internal (or legal) and external components.

It is precisely this sort of work that distinguishes the culturalist school of critical theory in mass communication. Culturalist theorists borrowed formal semiological analysis to treat media messages as structured wholes rather than as quantified fragmented parts.

Mass media was approached as a means of producing and articulating "messages within specific signifying systems, the rules and meanings of which we tend to take for granted." From the culturalist perspective, media messages are both created and interpreted pursuant to definable rules or codes. Thus, artifacts of communication (such as films, books, letters, and speeches) are viewed as means of discourse rather than as the sum total of the communication itself. As discourse, an artifact is subject to the system of rules that governs that discourse.

In the culturalist vein, I approach the trial itself as a text, which may be read within the context of a structure which includes ideological and cultural attributes. Thus, criminal procedures gain their meaning not solely from legal rules and juridical principles, but also from their relationship to themes or codes established through the operation of culture. In other words, the matrix that gives criminal procedures their meaning is broader than that of the law. This matrix includes news reports and analysis, entertainment, common sense knowledge, and other communicative or educative processes. Like other artifacts of communication, the trial must be seen as discourse, which can be interpreted only within the latitude of those codes that govern communication about crime.

I do not want to look at criminal procedure as an abstraction or a "fractured part" of the whole. Instead, I envision communication about crime as a cultural production, consisting of interconnecting structured systems of which the criminal justice system and its attendant language and procedure are only part. Discourse about crime, then, takes place within a single, large system of signification made up of smaller systems that operate in the areas of popular culture, media, criminology, law enforcement, jurisprudence, and politics, to name just a few. It is this larger system that I will investigate in the next section.

Crime and the Creation of the Consensus

To comprehend the functioning of the criminal justice system within the interconnected matrix of culture, we must first come to terms with what it means to be a criminal defendant - a person who has been charged with committing an offense against the social order. This requires an understanding of "crime" as a social phenomenon. By investigating the meaning of crime, we can uncover the codes that also order our perceptions of the criminal trial process, the codes that in effect shape our notions of what adversarial criminal justice is.

What we have come to call "crime" serves a variety of social functions. First, as the "labelling" school of criminology has demonstrated, the concept of crime allows a community to determine its norms and "label" other conduct as deviant. This labelling power is not, however, shared equally. What makes a dominant group "dominant" is its power to define a subordinate group as deviant. Once conduct is labelled "deviant," it affects the interaction of those so labelled and the majority in real, concrete ways. In short, the majority has "the power to define the rules of the game to which everyone is required to ascribe...."

The power to define rules has obvious consequences. It is axiomatic that describing certain conduct as criminal permits the punishment and stigmatization of those who step outside of the norm. That is, "the labelling process serves to mobilize moral censure and social sanction against deviants." Establishing crime as a social category thus involves the critical function of deciding who shall wield state power, against whom, and for what purposes.

Crime also serves the purpose of "reinforcing the internal solidarity of the moral community." As crime creates and excludes "them" it also creates and strengthens "us." The focus on drug abuse over the past few years has certainly enhanced the social position of those who have not used drugs. Thus, struggles to criminalize the conduct of others can also be seen as struggles to validate one's own behaviour.

This notion of crime as a creator of community is enhanced by Stuart Hall's concept of the "consensus." The "consensus" is Hall's term for the prevailing ideology subscribed to by the public at large. The "consensus" consists of the accepted parameters of social conduct and the established view of the purposes and functions of the institutions of society. It may be said, then, that the consensus consists of the intersection of those norms which are not deemed criminal. But the consensus so formed is not simply an agreement to accept majority rule, as it were, in the area of social order. It is a consensus to "a particular kind of social order."

Crime engenders consent to the moral community of those with the power to define. To the extent consensus works, then, it works in the interest of those with power. Social order calls for "integration within and conformity to the rules of a very definite set of social, economic and political structures." As Hall emphasizes, the social order that arises from the designation of crime is articulated to that which exists: to the given dispositions of class, power and authority: to the established institutions of society."

Hall's "consensus," then, implies domination rather than freedom. Indeed, "it is the complementary face of domination." This comes as no surprise because the mere existence of the law, whether criminal or otherwise, has inherently coercive implications. The law relies on the ability of the state to exercise force to exact compliance. But the law is merely "the repressive and negative aspect of the entire positive, civilizing activity undertaken by the State"; that is, law is used by the state to accomplish certain ends. These ends may just as readily be achieved by noncoercive means as by force Coercion, then, is the flip side of consent and consent is the flip side of coercion. Power relies on the consensus to govern because without consent it cannot govern efficiently. But for power to govern in its own interest, the consensus must allow it to do so. Thus, power seeks to shape and direct the consensus.

Unlike social contract theories, Hall's consensus does not arise spontaneously from the formation of the body politic. Consensus, like other significations, is produced. The production of consent must be understood as a semiotic process. The reality of the consensus is the "result of a particular way of constructing reality." The parameters of the consensus must be arrived at through the process of articulation, the work of selecting those values which will become part of the consensus and excluding those which will not. As Hall puts it, "language and symbolization is the means by which meaning is produced." Thus, the consensus is produced or given meaning by the discourse of those who subscribe to the consensus. Clearly, within this discourse, some themes predominate and others fall aside. This raises the question of which meanings come to be those we view as regular or accepted. Hall answers this question as follows:

> Because meaning was not given but produced, it followed that different kinds of meaning could be ascribed to the same events. Thus, in order for one meaning to be regularly produced, it had to win a kind of credibility, legitimacy or taken-for-grantedness for itself. That involved marginalizing, down-grading or de-legitimating alternative constructions.

As I explained earlier, the consensus is determined by those who have the power to define. Although the meaning of the consensus is produced "democratically" through the process of signification, a process in which all may participate, this process is controlled predominately by the state through its control of educational and cultural institutions. The state, then, plays a key role in the production of consent:

> It organises ideologically, through the cultural sphere and

the education system and... through the means and media of communication and the orchestration of public opinion. Increasingly, it organises the civil and social life of society - especially of the family and the poor, through the "mediated" structures of the Welfare State. Above all, it organises through politics, the system of political parties and political representation: through the "maintenance of order in political class conflict."

Crime represents more than simply the opposite of the consensus. The concept of crime can be enlisted by the state to aid in its production of consent. Crime plays a crucial defining role in the construction of the ideological representations of society. Crime lies within a structured discourse that places crime on one side and law abiding on the other. Crime is part of a dialogue about right and wrong, order and disorder, violence and peace. This emotive power endows "crime as a public issue" with a tremendous mobilizing force. The support of the community "can be rallied to a campaign against it, not by presenting it as an abstract issue, but as a tangible force which threatens" home, family and stability. In this way, crime "allows the construction of a false unity out of... very different social conditions...."

Hall's concept of the consensus is useful because it exposes the cultural and political supremacy of the elites. It shows how their views of reality come to be the accepted views of reality and how accepted views of reality are connected to the instrumentalities of domination and of force. Moreover, the consensus demonstrates how the accepted view of reality itself operates as an instrument of control, limiting (although not eliminating) the ability of the subordinated to challenge authority and power. In sum:

What the consensus really means is that a particular ruling-class alliance has managed to secure through the state such a total social authority, such decisive cultural and ideological leadership, over the subordinate classes that it shapes the whole direction of social life in its image.... But, because this domination has been secured by consent... that domination not only seems to be universal (what everybody wants) and legitimate (not won by coercive force), but its basis in exploitation actually disappears from view.

Furthermore, Hall's consensus makes this connection between the prevailing ideology and the domination of the ruling class without the determinism characteristic of Marxist theories of the state or conspiratorial views of history. Hegemony is not imposed, as it were, by the authority and power of the state. The masses are not dupes. Hegemony results from the coalescence of a consensus, produced by the semiotic process of signification - a process in which the state has distinct advantages, although no monopoly.

THE DEFINITION OF CRIME

The commission of a crime marks one as a deviant. It places the criminal outside of the consensus and identifies him as an enemy of the state. However, because the criminal is outside the consensus, he also may be described as an enemy of the people. Thus, crime as a category helps determine the borders of the consensus and the consensus helps provide legitimacy to the state's definition of crime. In this way, crime "provides hegemonic services for the state." The extent of these hegemonic services, however, is limited because the definition of crime is politically contested. Crime is not just what the state wants it to be, but what it comes to be signified as.

While there is general agreement that criminal acts are wrong, not everyone agrees on what acts should be criminal. Traditional or mainstream views of crime tend to focus almost exclusively on acts of individuals that threaten violence to persons or property.

This mainstream or state definition of crime is criticized by those who note that, under this view, harmful conduct of the wealthy and powerful is either not conceived of as crime or, if so, rarely prosecuted or punished.

These critics would propose an alternative definition of crime, one which would define a broad range of human rights violations - e.g., racism, sexism, economic exploitation - as crime. Even within these two general camps there is wide disagreement over which specific acts ought to be criminalized.

This is true because in the most fundamental respect the definition of crime is politically determined. Its definition derives from the political give and take generated as various interests compete for control of the state apparatus. The formal definition of crime, then, will vary as different interests gain power or as groups in power redefine their needs in response to changing social conditions.

Viewing crime as politically contingent only partially explains why the state definition of crime is so prevalent. It prevails because the functional definition of crime (i.e., the definition used to determine the imposition of punishment, whether from mainstream or alternative formulations) is built from deeper, more fundamental concepts of criminality. The fundamental definition of crime is not found in criminology courses or in criminal law texts. When people talk about crime, they draw on social images from "the available field of practical ideologies." These images provide the structure for any discourse about crime.

When the journalist, or the judge, or the members of the ordinary public have to respond to, or explain, troubling events, like "mugging", they tend to draw, often in a piecemeal and unreflexive manner, on the social images, the "ideas of society", the sources of moral anxiety, the scattered meanings which frame their everyday experience in order to construct, out of them, social accounts which carry credibility.

These fundamental images build up slowly over time, accruing from society's total experience with crime and its ideological reaction to it. These images are the result of politically contingent, functional definitions of crime percolating in the public consciousness until they reach the level of "truism." When definitions of crime enter into the social reservoir of ideas, they retain their political and ideological character.

Thus, the limited range of explanatory paradigms within which we structure our thinking about crime is greatly influenced by those who inject ideas about crime into the public consciousness, or those whom Hall refers to as the "definers" of crime.

Hall distinguishes between primary and secondary definers of crime. "Primary definers" are authority figures in powerful and high status positions. They are considered to have greater expertise and to have "access to more accurate or more specialized information on particular topics than the majority of the population." As a consequence, it is primary definers who are able to provide the primary definition or the most widely accepted "take" on crime.

"Secondary definers" are those who reproduce as secondary sources the definitions established by primary definers. In industrialized countries, these are primarily the media. Hall points out that the media are forced into heavy dependence on the statements of primary definers by their desire to produce an "impartial" and "objective" product under constant deadline pressure, since primary definers provide a readily accessible source of authoritative opinions.

The realities of news production, then, work to create" a systematically structured over-accessing to the media of those in powerful and privileged institutional positions." This means that the opinions and viewpoints of primary definers are much more likely to be widely disseminated than those of others. They will be credited as authoritative by the media, and ultimately accepted by the majority of the public.

Over time, as these opinions work themselves into the social reservoir of ideas, they will exert a greater and greater influence over all signification about crime that takes place within that culture. I do not mean to suggest that alternative perspectives on crime cannot be expressed.

Indeed, there are alternatives to the mainstream view of crime both at the functional and the fundamental level. But these alternative views generally lack credibility." Counter-definers," or those who produce alternative definitions of crime, are severely handicapped in their ability to influence the production of meaning. It is difficult for most counter-definers to gain access to the media and thereby participate in the defining process.

Those that can, by reason of the fact that they have won some degree of legitimacy from the system (such as law professors or criminal defence attorneys)," must respond in terms pre-established by the primary definers and the privileged definitions, and have a better chance of securing a hearing and influencing the process precisely if they cast their case within the limits of that consensus." Counter-definers who fail to respond in the familiar framework established by the primary definers run the risk of having their opinions de-authenticated and dismissed as" radical" or" extreme."

Thus, it comes as no surprise that a close inspection of the way that crime is reported reveals a heavy reliance on the statements of police, prosecutors, government officials, and other spokespersons of the established institutions of criminal justice.

To the extent that lay opinion is represented at all in this field, it is represented by the advocates of victims. Rarely are the opinions of those perceived as criminals solicited, unless they are the views of reformed lawbreakers, employed now as consultants to crime control organizations.

The alternative perspective is offered, if offered at all, by a small coterie of criminal defence attorneys and civil libertarians, whose opinions are made to seem more and more nonsensical, even though they are always careful never to challenge the fundamental assumptions of the criminal justice system.

In this section, I have shown how the meaning of crime is produced through a semiotic process of signification. Crime determines the consensus, but the consensus also determines crime. At the raw functional level, the meaning of crime is determined through a process of articulation as competing interests vie to establish their own self-interested definitions of crime. Thus, the working definition of crime is politically contingent and therefore relational.

The meaning of crime is also relational in the sense that the working, or functional, definition of crime is constructed from deeper, foundational notions that have been cloaked in the veneer of common sense. These common sense notions are themselves the result of a semiotic process at work. They are but distilled and refined versions of politically contingent, functional definitions of crime that have been worked and reworked through an extended process of signification. These fundamental views of crime comprise a cultural inventory of basic assumptions that structure all discourse on crime.

In the next Part, I examine the way that crime is signified in popular culture in order to reveal the basic assumptions about crime and criminals that are at work.

Making Meaning: The Depiction of Crime In Popular Culture

Investigating the way that crime is signified in popular culture can show how the image of crime is worked into the popular consciousness.

Exploring popular culture, then, can expose the codes that govern the way that significations about crime take their meaning, since it is from this deep level that all subsequent discourse about crime is structured. The popular culture serves as a window into the shaping of the consensus. It is the means through which the consensus expresses itself, as well as the means via which key definers can shape the consensus. The term" popular culture" can cover a lot of ground. For my purposes, I am concerned mainly with television as a representative of popular culture. I choose television because television is the primary means through which we learn about and make sense of our world. Whether offered as" fact" or" fiction," representations of crime invade all aspects of television programming.

For convenience, I divide my comments into:

- Observations about dramatized accounts of crime
- Non-fiction reporting of incidents of crime.

Crime on Prime Time Television

Crime is a staple of prime time television. A 1985 survey revealed that more than forty per cent of prime time hours during the 1985-86 television season were devoted to shows featuring police officers, detectives, private investigators or other law enforcement agents.

There is substantially more crime on the nation's television screens than on the nation's streets. The principal investigator in a two decade-long survey of prime time television claims ten times more crime is depicted on television shows than occurs in real life.

The average viewer watches six violent crimes during each hour of prime time viewing and two-thirds of all major dramatic characters are involved in some violence, typically brought about by the commission of or the consequences of a criminal act. As a result, television viewers are immersed, hour after hour, in a world where crime takes on exaggerated importance.

Not only is the amount of crime on television dramas exaggerated, but also the types of crime depicted are exaggerated. Television crime is bloodier and more violent than crime is in reality. As flawed as known indicators of crime are, it is clear that the vast majority of serious crime is directed at property.

Yet, the type of crime most frequently depicted on television dramas is murder. On television, the bulk of crime depicted is crime against the person, and the victims of crime are disproportionately white and female. The perpetrators of crimes are also portrayed unrealistically. Surprisingly, criminal characters on prime time shows are frequently played by white middle-class males. While real criminals are disproportionately poor, television criminals are often rich and greedy. Such a stereotype makes little sense, as white collar or victimless crimes are seldom the focus of television dramas.

Criminals are generally presented unsympathetically. Rarely are they depicted as victims of circumstance or motivated by concerns or needs, other than greed, with which the average viewer can empathize.

In the world of television crime, there are only two acceptable motivations for criminal behaviour: greed and insanity. When crime cannot be explained by these two factors, it is presented as just senseless - the consequence of an uncontrollable evil will. In short, instead of real people with histories, personalties, and relationships that frame and explain their conduct, criminals are represented as one-dimensional demons to be feared and destroyed. Viewing crime presented in a manner that suggests that it cannot be explained discourages us from looking for its causes.

The structure of television drama does not allow for the accurate representation of criminal defence attorneys, nor does it permit an adequate explanation of their function and/or necessity. Since most crime dramas end with an arrest, "[a]rraignments, pretrial hearings, jury selection, bonding, plea bargaining, trials, sentencing, and other postarrest processes are rarely shown." Furthermore, since we typical see the perpetrators as they commit their crimes, television criminals are, of course, almost always guilty. Consequently, criminal defence attorneys are either superfluous or corrupt. According to legal ethics scholar Steven Stark, "`criminal defence lawyers are usually depicted on crime shows as figures of derision and betrayers of the public trust.'"

Contrasting sharply with the image of the criminal and the criminal defence attorney is the image of the television "crime-fighter." Law enforcement agents are central heroic figures in prime time crime dramas. Whether police officers, detectives, private investigators, federal agents (FBI, DEA, Treasury) or even medical examiners or attorneys, the common characteristic shared by crime-fighters is their archetypical role as instruments of crime detection and enforcers of the established order.

Police officers are represented in particularly glamorous, but unrealistic ways. Their role as fighters of crime is exaggerated and other mundane, but more common aspects of the police officer's role are diminished. The life of a television crime-fighter is exciting. He rarely makes mistakes, and seldom makes a false arrest.

Crime dramas rarely focus on complaints of police brutality. When they do, the complainant is belittled and the brutality characterized as necessary. Studies have repeatedly disclosed that the constitutional rights of those suspected of crime are routinely violated on television crime shows. Not only are witnesses assaulted, but homes and offices are routinely broken into without warrants, highly suggestive identifications are solicited, and confessions are flagrantly coerced.

Notwithstanding the blatant illegality of fictional police conduct, the television representation of crime-fighters is generally positive and presumably perceived as such by much of the audience. Several studies indicate that police officers are held in high regard by members of the general public. The illegal conduct of television cops is accepted, even encouraged, in large part because in the context of such shows, illegal conduct is framed as pragmatic and necessary. In the words of one researcher:

In most crime shows the audience sees the crime committed, so they know who committed the crime, a position the television police do not enjoy. So when the police violate the Fourth Amendment and conduct an illegal search, it seems acceptable because guilt has already been established as far as the audience is concerned.

Police violence and illegal conduct are presented on television as an effective, quick, and simplistic solution to society's crime problem. Constitutional guarantees are presented as obstacles to effective law enforcement, causing more harm to citizens if taken too seriously. Police officers are frequently portrayed in a highly romanticized manner as macho individualists, who are not afraid to do whatever it takes to get the job done.

Since on television, the real threat to a prosperous life comes from criminals and not from a faceless government, the viewing public is encouraged to place their trust in the hands of violent, but effective, law

The ideological impact of the way crime is signified on television dramas was pointed out by George Gerbner over twenty years ago, in a study prepared for the Surgeon General's Scientific Advisory Committee on Television and Social Behaviour.

Gerbner's research disclosed that the vast majority of dramatic themes represented on television "revolved around threats to and the preservation of the moral, social and global order." Violence, including crime, is used in these contexts because it is an inexpensive and emotionally charged way to communicate messages about appropriate and inappropriate social behaviour and the consequences of each. "The typical plot," notes Gerbner, "ends by reaching a reassuring and usually foregone conclusion about who is the better man."

Violence operates symbolically to show us how it may be used to advance our causes and to avoid being hurt. Violence demonstrates who is heroic or empowered and what values should triumph over others. In this way, "symbolic violence is one of society's chief instruments for achieving the aims of real violence without having to commit any."

Gerbner found that "the lion's share Of representation went to types that dominate the social order...." Not surprisingly, "less... representation was allocated to those lower in the domestic and global power hierarchy....". This uneven representation of character types, combined with their placement in television's matrix of violence and crime, encourages the reproduction of dominance and rigid social order. Gerbner concluded:

The pattern of allocation of violence appears to project the fears, biases, privileges, and wishful thinking of dominant institutions onto a cosmic canvas.... The fundamental function and social role of ritualized dramatic violence is, then, the maintenance of power. The collective lessons taught by drama tend to cultivate a sense of hierarchical values and forces. Their conflicts expose the danger of crossing the lines, and induce fear of subverting them.

More Crime at Eleven: Television News and the Signification of Crime

Because television news ostensibly deals with the portrayal of reality, one might think that the representation of crime in the news would differ significantly from that offered in the fantasy world of entertainment television. But the distinction between television news and television entertainment is not sharp. The "reality" of television news broadcasts is highly selective. In fact, television news "is much closer to definitions of narrative construction than unmediated experiences or conceptions of real life." In this way, its reality mirrors the reality of television drama.

Both real and dramatic television are significations produced by an external and active will. Both reproduce the conventional cultural pressures of the existing social order. Consequently, both "compliment and reinforce each other as they repeat the same propositions about life and society."

Television's selective eye makes it all the more persuasive. Television has the power to concentrate its attention on one or two themes and strengthen its message through repetition. Crime reporting is a major feature of television news programs. This constant focus on crime, its frequency and its danger, reinforces the perspective on crime generated by television crime dramas.

The news media does not create its discourse about crime from whole cloth. It recycles concepts and terms already in the cultural lexicon. Thus, while a newscast may be furnishing information cast as facts, it is also constructing a tale that either "fits" or contradicts broader and deeper concepts of crime that operate as "myths."

Most news accounts of crime (whether reports of specific incidents of crime or more general accounts of crime statistics and trends) come from official government sources. News reporters and editors work closely with the police. Television stations routinely report bulletins, lookouts and warnings about criminal activities. While such activities lend an aura of respectability to television newscasts, they also reinforce the credibility and authoritativeness of the official sources upon which they rely.

Media reliance on official sources, in the end, permits police officials to shape the nature of news coverage of crime.) It gives government authorities input into the decision of which stories will be covered and which will not. Ultimately, the offenders and victims selected as newsworthy will tend to be those fitting established preconceptions.

Television news reinforces the perception that we are living in a "mean and dangerous world." A prominent place in each evening newscast is reserved for reporting some serious and violent crime - a shooting, robbery, carjacking, abduction, or rape - or the efforts of some law enforcement agency to control crime - a drug bust, increased street patrols, or a similarly newsworthy event. Those who are arrested, accused or convicted of crime are represented as malevolent and incorrigible outcasts.

Unlike the wealthy criminals depicted on prime time shows, criminals shown on the news are, more often than not, poor members of racial or ethnic minority groups arrested for crimes of violence. Newsreporting can thus interact with and feed on racial stereotypes, promoting a further deterioration in already strained race relations.

The exploitation of stereotypes is even more exaggerated on so-called" reality" programming such as Fox Network's" COPS" or NBC's" Rescue 911." These shows present a highly emotional and sensational product that is even more objectionable because the shows exploit a format that has become associated with objective reporting. Shows such as these blur the distinction between entertainment and news even further.

Television news influences society's concepts of order and normality in a manner which often goes unnoticed. Through its coverage and presentation of crime, television news signifies that violent crime is increasingly the norm and that greater imposition of state control and police intervention are necessary to maintain some semblance of order.

The end result is that television news coverage encourages the impression that we are living in a society that is under siege by the forces of crime and that it is only through the efforts of our local police forces that civilization as we know it endures. Through television news, crime works to reintegrate society, to reinforce notions of who is inside the" thin blue line" and who should be cast outside it. Media coverage, then, provides a vehicle for communicating" the necessity for strong social control." In this way, the news media have assumed the functions of ideological reproduction previously performed by public punishment. Where once public hangings were necessary to develop a sense of community and obeisance to authority, now nightly broadcasts of crime serve much the same role.

The Attitudinal Effects of Television Crime

Attempts to measure the effects of television viewing on attitudinal change have always been controversial. Given the pervasiveness of the medium of television and the difficulty of controlling for other influences that might interact with watching scenes or shows, opinion research based on exposure to television has always been qualified. Nonetheless, an impressive number of studies suggest that not only are the effects of television viewing measurable, but that television plays a tremendous role in the socialization process and in the formation of attitudes and opinions.

Several studies have concluded that exposure to television fosters the belief that we are living in an increasingly dangerous and violent world. Heavy television viewers tend to believe there is a greater incidence of crime than light viewers do. Heavy viewers are also more likely to fear victimization as a result of crime than are light viewers. Consequently, heavy viewing of television contributes to the development of a sense of distrust towards others, a factor which may make it difficult for a criminal defendant to convince jurors of the sincerity of a defence.

Another disturbing consequence of television's portrayal of crime is its tendency to undermine the rights of criminal defendants. Heavy television viewers are more likely to think that a person who has been arrested of a crime is guilty of something. Several studies have demonstrated that, on the whole, viewing television crime shows discourages support for civil liberties. Carlson concluded that" while crime show viewing does not explain a large proportion of the variance in attitudes toward civil liberties... its contribution is significant and greater than many other factors which presumably are important in the socialization of democratic values such as social status, achievement in school, and family structure."

Findings such as these support Gerbner's conclusion that" television profoundly affects the social and political climate and the institutional setting in which courts work." While most empirical studies have focused on crime drama viewing, the viewing of news programs," reality" shows, and televised trials can only exacerbate the effect.

Because the media tends to report only the most dramatic and spectacular crimes, news (and pseudo-news) coverage of criminal trials can only" warppublic understanding of the judicial process." Furthermore, the depiction of crime on television encourages the widespread belief that Blacks and other people of colour are the source of crime. Adeno Addis makes this point about the effects of the" media's daily narrative about crime":

The media paints a picture of the black criminal threatening the innocence of white America. Indeed," crime" has virtually become a metaphor to describe young black men. Not only does the mainstream media present news stories about African Americans that" are more often negative, focusing on crime or other negative attributes than are stories about whites," but also quite often the media, especially television, uses the picture of young black men to illustrate a point about the pervasiveness of crime and drug abuse in the society.

Television's linkage of crime with race may lessen any public concern over racial abuses in the criminal justice system and make it more difficult for people of colour to receive a fair trial.

Consequently, all television's offerings having to do with crime, whether designed for purposes of entertainment or information, are both creatures and creators of the consensus. Operating through the consensus, television contributes to the "exploitation of popular prejudices and the cultivation of public support for the suppression of threats and challenges to the social order." Television works, then, to extend hegemony and to create a populace that is more respectful of authority and power. Thus, heavy television viewers, while subject to varying ideological influences, tend to take unmistakably conservative positions on issues. insofar as crime is concerned, television viewing "can... be expected to contribute to receptivity to repressive measures and to apparently simple, tough, hard-line posturings and 'solutions.'"

Television draws its images from a cultural reservoir stocked by and large with images of dangerous criminals, shady defence attorneys, and virtuous prosecutors and police. What television takes from the cultural reservoir, it also replenishes through the process of signification.

Thus, as television is influenced by the consensus, television also influences it. Television teaches that a particular type of social order is appropriate and normal, a social order that is conservative, dominant, racially-biased, and rigid. Television represents a social order that excludes and vilifies not only criminals, but also those who are merely charged with crime. Television teaches us that these people are already guilty. They have only yet to be provided with the formality of a trial.

In the next section I discuss how the images of crime and justice represented on television, structured as they are in conservative notions of law and order, are replicated and reinforced in the criminal trial.

The Trial as Text

The trial is a highly ritualized formal narrative that is the culmination of the adversarial process. Like the image of the criminal, the trial too is socially constructed. Our ideas of what rights are fundamental, what procedures are fair, indeed the very notion of fairness itself, all spring from the same cultural reservoir as do the images that are represented on television. The consensus influences and is influenced by the trial just as it influences and is influenced by television. In a word, the trial is a "text."

The ostensible purpose of the trial is to determine the guilt or innocence of the accused. This determination is reached by a jury made up of lay persons drawn from the community and is based on highly abstracted and formulaic presentations of evidence made by the state and the accused. From these highly abstracted presentations it is the job of the jury to ascertain the facts. Indeed, there are no facts before evidence is presented to the jury; it is the job of the jury to find them.

The trial, and as a result the jury's verdict, function "as if legal proof, which is largely a matter of formal procedure, and knowledge, which is largely a matter of the substance of the facts, are the same thing." Consequently, the verdict is treated as realistic: not as just one version of the truth, but as "the whole truth." But legal proof is not knowledge and verdicts can never embrace the whole truth. The realism of the verdict is, at best, "belief" masquerading as "truth." "As realism, the trial does not embody real social relationships but cultural mythologies about those relationships." The verdict of the trial is as constructed as the trial itself.

The consensus on crime reaches its ultimate expression in the device of the trial. The trial is where society both assesses and responds to behaviour it marks as deviant. The cultural mythologies that work to produce the verdict are forged in an environment that can best be described as a "metaphorical morality play." As a morality play, the trial has its own stage or setting, players, and conventions as to how the script is to unfold.

As in any morality play, the actors in the criminal trial play symbolic roles. The adversarial posture of the parties symbolizes the clash of good and evil. But in the allegory that is the trial, good is supposed to triumph over evil. The adversary nature of the criminal trial must be reexamined in this light. If good is to win over evil, good must be more powerful then evil. For the trial to play out its symbolic mission, the prosecution and defence cannot be two evenly matched adversaries. The prosecution must have the upper hand. The criminal trial can only be adversarial in the sense that the prosecution and defence oppose each other as the symbolic representatives of good and evil.

Here we have a departure from the typical notion of what the adversarial process is all about. The common view depicts the adversarial process as a contest waged between two opponents who have a roughly equal chance of convincing the fact finder that their version of events is true. While the trial does proceed in this way on its surface, at a deeper level, the notion of "trial as morality play" works at cross purposes to the "trial as fair contest" ideal.

In the remaining sections of this Part, I review those attributes of the trial that make it resemble a morality play. My analysis of the setting, participants, and staging of the trial reveal the working of the same ideology that pervades popular culture and that is made manifest in television's representation of crime.

The Setting

Trials typically take place in buildings with imposing architectural designs. It is not uncommon for courthouses to evoke associations with glorious empires of the past. The courthouse is represented as a place where justice in the philosophical sense is done. To underscore this projection, quotations from great moralists, esteemed jurists, or classical works of morality or law are frequently inscribed on courthouse walls.

The courtroom, where the trial actually takes place, is a familiar venue to most as a result of its frequent appearance on screen and description in print. A courtroom is formal space.

Stately and ceremonial, the design of a courtroom is intended to provide a dignified setting for the trial. Adding to the courtroom's sense of decorum are emblems and symbols of state authority and power. Through items such as these, the courtroom and all that occurs in it are stamped with the mark of officialdom, evoking all the prestige and supremacy of the state.

The typical courtroom shares much in common with a playhouse, further accentuating the trial's relationship to theater. The well of the courtroom serves as the stage. On this stage are the props around which the drama will revolve: tables and chairs for the prosecution and defence and, often, a podium.

In many courtrooms, the table closest to the jury is reserved for the prosecution. The judge sits on a podium overlooking the well of the court, as if to direct the drama that is to unfold on the stage below.

The immediate audience for the story is the jury, which is seated in a bleacher-like jury box to the side of the well of the court. More removed is an area of auditorium-style seating for the general public. These seats are normally separated from the rest of the courtroom by a barrier or "bar," which emphasizes to those that sit behind it that they are spectators, not participants.

The setting of the trial not only suggests the presence of theater, but it also sets up a commanding "environmental resonance," or atmosphere, of authority and power. Within this space the state is on home turf. All others are made to feel uncomfortable and out of place. The defendant is not the beneficiary of the courtroom's formality and sterility. Instead, the defendant stands out as an object to be regarded and examined. The very structure and design of the courtroom works to legitimate the prosecution and delegitimate the defence.

THE PLAYERS

There are many participants in a trial. However, the defining characters in any criminal trial are the judge, the prosecutor, and the defence attorney or public defender. They are the ones who will ultimately determine how the story is told.

- *The Judge*: The judge is the representative of the state's judicial power. The judge serves as the ultimate legal authority, decisionmaker, and referee over the adversarial contest that takes place during the trial. During the course of the trial, the judge is responsible for governing the conduct of the trial. In this sense she is like the director of a play. At the conclusion of the trial, the judge instructs the jury as to the law they should apply during their deliberations.

  The judge is treated with utmost dignity and respect. Her demeanor is authoritarian and aristocratic. Like any other autocrat, the judge commands an entourage of aides and assistants. Indeed, the judge personifies hierarchical power. The judge's authority comes from a number of ancient and well-entrenched sources: the prestige and prominence of the clan leader (from whom the role of the judge evolved); the special authority traditionally afforded to the landed gentry and/or aristocracy in European cultures; the might and supremacy of the state; and the stature and distinction of the judge's age and social status. The judge carries all of this elite-based power and privilege into the courtroom to aid her in her functions. Of the trial's three key participants, the judge is by far the most prestigious.

The judge can use her power and prestige to influence the course of the adversarial process. Akin to a sports umpire, the judge is in a position to ensure a fair contest or throw the game in favour of one party or another. As creatures of the consensus, judges are more likely than not to favour the prosecution. Although the trial is itself weighted in favour of the prosecution, the judge polices this imbalance and works to insure that the outcome of the, trial comports with commonsense notions of justice - i.e., that the symbolic function of the morality play is realized.

- *The Prosecutor*: The prosecutor represents the state as a legal entity before the court and is the proponent of the state's case against the defendant. Prior to trial, the prosecutor decides what charges to bring and what penalties to seek. The prosecutor's power in this regard is enormous; although the decision to charge is subject to review in most states by grand jury or preliminary hearing, the meaningfulness of this review is limited since" a prosecutor seldom has any difficulty in making a prima facie case against a defendant." When trial commences, the prosecutor is responsible for presenting the government's case-in-chief. That is, the prosecutor tells a story that he urges the jury to accept as the preferred version of the facts.

After judges, prosecutors are the most important state government officials in the criminal justice system. Prosecutors have prestige not only because they are attorneys but also because they are representatives of the state. Prosecutors trade on the authority of the state. They are cautioned in trial manuals not to refer to themselves as" the prosecution" but rather as" the state," " the government," or, in the most extreme version of this practice," the, people." Thus, to the eyes and ears of the jury, it is" the state" that rests," the government" that alleges, or" the people" that object. The prosecutor, then, is not just some employee of the government; the prosecutor is the alter ego of the state - the government personified. To the extent that the state engenders authority, power, and respect, so too then does the prosecutor.

Prosecutors consciously position themselves in the mainstream. On the whole, prosecutors are cleancut and wholesome, representing the image of efficiency and professionalism. The image and appearance of the prosecutor is not happenstance. It is partially a function of seeking to reflect majoritarianism and to avoid identification with any" special interest group." But the prosecutor's grooming, dress, and demeanor are also intended to demonstrate an identification with generally conservative (or" moderate") political ideology. The image that the prosecutor projects embraces and endorses the mainstream, and thereby, embraces and endorses hierarchy and power.

As the judge can use the authority and prestige of her office to influence the conduct and outcome of a trial, so too can the prosecutor. By determining whom to charge with crime, prosecutors engage in the labelling function that crime in its social role permits. More importantly, prosecutors draw on the moral superiority that is theirs as representatives of the consensus. Their role as definers of crime allows them to speak to the jury as one in a shared community. This permits a prosecutor to position himself and the jury as" us" and the defendant and his attorney as" them."

- *The Public Defender*: The public defender is most often a state or county employee retained or appointed for the purpose of providing free legal assistance to criminally charged indigents. Public defenders act as ombudsmen for their clients as they confront a hostile criminal justice system. Public defenders must employ a variety of skills to advance their clients' interests, including negotiation, bureaucratic maneuvering, and legal challenge. Although it is the most visible, representing his clients at trial is only one aspect of the public defender's job. It is, however, the most important in terms of the allegorical nature of the criminal justice process.

At trial, the public defender directly opposes the prosecutor. The public defender works to counter the government's case by offering the jury an alternative story, one that may conflict with the government's version of events, or one that may agree with the state's account but raises an affirmative defence. But, no matter which approach the public defender takes, the public defender is hampered by the restrictive discourse regarding crime that is produced by the consensus.

While public defenders have the prestige of being members of the bar - they are respected to that degree by court officials, witnesses, and laypeople - that prestige is tempered by two factors: they represent "criminals," and they are the opponents of the state. All defence attorneys oppose the state and thus oppose, in the minds of the public, all that the state stands for - security, order, justice, and consensus. Retained attorneys may compensate for this negative identification by the positive force of their own public image or that of their comparatively well-to-do clients. The public defender cannot. Further-more, the public defender's clients are the epitome of the class of individuals that the public is convinced is the cause of crime. Public defender clients are uniformly poor, mostly Black, and routinely perceived as social outcasts.

Unlike the case with prosecutors, it is not unusual to find flamboyant and eccentric personalities among the ranks of public defenders. Many take pride, in maintaining an appearance that is out of the ordinary and a little risky. Rather than embrace the status quo, the public defender purports to stand somewhere outside of the mainstream. The public defender projects the image of the anti-establishmentarian rebel more so than that of the efficient and professional public servant.

STAGING THE TRIAL

The trial begins, appropriately enough, with opening statements from the prosecution and the defence. In these, the parties outline their respective cases to the jury by summarizing what they expect the evidence to be. Through their opening statements, the attorneys inform the jury of their theory of the case and explain how they expect to prove it. Although it is important that the jury receive a "roadmap" of what to expect when the evidentiary portion of the trial commences, it is equally, if not more, important for the attorneys to use this opportunity to establish rapport with the jurors.

"First impressions," so the saying goes, "are lasting impressions." As a result, it is significant that the prosecution gives its opening statement first. The prosecution gets the first opportunity to make a lasting impression in the minds of the jurors. The prosecution's theory of the case and "take" on the evidence will be the yardstick against which all others' will be measured. After all, the government can make a compelling case. The prosecutor represents the state - the state that we all expect to protect us from crime. And it is the state that accuses the defendant, the state that tells us all of its resources have identified this defendant as the perpetrator, and the state that tells us, in its disciplined and professional way, how it will prove the defendant's guilt. From the very beginning of the trial, the government is able to bring into play all of the myths and symbolism that the jurors have already learned about crime. The defendant, especially, appears dangerous and antisocial. Thus, the government's accusations seem reasonable, even common-sensical.

The prosecution starts with much more legitimacy and credibility than does the defence. To the jury, every word the prosecution utters is suspended in a web of meaning that has been spun and re-spun every day of their lives. Every teacher's mention of "Officer Friendly," every parent's caution not to trust strangers, every book, every television show, every newspaper report of crime, collectively work to suggest a guilty defendant and an earnest prosecutor committed to justice.

The prosecution draws on its credibility to strengthen and mobilize the consensus. The jury can be addressed as a community of law-abiding citizens who share, along with the prosecution, a common interest in eradicating crime. This legitimates the prosecution's narrative and invests it with a persuasive power that the defence cannot muster. As a consequence, "guilt" and "innocence" are determined more by the definitional work of the consensus than by the arguments of either the prosecution or the defence.

The public defender has a tremendous hurdle to overcome, even before he or she utters a word about the defense's case to the jury. The public defender must work to overcome the jurors' natural biases and suspicions against his client, which have just been reinforced by the prosecutor's opening remarks. Somehow, the public defender must counter the prosecution's advantage and establish a rapport with the jurors. The first task of the public defender is to quickly raise some doubt in the minds of the jurors about the tightness of the government's case. Then, the public defender must go further and attack the jury's tendency to stereotype his or her client as a "criminal." The public defender must personalize the defendant, establish him or her as a human being, separate him from the demonic image that the jurors carry ready-made in their heads. This can be done, and it often is, but it is a decidedly uphill battle. Despite the supposed level playing field, it is the government that claims the jurors' allegiance and has every opportunity to keep it.

After the opening statements, the trial proceeds to the presentation of evidence stage. As with opening statements, the prosecutor goes first. The prosecutor is not content to just let his or her witnesses tell their stories. Like any trial attorney, the prosecutor meticulously prepares the witnesses he or she intends to call. What is recounted at trial is not "reality," but rather a rigidly structured narrative, the telling of which is accomplished through question and answer.

By the time a witness testifies at trial, every question and every answer has been crafted and practiced to bring the utmost advantage to the prosecution. The skillful prosecutor uses this opportunity to rework each witness's testimony so it "fits" the expectations created by the consensus. For the prosecution this is a relatively easy task. The fit is natural because jurors have already been educated to place each element of the trial, whether symbolic or real, into its proper place.

Not only is the content - of a witness's testimony scrutinized, but much energy is expended on its presentation as well. Witnesses are primed to look good and to be believable. It is important that witnesses appear sensible and sympathetic. Attorneys intuitively know that aesthetic factors such as these greatly influence a juror's decisions at trial. Prosecution witnesses are generally respectable police officers, doctors, ballistic and forensic experts, and average citizens. A defence attorney attempting to cross examine witnesses such as these may find it difficult to undermine their credibility with the jury. This is especially true when the attorney is an anti-establishmentarian public defender, who lacks the authority of the prosecutor and represents a suspected criminal.

Notwithstanding the fact that the state has brought the charges and bears the burden of persuasion, permitting the prosecution to present its case first, like permitting the prosecution to deliver its opening statement first, allows the government to establish its story as the story. Within the context of the adversarial trial, the prosecution determines which account becomes the preferred version of events, a version which, once accepted as the status quo, can shape the remainder of the jury's deliberations and limit the way in which the defence can respond. If the jurors were to have any doubts about the importance of the evidence to be relied on by the state, the fact that it is presented by the prosecutor organizes it in a way that makes it more believable.

The prosecution's story is invariably conservative. In its telling, the prosecutor focuses on the "facts," which are presented as "objective" and "immutable." By so doing, the prosecutor shifts the contest from the courtroom to the consensus where the prosecution is more apt to win out. This strategy can be observed in the prosecution's constant appeal to the "common-sense" of the jurors. By asking the jurors to trust their common-sense, the prosecutor is telling them to rely on that which they already have accepted as true via the operation of the consensus.

At the close of the prosecution's case the defence has two choices: the defence may present evidence of its own, or the defence may present no evidence and argue that the government failed to meet its burden of proof beyond a reasonable doubt. Typically, the defence will present evidence at the close of the prosecution's case. The defence can cast doubt on the government's case-in-chief by seeking to undermine the credibility of the government's witnesses or by attacking the prosecution's logic. On the other hand, the defence may bypass a direct assault on the validity of the government's version of events and, instead, attempt to establish an affirmative defence. Whatever course the defence chooses, it is of equal importance that the defence construct its case in a manner that will humanize, as well as generate sympathy for, the defendant. Given the way the defendant is constructed in popular culture, this is not an easy task.

Like the prosecution's case, the defense's case is also a highly stylized and structured narrative. Witnesses for the defence are also carefully selected, and their testimonies are painstakingly rehearsed. But this preparation does not endow defence witnesses with the kind of credibility that prosecution witnesses have by virtue of association. Instead of working with the consensus, the defence must work against it. While public defenders would like to present attractive and sympathetic witnesses, this rarely occurs. Public defenders are constrained by the class position of their clients.

Furthermore, police officials will not ordinarily be available to testify in favour of a criminal defendant, or they will be reluctant to do so. Rarely will witnesses with equivalent high status, such as professionals and members of the clergy, be among a criminal defendant's social contacts.

It is more likely that the defendant's witnesses will be like the defendant - poor people, working class people, racial minorities, or members of the defendant's family. If the defendant is involved in criminal activity (which is often the case in criminal trials), or has been so in the past, then the defendant's witnesses will more often than not be tainted with a criminal past. This makes it all the easier for the prosecutor to impeach their testimonies.

The most unattractive witness in the defendant's case may be the defendant himself. Of course, the defendant need not testify, but that is a course that is itself fraught with danger. Jurors frequently wish to hear the defendant testify, if only to hear the defendant's denial of the charges from his own mouth. But whether the defendant testifies or not, the jury will silently evaluate his demeanor and appearance.

The defendant, the jurors will often be reminded, looks the way they would expect a criminal to look. It is the congruence of the defendant's image with the socially constructed image of the criminal that ultimately convicts. If the defendant is a "criminal," then, so the reasoning goes, he cannot be trusted, his defence is merely a scheme to evade justice, and he is certainly capable of all that which the prosecution accuses him.

Thus, as the defence presents its evidence, it must attend to the double duty of both contradicting the established, official story of the prosecution and lessening the negative socially constructed conceptions that jurors may already have of the defendant or of defendants in general. At the close of the defendant's case the prosecution has an opportunity for rebuttal. Thus, the prosecution has the opportunity for the last word at the presentation of evidence stage, as it does when opening statements are delivered to the jury. While the opportunity for surrebuttal is available to the defence, as a practical matter it is rarely invoked.

The prosecution also gets the last word at the argument stage of the trial. At argument, the parties may give their opinions of the evidence and attempt to persuade the jury as to how it should vote. The usual procedure at closing is for the prosecution to go first, followed by the defence, leaving the prosecution an opportunity for rebuttal.

Closing arguments are critical to the outcome of the trial. Often, at the conclusion of a trial, jurors are left with a mass of conflicting testimony and confusing instructions from the judge. Closing arguments can help the jury place this evidence in perspective and can supply common sense interpretations of arcane legal rules.

A good closing argument should tell a jury why it should vote a particular way and how it can do so. While a closing argument is not likely to persuade a jury to convict or acquit in the face of overwhelming evidence to the contrary, a closing argument may provide the margin of victory in a close case.

In a close case the prosecution has a distinct advantage. If confronted with two equally plausible stories, the jury will naturally gravitate toward the prosecution's version of events. The prosecution has the upper hand because its version is the one stamped with the authority of the state, and the jury has simply heard the prosecution's story earlier and with greater frequency than it has heard the point of view of the defence.

The closing argument is opinion, and the prosecutor's opinion is apt to have greater weight with the jury than the defense's opinion. To a jury, the prosecutor's argument is likely to appear more attractive. It implies that the system works, that the right suspect is in custody, and that the government is taking steps to reduce the threat that crime poses to the community at large. The defence, on the other hand, must rely on the discomforting contention that the system cannot be trusted to do anything about crime, and that, in this case, the government has arrested and prosecuted the wrong person.

Following closing arguments, the court instructs the jury on its deliberations about the case. The instructions tend to be worded in a technical and archaic prose that is hard for the uninitiated to comprehend or understand. Because jurors do not understand the very instructions that are supposed to guide them in carrying out their responsibilities, it is difficult for a defendant to receive the theoretical benefits of a trial by jury. Instead, jurors are more likely to fall back on common sense notions of crime - common sense notions that unavoidably favour the state.

Even when jurors do understand them, instructions are often slanted in favour of the prosecution. Sometimes this bias results from the legal rule or element that is addressed by the instruction which may itself favour the prosecution. On other occasions, however, bias occurs as a matter of emphasis - either in the words chosen to express the legal principle or how those words are delivered by the judge. As representatives of state authority, judges are more likely to sympathize with the prosecution, and their instructions to the jury are apt to reflect their pro-prosecution orientation. Rarely are judges pro-defence.

The requirement that the state prove its case beyond a reasonable doubt is often viewed as a heavy burden for the state to meet and a rigorous line of defence for the accused. In reality, it is neither.

First of all, it is notoriously difficult to arrive at a precise definition of what proof beyond a reasonable doubt is. Absent any meaningful direction from the court, jurors are at liberty to apply their own idiosyncratic views of the matter, which are likely to be at variance with the defendant's expectations. Moreover, no matter how the standard of proof might be interpreted, a number of evidentiary presumptions help the prosecution meet its burden of proof. Finally, and most importantly, jurors are generally reluctant to acquit defendants whom they believe to be guilty, although the state's evidence may be insufficient to erase all reasonable doubts. Thus, from the beginning to the end of the trial, the advantages lie decidedly in favour of the prosecution. The jurors come to the courthouse already biased in favour of the government. The prosecution gets the first opportunity to confront the jurors with its "official" view of reality. Throughout the trial, the defence must labour to contradict this established version of events, a version cloaked with the credibility of the state.

The prosecution has better resources at its disposal - more thorough investigation, more attractive witnesses, greater respect and deference from the judge. The trial even takes place in a venue that reinforces the state's prestige at the expense of the defendant. In the face of such concrete inequities, physical as well as psychological, the advantages supposedly conferred on the defendant by a mostly theoretical presumption of innocence and a seemingly high, but ephemeral, burden of proof are quickly overwhelmed.

The Trial in Context

The adversarial criminal trial, when examined in isolation, presents a majestic facade. Justice is served, it appears, because the state's accusation of crime is not taken for granted.

The government is first required to prove its case beyond a reasonable doubt before a jury of the defendant's peers. The defendant is given an opportunity to contest the government's charges and is provided with an attorney, if he cannot afford his own, to help make his case. In addition, the defendant is provided with a panoply of rights that regulate the trial process in a fair manner and protect the defendant from government overreaching.

But it is misleading to analyse the trial as a free-standing institution. A more revealing way to approach the trial is as it actually functions in its social context. That is, the trial must be viewed as the result of a semiotic process - a text - a medium through which the reader can signify, drawing on a long chain of significations that reach deep into the recesses of culture.

As text, the trial is the property of no one. All are free to signify through it. But all significations, all attempts to make meaning manifest, are constrained by he significations that have been produced before. Thus, the genealogy of significations - of things, ideas, and institutions - can be traced.

The criminal trial cannot stand apart from the images of crime that are at work in the popular culture. The very same process of signification that produces these images also produces the notions of justice, conceptions of rights, and patterns of rituals that make up the criminal trial.

That is, the trial is linked to a specific system of signification that is governed by particular themes and codes. These themes and codes structure all discourse, including the adversarial criminal trial, in ways that make some interpretations of meaning appear more appropriate and others less so. A general ideology or "consensus" arises from this interplay of structured meaning. Since the process of signification is dominated by powerful elites who can give their articulations wider circulation, a consensus is produced that vilifies the defendant while it glorifies social order.

The adversarial criminal trial is a social construction and, like any other social construction, it is made out of bits and pieces produced through the consensus. The consensus on crime structures the trial in ways that favour the prosecution. No matter what formal rights the defendant may have, in practice, procedures are adopted, rights interpreted, judgments made, and meaning determined in ways that disadvantage the defendant in the criminal trial.

Consequently, both judge and jury perceive the defendant negatively; jury instructions and court procedures are biased in the prosecution's favour; the Iegitimacy of the prosecution's case is reinforced by the authority of the state; and the prosecution's case is strengthened through repetition and strategic positioning at the beginning and end of the presentation of both argument and evidence. Through the working of the consensus, these disadvantages, and others, are made to seem "fair."

Consequently, the trial as "text" follows a tried and true formula. Upon reading the text, one can see that the criminal trial is not constructed in such a way as to match its formal signification as an institution of even-handed justice. The "rights" of the criminal defendant are not fully enforced, and as a result, the adversarial system is not all that adversarial. More importantly, no matter how secure a defendant's rights may be, the entire criminal justice system is permeated by an ideology that frustrates their realization. Within the structure that culture provides and the consensus shapes, the moral of the story told in the criminal courtroom - and the meaning of the allegory of the trial - is that the defendant is guilty and deserves to be punished.

The foregoing is not meant to suggest that the defendant is never capable of winning at trial. Instead, it is offered as a realistic assessment of the obstacles that stand in the way of acquittal and that create imbalance in the adversarial process. The possibility exists, of course, that an especially competent defence attorney may be able to overcome these obstacles, or that an inept prosecutor may fritter away the advantages that flow from representing the state. That defendants are disadvantaged by the adversarial trial process would be of little significance if their attorneys were in a position to reasonably compensate for the imbalance. In the next section, I ask whether public defenders are prepared to handle the extra burdens that the ideology of crime places on them in the adversarial process.

PUBLIC DEFENDERS: CREATURES OF THE CONSENSUS

The myth of criminal justice suggests that the state acts as a civilizing influence on the expression of public outrage about crime. It is assumed that the state, through its ordered system of criminal justice, prevents vigilante behaviour and mass tyranny. Justice is supposedly above culture and popular sentiments. Although culture may influence the criminal justice system, the state compensates for this by providing counsel and a protective regime of rights. Thus, whether the myth of criminal justice is truly a myth depends to a large extent on the effectiveness of counsel. Good legal representation may be able to help ameliorate the influence of negative cultural attitudes toward the defendant. In this section, I concentrate my analysis on the type of representation that the state provides to criminally charged indigents: public defenders. I focus on public defenders for a variety of reasons. First, they serve a vast majority of the nation's population. Second, in most cases they are professionals, devoting full-time service to indigent defence. Finally, as governmental agencies, public defender offices may be readily compared to prosecutor's offices.

Public defender agencies are a relatively recent addition to the criminal justice system. A public defender system may be defined as an organization "in which salaried lawyers devote all or a substantial part of their time to the specialized practice of representing indigent defendants." The first publicly supported, indigent defence programme was established by the city of Los Angeles in 1914. Public defenders did not become commonplace, however, until several decades later, in the 1940's and 1950's.

There is a great deal of diversity in the way that public defender offices are organized and structured. Most are organized at the local level and depend on local finances. In 1982, only 13 states operated public defender systems organized exclusively at the state level. Several states provide some support to local budgets, but the vast majority of public defender offices in the country are either part of county government or are organized by local trial courts.

Public defender systems should be distinguished from the two other major means of providing for the defence of indigents: assigned counsel systems and contract systems. Assigned counsel systems utilize private counsel, who are appointed as needed from a list of available attorneys. Assigned counsel programs are the most widely used form of indigent defence services. Contract systems rely on one or more private attorneys to provide indigent defence services, but these attorneys are not appointed on a case-by-case basis by the court. Instead, they provide representation pursuant to contractual arrangements with the appropriate state or local governmental entity.

Many public defenders are hard-working professionals who are committed to their work and concerned about their clients. This is not to say, however, that the typical public defender agency is sufficiently equipped to carry out its formal role as worthy adversary of the prosecution. Indeed, most public defender offices are vastly outgunned by the prosecution, in terms of both the tangible and intangible resources at their disposal.

Material Disparities

In comparison with other governmental expenditures, very little is spent on criminal justice programs, whether for prosecution, defence, police protection or the courts. No matter how inadequate support for criminal justice programs may be generally, funding for indigent defence is abysmally low. There is a great disparity between the level of support provided for indigent defence and that provided for the prosecution of crimes. In 1990, only slightly more than two per cent of all criminal justice expenditures nationwide was spent on indigent defence. By comparison, prosecution agencies received more than three times this amount. Virtually every public defender office in the country is vastly underfunded. Numerous studies have concluded that the level of support for indigent defence is entirely too low.

This low level of financial support translates into lower salaries, higher caseloads, and less secretarial and other basic support for public defenders than their prosecutorial counterparts receive. Because of low funding, public defenders may not be able to adequately prepare their cases for trial due to nonexistent or overburdened investigative services, inadequate libraries or insufficient office space. Dean Norman Lefstein spoke to the importance of the funding issue in a 1982 study he conducted for the American Bar Association. As Dean Lefstein succinctly put it:

Criminal defence services for the poor must be adequately funded in order for comprehensive and effective representation to be provided. Experience teaches that when funding is insufficient, some defendants are not represented at all, despite having a constitutional right to counsel. If representation is by public defenders, their numbers must be adequate to avoid excessive caseloads, and they must be paid salaries that are competitive with those earned by prosecutors and by lawyers in private practice.

Unfortunately, few jurisdictions have heeded Dean Lefstein's admonition. Salaries remain low, caseloads remain high, and, consequently, many clients of public defenders continue to receive less than adequate representation.

Generally, there is a considerable gap between the typical public defender's salary and that of the average prosecutor. For example, in Gainesville, Florida, the entry level salary for public defenders is $23,000. Entry level prosecutors earn $25,000. Prosecutorial duties in the District of Columbia are the responsibility of the U.S. Attorney for the District of Columbia. The starting salaries for beginning Assistant U.S. Attorneys is $47,670.

By comparison, attorneys at the Washington D.C. Public Defender Service with comparable experience earn only $39,048. Why these differences? Is the rationale that prosecuting is that much harder than defending, or that there is a need to attract better talent to prosecution offices, or that the market for prosecutors demands that they be paid more?

These assumptions can be justified only if one thinks that defence work is somehow less important than prosecutorial work. There is little reason why public defender salaries should be so much lower than prosecutors'.

The responsibilities of the individual line prosecutor are not substantially different from those of trial attorneys employed by public defender offices. For every investigative, research, or litigation task performed by prosecutors there is a substantially parallel task that must be performed by public defenders. The practical effect of the salary disparity between these positions is that it becomes more difficult for defender programs to attract talent.

Thus, indigent defence is left to those who cannot find other employment or to those ideologically committed individuals who can afford to forego the economic considerations of maintaining a middle-class lifestyle or supporting a family. It is not uncommon for many students who are interested in criminal litigation to choose to begin their careers at the state or district attorney's office rather than the public defender's office because the salaries offered by the public defender are too low.

Another problem with low salaries is that they make it difficult for the public defender to retain employees for the period of time necessary to develop expertise.

Consequently: where the salary is low the staff attorney is likely to be a young lawyer who will leave for a better job within two or three years, for example to join the staff of the prosecuting attorney. Like any other lawyer, the defender will usually do a better job of representation as he gains experience. But if the experienced lawyer is replaced by a beginner within a fairly short time, the quality of representation afforded the indigent is bound to be different from one year to the next.

After reviewing the low salaries present in the mid 1960's at the time of his report, Silverstein concluded that a large proportion of the reported salaries were not" career" salaries," even if one allows for differences in the cost of living and in a lawyer's income in communities of different sizes...."

If an insufficient number of attorneys is hired, then those present in the office will naturally have to labour under heavy caseloads. An excessive caseload is a frequently cited problem for public defenders; nonetheless, it remains pandemic in the defence of indigents.

Low funding also restricts the number of cases that receive pretrial investigation and the degree of investigation provided to those cases that are lucky enough to receive any investigation at all.

Misdemeanor cases suffer especially, but felony cases are also vulnerable, particularly if other, more complex or more serious cases are being tried at or around the same time. Inadequate investigation is a common occurrence for criminal trials. It is at this level that defenders and their clients are most at a disadvantage in comparison with the prosecution. The prosecution is usually able to avail itself of the comparatively well-funded and extensive investigative resources of the police.

Poor funding can also be made manifest in other, less dramatic ways. Often, public defenders are unable to obtain decent secretarial support. This means that, instead of concentrating on providing legal assistance to their clients, many public defenders must spend their time typing motions or handling other clerical duties. As a general rule, this of course means that the unsupported public defender will ultimately file fewer motions and less vigorously represent his or her client. In many offices, it is not uncommon for public defenders to have to furnish their own office supplies. Frequently, public defenders are forced to work in cramped, run-down quarters that make it difficult to interview clients in privacy or store files or other needed materials.

Systemic Disparities

To the extent public defenders lack independent and adequate funding, they remain subject to the whims of the funding sources they do have: typically county governments and courts of general jurisdiction. One of the most frequently raised critiques of public defender programs, from their proponents and detractors alike, is their lack of autonomy.

This lack of autonomy can manifest itself in two ways. First, lack of funding independence can have a chilling effect on the public defender agency's interest in providing vigorous representation.

Public defenders may be reluctant to undertake unpopular forms of representation that might jeopardize funding sources. After studying the operation of public defender offices in three jurisdictions, sociologists James Eisenstein and Herbert Jacob concluded:

Public defenders become adept at modifying office policy in anticipation of possible consequences and reactions of their governing boards.... They cannot forget that actions which disrupt the felony disposition process may generate opposition from the governing board and appropriating agencies. A public defender office that demands jury trials in all of its cases is likely to experience swift budget cuts and attacks on its personnel.

Second, outside funding sources may acquire direct or indirect control over a public defender's practices or policies by virtue of their control over finances. For example, if the court oversees the public defender's expert witness funds, then the court can exert influence over litigation strategy and policies by simply agreeing or not agreeing to allow expert witnesses to be used in certain cases. In a case that addressed whether public defenders acted" under colour of law" for purposes of permitting suit under 42 U.S.C. [sections] 1983, Justice Blackmun noted:

The county's control over the size of and funding for the public defender's office, as well as over the number of potential clients, effectively dictates the size of an individual attorney's caseload and influences substantially the amount of time the attorney is able to devote to each case. The public defender's discretion in handling individual cases - and therefore his ability to provide effective assistance to his clients - is circumscribed....

The lack of autonomy observed in the operation of most public defender offices implies a lack of adversariness or a failure on the part of the public defender agency to vigorously advance the interests of its clients. The more extreme version of this theory would condemn the public defender as a" police state" tactic simply because it is not believed possible for the state to both prosecute and purport to defend the accused at the same time.

A more widely held belief is that the institution of the public defender is a poor method for insuring the vigorous representation of the rights of indigents because the public defender's office cannot help but settle into a form of institutional entropy with the prosecuting agency that is its regular opponent. Because of the close cooperation between prosecutor's offices and public defender agencies, the reasoning goes, public defenders are conditioned to not make an issue of the morality of the police, the criminal justice process, or the courts. In exchange, the defendant's guilt is treated in a matter-of-fact fashion. What results is a criminal justice system that does not operate along ideological lines - such as due process ideals or retributionism - but instead functions as "a system of 'bureaucratic justice' - a system in which discretionary actions are governed by fairly rigid adherence to informal means and procedures designed to pigeonhole defendants into a few rough groupings with as few exceptions as possible."

Many observers have noted this tendency, but whether the alleged nonadversariness of public defenders actually harms their clients is a point of view that has been challenged. Most of the researchers who have studied the problem have failed to find any relationship between the fact that a defendant was represented by a public defender and the ultimate outcome of the case. But this could very well result from the fact that excellence in the provision of defence services is hard to quantify and that case outcomes may not provide the best measure of the quality of representation.

These findings may also be skewed by the fact that public defenders, by virtue of the numbers of cases they handle, may "lock in" all other practitioners. As Peter Nardulli described it, public defenders and other courtroom regulars (or "insiders") act "as creators and protectors of the status quo. In this view... insiders play a crucial role in the formulation and evaluation of norms which govern particular types of cases. Once established they affect cases involving both insiders and outsiders on a routine and systematic basis." The sad fact may be that - except for that rare criminal attorney who brings outside clout - the type of representation provided by the public defender, although deficient, may be typical.

Finally, although much insight may be gained from quantitative analyses of criminal justice processes, one should not expect too much from statistical depictions of reality. The limits of quantitative inquiry have been widely debated in the social sciences. Particularly in the case of criminal court research, one should be wary of focusing on case outcomes. Researchers, such as McIntyre, who conclude that social science research has discredited the claim that public defender clients receive less effective representation greatly overstate their case. The burdens that the typical public defender must labour under do have an effect, although one that may not be easily quantified. They would do well to remember that: discussions with criminal court veterans who have watched these changes unfold over the years reveal the salience of environmental factors for courthouse communities. Students of criminal courts who ignore them because they fail to have a "statistically significant effect" upon case outcomes do so at great peril and at great cost.

When we look at the criminal trial process in its larger context, the fact that there are glaring disparities between the public defender and the prosecution is inescapable. There are disparities in funding, salaries, resources, training, and physical facilities. These disparities cause or contribute to the way that public defender clients are disadvantaged vis-a-vis other criminal defendants and the state. While statistical evidence suggests that the claim that public defenders lack adversariness and autonomy is false, at best these data simply show that public defender clients do not fare any worse than do criminal defendants generally. Comparisons of case outcomes alone, then, cannot measure the ways that criminal defendants as a class are handicapped in their ability to contest the state's accusation of guilt.

The Symbolic Importance of Material and Systemic Disparities

To expose the way that defendants in general - and public defender clients in particular - are poorly equipped to compete for the hearts and minds of jurors in the adversarial arena of the criminal trial, it is helpful to consider how the material and systemic disparities discussed above work symbolically. What cultural values are implicit in the ways that criminal defendants are treated and what meaning can be extracted from the way that the role of the public defender is constructed?

Money takes on a central importance in this culture. It is not simply a matter of "getting what you pay for" (which presumes a sellers market), but it is also a matter of "paying what one thinks things are worth." When public defenders are offered salaries that are thirty per cent less than those offered to state's attorneys, obviously this signifies a belief that the services of public defenders are worth less than those provided by prosecutors. According to a commission charged by President Johnson to investigate the administration of justice in the nation's courts, low wages unavoidably impose a stigma of inferiority on the defence of the accused. If the status of the defence bar is to be upgraded and if able lawyers are to be attracted to criminal practice, it is undesirable to perpetuate a system in which representation for the poor seems to be obtained at a discount.

The lessened importance that the public attaches to providing defence services to indigents can be measured by the fact that over three times as much is spent to support prosecution agencies than is spent on all forms of indigent defence. If the prosecution and the defence were truly seen as evenly matched counterparts of one another, then the nation would not be spending a fraction of what it spends to prosecute crimes on the defence of crimes.

Nothing underscores this point more than the disparity in facilities and physical plant that is often a feature of public defender offices. The objective needs of the prosecution and the defence are pretty similar in respect to facilities. They both need offices with sufficient space for filing and support services to allow the attorneys to ply their trade with a sufficient amount of dignity. There is no particular reason why prosecutors would need larger or more modern offices or facilities that are more pleasing to the eye. Yet, in virtually every jurisdiction, there are readily observable differences in the quality of the work spaces afforded the prosecution and those afforded the defence. The commentary to the A.B.A. Standards for Criminal Justice points out why this discrepancy is harmful:

It is essential to the efficient operation of the defender programme that facilities be provided in which clients can be interviewed in privacy. Without offices and facilities befitting the nature of a lawyer's professional calling, the accused may very well lack confidence in the defender and, ultimately in the system of justice itself. Appropriate facilities are also necessary to attract and retain career personnel.

Where appropriate facilities are not provided, is this not an indication that society does not view public defenders as entitled to display "the dignity of the legal profession"? The fact that public defender offices are almost uniformly less desirable than prosecution buildings and workspaces may be taken as clear evidence of the public defender's lower prestige and authority.

The differences in salaries and work facilities that exist between defenders and prosecutors cannot be explained by differences in either the market conditions or the required functions of each job. Instead, these disparities are clearly representative of the opinion that the majority of society holds about the type of work that is done by public defenders and prosecutors. Whether public defenders can be conclusively shown to be less effective than other attorneys or not, "it is clear that those that represent the poor are not generally held in high esteem, either within the legal profession or outside of it." It is a commonplace observation that "a lack of respect and influence is a common characteristic of public defenders.

Within the courthouse, public defenders are at the end of the pecking order." The truth of this observation may be emphasized by the following comments made by a public defender in Chicago:

We are the gophers sic, we run for things. Whenever there's something the judge needs done, if there is not a clerk available, the judge gives it to the public defender and has him do it. They would never think of having a state's attorney do it. But public defenders have to do this silly stuff. The problem runs deeper than is demonstrated by the treatment public defenders may receive at the hands of autocratic judges. Public defenders are not perceived as "real" lawyers by the public, their peers, or by their clients. The professional life of public defenders is characterized by their attempts to cope with the deep stigma attached to the work that they do. Yet, the stigma is hard to escape. Even in Washington, D.C., which is serviced by what is arguably the country's best public defender organization, defendants often pass up representation by the public defender in favour of less-experienced and much more costly private defence lawyers. Trained professionals, who ought to know better, offer no greater support for public defender organizations. As the A.B.A. Special Committee on Criminal Justice in a Free Society concluded in its 1988 report, "the criminal justice system is shunned by the mainstream bar, and it will never be able to attract funds and public support if it cannot even garner the respect and support of the bar."

Considerations such as these have led many to conclude that "the pivotal concern" that led to the establishment of the public defender was not justice, but "judicial economy," or "efficiency, particularly as it affected the smooth flow of guilty pleas." Also, as Lisa McIntyre has pointed out, public defenders increase judicial legitimacy by encouraging public confidence in the administration of justice. Yet, neither of these rationales for the establishment of defender programs necessarily calls for a viable, wellfunctioning and adversarial enterprise. All that is needed to account for judicial economy and legitimacy is a public defender who appears competent, no matter how rough an appearance it may be. If the motivation for the creation of a public defender organization is anything less than supplying equal justice under law for its own sake, then a "paper tiger" public defender may be just as good as the real thing.

It is certainly true that if public defenders were more successful and "won consistently and often, their successes would undermine the legitimacy of the courts and ultimately jeopardize support for them." Indeed, the entire criminal justice system is premised on the expectation that defendants will be proven guilty and locked away. There is no room for the proposition that an adequately functioning criminal justice system might result in the release, without sanction, of a majority of those who have been charged with crime.

Of course, such a state of affairs might suggest that something is terribly wrong with the criminal justice system, something overlooked in the midst of the commonly heard anti-crime rhetoric. Such a situation might demonstrate that the state is intervening in the lives of too many of its citizens via unjustifiable arrests and prosecutions. However, this possibility is never seriously considered. It is easier, both politically and economically, to simply validate what the police and courts are doing by gutting the ability of the public defender to defend his or her client. In a society that excludes "criminals" from the consensus, and that, in fact, uses crime to shape the consensus, the inadequacies of public defenders appear normal.

DEFENDER GENERAL

Remedies and Ihe Importance of Reform

I have attempted to demonstrate that the mere identification of formal rights for criminal defendants does little to ensure a fair trial. Instead, as I have explained, the difficulty is external to the legal system and lies, rather, in the way that the community at large seeks to define crime and the type of justice to which criminal defendants are entitled. Because the disparity in the criminal justice system is culturally based, one could argue that it presents an unsolvable problem. The difficulty is that any attempts at reform are likely to be subverted by the very cultural processes that led to the imbalance in the adversary system in the first place. But this is a point of view that can lead to paralysis. Notwithstanding my broad critique of the criminal justice system, I feel compelled to offer something in the way of a concrete and pragmatic solution.

A factor favoring reform is that the process of signification is, in a sense, democratic; that is, the state or dominant social groups cannot monopolize the production of meaning. There is always room for alternative interpretations and resistant readings and recodings of texts. It is possible that, through disciplined and rigorous cultural work and the raising of consciousness, the allegorical meaning of the criminal trial could be changed, or at least contested.

Admittedly, the ostracism of the criminal (and the subsequent failure to take the rights of criminal defendants seriously) is a deep and pervasive problem that is not subject to easy, instrumental solutions.

However, the government can still be expected to do what it can to improve the adversarial process and, at the very least, prevented from taking actions that aggravate the situation. If the state were to take the role that the public defender plays in the adversarial process seriously, then perhaps the public would too.

The first step, then, to improve the adversarial criminal trial process is to infuse the criminal defendant's right to counsel with new meaning. Having argued that the problem lies outside of the formal legal structure and its collection of rights, it would seem to make little sense to retreat into the rhetoric of rights in order to resolve it.

Yet, that is what I propose to do here. While the designation of something as a "right" does not necessarily ensure justice, greater importance can be attached to how a "right" is interpreted, both by courts and by the broader culture.

The creation of rights and their subsequent treatment by the state can play a significant role in the shaping of the consensus, and this in turn can play a role in constructing the meaning that is attached to rights.

BEYOND ASYMMETRY

As I see it, the core of the problem with the adversarial system is the current imbalance in the degree of attention the government pays to the act of prosecution as opposed to its obligation to provide for the defence of citizens whom it accuses of crime. While it cannot be argued that prosecuting crime is one of the central concerns of government, there is no legitimate reason for the current excessive focus on prosecution at the expense of individual rights (other than illegitimate reasons of social control). If there is to be balance in the adversarial process, there must be balance in the role that the state plays within that system.

The state's commitment to prosecution is institutionalized in the office of the attorney general. At both the federal and state level, the attorney general is a high government official responsible for supervising the state apparatus for the prosecution of crimes, in addition to rendering formal legal opinions and advising government agencies.

The attorney general also has an important political role and may have significant input in the formation of national or state policy.

The federal Attorney General, often referred to as "the nation's chief law enforcement officer," has the greatest symbolic importance. The Attorney General for the United States heads the Department of Justice and is the fourth ranking member of the President's Cabinet.

The U.S. Attorney General provides legal advice to the President and the various executive and military departments of the U.S. government. Moreover, the Attorney General "has overall responsibility... for representing the United States in all state and federal courts." The duties of the Attorney General include the "supervision of United States Attorneys and other government counsel" in, inter alia, the investigation and prosecution of crimes against the United States.

In addition to these criminal litigation functions, the U.S. Attorney General is also charged with investigative authority, chiefly through the Federal Bureau of Investigation and the Drug Enforcement Administration.

While the commitment to the act of prosecution is institutionalized, the commitment to defence is haphazard. There is no defence counterpart to the Attorney General. Perhaps there should be. In addition to prosecuting crimes, the government also has an overriding duty to provide for the general public welfare.

In theory, this duty would require the government to expend as much effort on preventing erroneous convictions as it does on obtaining justified ones. Certainly, the governmental undercommitment to the defence function has deep symbolic import. What the public sees stamped with the authority of the state is the act of prosecution - this is what has allegorical power, and this is what skews the defendant's ability to obtain a fair trial in an adversarial context.

Conceptualizing a Federal Defender General

In order to balance the government's symbolic relationship to the criminal justice system, I would propose the creation of a "Defender General" at the federal level. Like the Attorney General, the federal Defender General would also be a high government official, although not necessarily a member of the President's Cabinet.

However, there are many differences in the way that cases are prosecuted and the way they are defended that would call for the Defender General's Office to be structured somewhat differently from that of the Attorney General.

First, there is no uniform system for the provision of defence services comparable to the network of U.S. Attorneys and local state prosecutors.

Secondly, although assuring that criminal defendant's receive the effective assistance of counsel is a governmental concern, the actual representation of criminal defendants is not primarily accomplished through the state's employees. Third, and most important, while all prosecutors theoretically represent the state, each defence counsel represents the unique interests of his or her own client.

Perhaps the Surgeon General would provide a better model for a Defender General than would the Attorney General as that office is presently conceived. The delivery of medical services is, quite possibly, even more fragmented and diversified than is the delivery of defence services. Although the Surgeon General does provide some direct medical care through the Public Health Service and its Commissioned Corps of doctors, most Americans receive their medical treatment from private physicians.

And, while government plays a substantial role in paying for the health care of many people, doctors, like defence lawyers, consider their primary duty to be to their patients, not the government.

Prior to the reorganization of the Executive Branch in 1966

the Surgeon General was responsible for the administration of the Public Health Service and the promulgation of "regulations necessary to the administration of the Service."

In addition, the Surgeon General was required by statute to "encourage, cooperate with, and render assistance to other appropriate public authorities, scientific institutions, and scientists in the conduct of... research... and studies relating to the causes, diagnosis, treatment, control, and prevention of physical and mental diseases."

In carrying out this responsibility, the Surgeon General was given broad authority, including the ability to issue publications, provide research facilities, maintain research fellowships, and "make grants in aid to universities, hospitals, laboratories, and other public or private institutions." Even though the Surgeon General no longer exercises the same authority, he is still recognized as the symbolic leader of the medical profession and, when it comes to health matters, continues to exert great influence.

A Defender General patterned after the Surgeon General (as the office was originally envisioned in the Public Health Act) could serve as the symbolic leader of the criminal defence bar and enable criminal defence lawyers to claim more prestige vis-a-vis the prosecution.

The Defender General could also serve as a source for necessary training and as a catalyst for improving the delivery of defence services.

By committing its resources to the establishment of a viable and vital Defender General Office, the government would be signaling the importance and significance of the right to counsel.

By improving the ability of criminal defendants to compete for the hearts and minds of jurors, the government would increase the chances that those accused of crime would receive a fair trial.

Thus, the federal Defender General I propose would have the following responsibilities:

- Give leadership and direction to the nation's criminal defence programs and practitioners.

- Contribute to the advancement of criminal defence techniques through research and clinical programs.
- Disseminate that knowledge to legal professionals and the general public.
- Assure the adequate training and personnel development of criminal defence practitioners.
- Improve the organization and delivery of defence services in the communities. In order to carry out these responsibilities, the Defender General would be empowered to make grants in aid to public defender organizations, law schools, universities and other public or private institutions; offer fellowships to promising or renowned defence attorneys; offer scholarships to deserving students in exchange for a commitment to practice criminal defence for an appropriate time; retain experts, scholars and consultants; issue publications; and provide technical advice and assistance to appropriate public and other nonprofit organizations and institutions.

Obviously, many details remain to be worked out before a federal Defender General could ever become a reality - such as whether the Defender General should be a part of the Justice Department, the Department of Health and Human Services, or an independent agency in the judicial branch.

But what is important about the concept of the Defender General is the idea of committing the state to the provision of defence services in a way that parallels the government's commitment to the act of prosecution. By committing the government to the defence of accused persons in such a concrete and substantial way, the Defender General would make an important symbolic statement.

It would teach respect for individual rights and infuse the presumption of innocence with real meaning. A Defender General would help make the right to a fair trial and the right to adequate counsel more than just empty promises. As a result, this country would go a long way toward making the myth of criminal justice a reality. The functioning of the adversarial criminal trial cannot be determined solely by reference to the ideals that are set forth in the Constitution, the mandates found in statutes, or the guarantees that are promised in court opinions. The adversarial trial takes its real meaning from the culture from which it springs, after it has been worked and reworked by the play of semiotic processes.

The adversary system has been socially constructed so that its requirements may be easily met by the provision of an overburdened and undertrained public defender, who has a scant chance of providing his or her client with a fair trial. If the trial is to be made more than a simple way station on the road to a sure conviction, then public defenders must be given the ability to contest the government's case from a position of equality. To facilitate the task of re-envisioning and reconstructing the allegory of the criminal trial, the state must afford the defence the same dignity and resources that it affords the prosecution.

Chapter 4

Politics on the Couch

The intention is to test and explore the boundaries that exist (we have been told) between therapy and politics, between the inner world and the outer world, between being and doing, and even between what people still call "feminine" approaches to life and "masculine" approaches to life-no matter how problematic those words are.

This paper is divided into a number of sections. It begins by addressing the questions, Why me? Why here? Why now? Then there follows a discussion of how, particularly after the 2004 U. S. presidential election, politics in the West can be understood as changing in the direction of what I call "transformative politics." Third, the question, "Can therapists really make a difference in the world today?" is asked. Fourth is a markedly experiential section entitled "The Inner Politician." I conclude with a few reflections on therapy, politics, and spirituality.

Introduction: Why Me, Why Here, Why Now?

The bases for these remarks, which are grounded in clinical work with individuals, also lie in my involvement with a number of political organizations and recent political developments. I have carried out consultations and conducted workshops in Britain, Europe, the United States, Japan, Brazil, Israel, Australia, New Zealand, and South Africa. These activities are designed to see how useful and effective perspectives derived from psychotherapy may be in forming policy, in creating new ways of thinking about the political process, and in resolving conflict. It is difficult to present therapy thinking so that mainstream politicians-for example, a senior U. S. Democrat senator or a British Labour Party committee-will take it seriously. And the problem is only slightly reduced when the politicians and organizations are alternative or activist.

I have also been involved in the formation of three organizations in Britain that are relevant to the themes of the paper. One is Psychotherapists and Counselors for Social Responsibility, an organization intended to help therapists and counselors use their knowledge and experience to intervene as professionals in social and political matters. The second organization is Antidote, a psychotherapy-based think tank cofounded with Susie Orbach.

It fosters multidisciplinary work, and links are sought with people working in fields other than psychotherapy. Antidote has undertaken research into psychological attitudes toward money and economic issues and is also involved in trying to apply ideas about emotional literacy/intelligence to politics.

The third organization is called the St. James's Alliance. Based at a beautiful Wren church in Piccadilly in central London, it consists of individuals from diverse fields such as politics, economics, ethics, religion, nongovernmental organizations, activist and pressure groups, the media, and psychotherapy.

It attempts to incorporate psychological, ethical, and spiritual concerns into the political agenda and to facilitate dialogue between various single-issue and pressure groups.

In the past, these groups were unsympathetic to other groups' goals-poverty workers did not have time for animal rights activists, for instance, and neither group seemed interested in the problems of the Middle East.

But in a suitably facilitated environment, it has been possible to find whole areas of common ground in relation to politics, and there are so many emotional and spiritual similarities to share. This is an experiment in gathering and using the shards of political energy that are normally split up and dissipated. Politics in many Western countries is broken and in a mess; we urgently need new ideas and approaches.

Psychotherapists, along with economists, social scientists, religious people, environmentalists, and others, can contribute to a general transformation of politics.

Today's politicians leave many with a sense of deep despair and disgust. They seem to lack integrity, imagination, and new ideas. Across the globe, and in response to the challenge, a search is on to remodel politics. Psychotherapy's contribution to this search depends on opening a two-way street between inner realities and the world of politics. We need to balance attempts to understand the secret politics of the inner world of emotional, personal, and family experiences with the secret psychology of pressing outer-world matters such as leadership, the economy, environmentalism, nationalism, and war.

Our inner worlds and our private lives reel from the impact of policy decisions and the existing political culture. Why, then, do our policy committees and commissions not have psychotherapists sitting on them as part of a range of experts/This is not a call for a committee of therapists, but just as a committee will often have a statistician present (someone whose role may not be fully appreciated by the other members), there should also be a therapist at the conference table. We expect to find therapists offering views on social issues that involve personal and familial relationships or matters to do with mental health but they may also have ideas to contribute on the" hard" issues-war, violence, poverty, and the economy.

Is it possible to imagine a world in which people are encouraged to sharpen their half-thought-out, intuitive political ideas and commitments so as to take more effective political action? There are probably buried sources of political wisdom in many people, particularly those who do not seem likely to function in such a way. More and more, I have come to see that one does not have to be politically active or knowledgeable and talkative about politics to have something creative to say. Poets and mystics, introverts, those who eschew politics, and those who are ashamed at what they take to be their own ignorance often know something that the more overtly political do not. These anti-political citizens are a great aid in finding out how secret thingschildhood experiences, intimate relationships, fantasies (including sexual fantasies), dreams, and bodily sensations-may be reframed and turned to useful political ends.

Thinking about those who usually do not say much, I find that they make a profound contribution to what I call" political clinics." These are large-group events, often composed of persons who have nothing to do with therapy and psychology at all but come together to explore their emotional and feeling-based reactions to major political themes such as terrorism, the troubles in Northern Ireland, the conflict in the Middle East, racism, and homelessness.

I have discovered that those who say" I am not interested in politics" are often deceiving themselves, caught in a reaction formation. As the political clinic unfolds, it becomes clear that they are indeed extremely interested, knowledgeable, and wise about politics but have always doubted, because they have been taught to doubt, that the emotional reactions they are experiencing are a legitimate part of political process. We are taught, in the Western countries, not to deny that we have emotions about politics, because that would be impossible, but to put those emotions rather low on the scale of what we value in official political debate and political discussion.

Sometimes at the conclusion of these political clinics, we start to talk in terms of citizens as" therapists of the world" who have a large set of usable countertransferences to the political cultures in which they live. This idea constitutes an intellectual challenge to much psychological theorizing about citizens, especially in psychoanalysis, wherein the citizen is regarded as a kind of baby, who has a transference and a collection of fantasies toward the" parental" society in which he or she lives. Turning that around, so that the citizen is seen as a kind of therapist or parent figure for the society can have a radical, uplifting, and empowering effect, overturning the tradition-especially in psychoanalysis-in which the citizen is seen as the baby and society as the parent. This claim, that the citizen is capable of being the therapist (parent) of the world, is one that embodies many possibilities as we struggle to work out what functions citizens might perform in a society in which their voices are distorted by the mass media, and their internal lives unfold in a highly fraught political climate dominated by corporations and cartels.

TRANSFORMATIVE POLITICS

Politics is slowly changing in Western countries, and we are at a very interesting moment in political consciousness. What used to be an elitist insight about how everything is secretly political is now becoming an element in mass awareness. For years now, feminists, academics, intellectuals, and some therapists and analysts have lived happily with the idea that our personal, psychological, and private worlds are full of political tensions, dynamics, and energies. But actually this has been a superior form of knowing, a political gnosticism.

We knew that politics has expanded its definition to include all of the private stuff, but the masses did not. They have continued to be taught (but many now accept it less) that politics means official politics, party politics, congressional or parliamentary politics, power politics, the politics that money can buy, and so on. What helped to accelerate the democratization of the personal-is-political insight were the huge eruptions of feelings about certain events or political trends in recent years, turning those events into what can be called archetypal or at least numinous experiences: I am thinking of disparate phenomena, ranging from grief at the death of Princess Diana, to global anger at the role of the United States in world politics, to intense debates about the role of women in societies across the planet.

The most ruthlessly successful contemporary politicians (such as Tony Blair) have perceived this move into general awareness of the elitist, gnostic, private knowledge about how politics has changed, and they now couch their utterances in the language of the emotions.

Another way in which politics has changed is that it has become more of a transformative process. By this I mean that engagement in political activity and processes of personal growth and development are seen increasingly as the same thing, or at least as the two sides of a coin.

If one interviews persons active in post-Seattle politics, in the environmental movements, in certain sectors of feminism or the men's movement, or in ethnopolitics, one sees that what they are doing is in many respects self-healing in a positive sense that is familiar to psychotherapists. So politics starts to carry an overtly psychological, transformative burden. Sadly, this kind of transformative politics is not only progressive and left leaning, but it can also be spotted in many right-wing and reactionary movements, as the recent election showed.

A third way in which politics has changed is that there is now something that can be called" political energy" to be considered along with political power. Political power is what you would imagine it to be: control over resources such as land, water, oil-or indeed, information and imagery.

Especially today, the issue of who controls information and imagery (e.g., on the Internet and on television) is almost as important as the issue of who controls oil or water. Political power is held by those you would expect to hold it: men, white people, the middle and upper-middle classes, and those who run the big institutions of finance, the military, and the academic and professional worlds, including the world of mental health.

Political energy is different. It is almost the opposite of political power. Political energy involves idealism and an imaginative and visionary focus on certain political problems with a view to making a creative impact on those problems (not necessarily with the goal of solving them).

Political energy seeks more political energy, attempting to build to critical mass. It is different from political power because those who have political energy, imagination, commitment, idealism, and real compassion almost by definition lack political power.

Conversely, in contemporary societies, those who have political power tend to lack political energy. This is a fundamental and radical claim that I am sure will be much disputed. Indeed, the very idea of political energy will upset some intellectual applecarts, because most analysts cannot entertain this notion. In their view, energy does not exist; it is only a mechanistic 19th-century way of looking at things. But there seems to be a possible middle position in which energy, in the sense of psychic energy, is maintained both to exist and not to exist.

Jung suggested that, contra Freud's conception of libido, there is a neutral form of psychic energy that can run down various biological, psychological, spiritual, and moral channels. My proposal is that there is also a social channel and that a subset of the social channel will have to do with politics and political energy. As indicated just now, I use the term energy in both a metaphorical and a literal sense.

Jung's idea that there is a specifically moral channel for psychic energy is extremely interesting, resonating with much evolutionary, ethological, genetic, and psychoanalytic thought-Klein's idea of an innate superego, Winnicott's insistence that children have an inborn sense of guilt and hence are not born amoral, Milner's counsel that we stop seeing morality solely as something implanted in children by parents and society. Freud foreshadowed this train of thought with his remarks about the innate disposition of the self-preservation instincts to become more socially oriented.

People with political energy are doing something rather new and different in the Western world today in comparison with what those who have political power are doing. This thought can be liberatory if you are working in a small neighborhood group, in a social and political project with limited resources and support, or with people who have been abused, or if you are trying to build an environmentally informed movement for sustainable development and worldwide economic justice. If you are doing any or all of these things, then you probably do not have much power and it is very easy to judge yourself the way that the conventional political world might judge you-as a waste of time and space when it comes to real politics.

But the very notion of political energy is intended to shift this way of thinking. Very often when I talk about this, people say (as they did for example, at a conference in BeIo Horizonte, Brazil), "Yes, and we wonder what would happen if our country valued political energy as much as it values political power."

If political energy is not to be found in the sites of official politics, then where may we find it? Politics has left its home base and gone out into the world to redefine itself and find other and new places to settle.

I am not advocating removing political energy from moribund formal institutions; this has been happening in Western societies anyway over many years in one of the most significant sociocultural and collective psychological shifts to take place in the developed countries since the end of World War II.

A striking feature of the past 20 years in such societies has been the spontaneous growth of new social and cultural networks. More and more people are now involved in such networks, increasingly aware that what they are doing may be regarded as political.

The contemporary elasticity in our definition of politics is not something that has been worked out by intellectuals. Nor has there been a concerted effort to achieve such a shift, because the new social movements operate in isolation from each other.

Yet, as we have found in the St. James's Alliance discussed previously, they have something psychological in common. They share an emotional rejection of big politics-its pomposity and self-interest, its mendacity and complacency.

They share a Weltanschauung and set of values based on ideas of living intelligible and purposeful lives in spite of the massive social and financial forces that work against intelligibility and purpose.

Such new social changes include environmentalism; the formation of groups working for the rights of ethnic and sexual minorities, animal liberation, complementary medicine; spiritual and religious groups devoted to paganism and neo-paganism; rock and other kinds of music and art; finding God in the new physics; an explosive growth in the participation in sports; organic farming-and psychoanalysis, psychotherapy, and counseling.

Elsewhere, I referred to the social movements as participating in a "resacralization" of politics. Sacral means holy, and the intent was to pick up on the attempt to get a sense of purpose, decency, aspiration, and meaning back into political culture. When I consider attempts by analysts and psychotherapists to do their bit, I have no alternative but to count us as part of this general, worldwide resacralizing movement.

Psychotherapists may want to be different and special, but in our attempts to work the borders between psychotherapy and society, we are part of something bigger, even if the rhetoric sometimes feels too New Agey. Psychotherapists tend to share with other resacralizers a sense of disgust with present politics and politicians. In political clinics, this is often an actual physical disgust involving the gagging reflex, an ancient part of the nervous system that is absolutely necessary for survival in a world full of tangible and metaphorical toxins.

Let me conclude this section by accepting that a transformation of politics is not going to happen in any kind of simple or speedy way and may not happen at all. There is an impossibility to the whole project because the social realm is as inherently uncontrollable as the drives and images of the inner world and the unconscious. Once human desire enters a social system-as it always will-that system cannot function predictably. There are no final solutions to social questions. The social issues that face Western societies are as incorrigible, as unresponsive to treatment, as the psychological issues that individuals face.

Moreover, many will dispute that the cumulative public significances of these movements is positive. It can be argued that the proliferation of new networks and cultural practices is merely a further symptom of social malaise-a selfish retreat into personal, individual preoccupations, reflecting an abandonment of the aspiration to truly political values. It can also be pointed out that reactionary, fundamentalist, religious movements can be seen as attempting, in their own rather different terms, a form of resacralization. But what gets highlighted when religious fundamentalism is brought into the picture is the vastness of the energy pool available for the political reforms that are urgently needed.

Although I am enthusiastic about psychotherapy's role in the refreshing of political culture, I am also somewhat skeptical. So my answer to the question "Can therapists really make a difference?" is both "No" and "Yes." Let's deal with "No" first-with the pessimism. James Hillman and Michael Ventura wrote a book called We've Had a Hundred Years of Psychotherapy-and the World's Getting Worse. It is fairly clear what they were getting at-that psychotherapy makes little or no impact on an unjust world and that persons in therapy are cut off from taking responsibility for ameliorating injustice (cut off from their political energy by therapy, which takes all available psychic energy for its own project of personal exploration).

Yet I think that a much more accurate title for their book would have been We've Had a Hundred Years of Psychotherapy, Trying to Improve the World, But the World Has Stayed Pretty Much the Same, because it is not new for psychotherapists to want to do something in relation to the world. Freud wanted it, Jung wanted it, and the great pioneers of humanistic psychotherapy-such as Maslow, Rogers, and Peris-all wanted it as well. All of these people and their followers invited the world into therapy, but the world didn't show up for its first therapy session.

There are good reasons why the world didn't show up, other than mere resistance. One reason is that therapists so much want and need to be right. (Me, too-this shadow issue of the analyst's maddening rectitude is not one I pretend to have fully dealt with.) Therapists want to reduce everything to the special knowledge that they have. This kind of reductionism gives therapy a bad name when it comes to political and social issues. For example, I remember reading in the London Guardian an article-later the object of intense ridicule-by a Kleinian psychoanalyst about the phallic symbolism of cruise missiles going down ventilator shafts in Baghdad.

My Jungian colleagues are just as bad when they tell us that the military-industrial complex is all the responsibility of the Greek God Hephaestos. The world won't listen to that level of explanation from psychotherapists and is right not to. The priority for psychotherapists is to embark on multidisciplinary work.

But other issues besides therapy reductionism have stopped us from being useful outside a few specific areas such as psychoanalytically influenced social casework or, in some countries, child welfare legislation. Overall, there is a fairly bad record to own up to. Psychotherapists have colluded with oppressive regimes in Nazi Germany, the former Soviet Union, Argentina, and South Africa.

We have been involved in dubious activities such as sending soldiers suffering from shell shock and battle fatigue back to the line of battle in both world wars. There is also the ever-present collusion of many psychotherapists with all manner of normative and oppressive practices, ranging from the psychopathological stigmatization of lesbians and gay men.

And therapists all over the world easily join in right-wing politicians' attacks on father-lacking lone-parent families. According to the right-wing reading, these families-totally responsible for spoiling our wonderful world, only need a father or father figure to come back and sort them out. I love fathers and was one of the first to write about what good-enough fathers actually do, especially with their bodies, to further the sexual, aggressive, and spiritual development of their children.

But I utterly loathe the damaging idealization of fathers that so many Western politicians have gone in for, backed by complacent analysts, therapists, and other mental health professionals.

Then there is the problematic matter of psychotherapy's implicit claim that Western androcentric, middle-class values and ways of thinking hold and have value universally and are superior to/should be imposed on the values and ways of thinking of non-Western cultures.

Clearly, these unspoken assumptions reflect the typical caseloads of analysts and therapists, especially in private practice, in many countries. The treatment of women in much psychoanalytic thinking and practice has also been damaging to some. The rise of feminist and gender-sensitive psychotherapy has had an important impact in ameliorating this situation. And what a lot of therapists and analysts say about men is also beginning to receive the same kind of critique that definitions of and generalizations about women used to receive.

Another reason why people are not so likely to listen to therapists who want to make a difference in the world is that therapists are completely crazy in their own professional politics, and the way they organize themselves radiates that craziness. No profession has been quite as subject to splits as the therapy profession; no profession has so frequently used personal demonization and pathological pigeonholing to deal with and get rid of troublesome outsiders and those who question from within.

As I continue to look at why we world-oriented therapists do not have a client, I note that-for reasons I do not fully understand even now-the therapy world has tragically split its clinical project off from its sociocritical project. Frankfurt school writers and Lacanian theorists rarely talk of clients, or in an ordinary way about people: mothers, fathers, families, marriages, dreams, symptoms, sexuality, aggression, the inner world of the imagination. And when we read most clinical texts, the external world is hardly mentioned. Much therapy still seems (or claims) to take place in a political vacuum.

There are several delusional aspects of this virginal fantasy about what we do. One delusion is that there are no politics going on the session itself, whereas many clinicians know how the power dynamics and imbalances of the typical therapy setup cannot be wished away by reference to parental transference or the law of the father. These power imbalances often involve the denial of difference of any kind between therapist and client, the bending of the client to the moral will of the therapist, and the ongoing scandal of sexual misconduct.

Another delusion is that it is not possible to find a responsible way to work directly with political, social, and cultural material in the clinical session. There is not sufficient space here for a full discussion of this topic. Succinctly, my position is that it is time to think together about how we can change our practices and our thinking about clinical work in order to incorporate these taboo themes.

To explore empirically what has been happening at the interface of psychotherapy and politics in the actual session, I surveyed 2000 analysts and therapists of many schools worldwide about which political issues their clients mentioned in therapy, how frequently the clients raised such issues, whether such mentions were increasing or decreasing, and how the therapists reacted.

Approximately 700 responded: I also asked the respondents about their own political views and histories. The survey revealed that the therapy profession is far more politically sensitive than one would think, and that politics is a welcome theme in a significant minority of clinical offices.

It underlined the importance of shopping around for and interviewing a potential analyst or therapist. The answers to the questions about which political and social issues are raised also made it clear that clients are raising economic, environmental, and gender-political issues (including issues that do not seem to affect them personally) in their therapy sessions much more than they used to.

The respondents clearly wanted to honour and respond to this development, but almost all admitted that they lacked training, helpful texts, and general encouragement to do it on a regular, professional, reputable basis. In fact, many felt that it would be regarded as bad practice even though they wanted very much to engage more expertly with such material when clients bring it to the session.

There is a big difference between a mutual exploration of some huge external event that has dominated everyone's lives (such as the terrorist attacks on September 11, 2001) and struggling to develop ongoing, ordinary ways of working in the session with the client's political selfhood (and that of the therapist) as it has evolved over a lifetime.

Though it can be a fascinating and important moment in any therapy, responding to the impact on the analysis of a moment of high political drama that has affected everyone is not the same as extending what we regard as contemporary good practice to include all aspects of work on the political dimensions of experience.

For example, the Psychoanalytic Dialogues symposium entitled "Reflections on September 11, 2001" (2003, 13/3), though moving, and insightful, did not refer to an ongoing need to develop clinical principles by which to explore the transformative aspects of what I call political discussion within the sealed vessel of an ordinary therapy relationship.

Such work might include (but not be restricted to) the following:

- Exploration of the role played by the joint immersion in the social order on the part of analyst and client in making relationality possible in the first place, whether at a conscious level or at that of unconscious-to-unconscious communication: citizenship facilitating countertransference;
- Considering the functioning of nonpersonal fields that cause distress in individuals who are not personally affected-for example, economic injustice, species depletion, domestic violence (my experience being that the strongest imaginable affects, disturbances in self-image, and psychological conditions-such as depression-involve etiologies at least partly rooted in such nonpersonal fields); and
- Refining technique so as to work out ways of managing states in the analyst that are difficult to manage due to the presence of political viewpoints in the client that feel offensive, upsetting, or disagreeable to the analyst (we all work with people whom we sometimes find unpleasant, and we can build on this capacity so as to encompass our

responses to what we find personally unpleasant in the political positions held by the client).

The Inner Politician

Where did your own politics originate? I think this is a question worth asking. What influence did your mother have on the politics you now have? Or your father? And what about differences between your parents in political outlook? Some people have been influenced in their political development by significant others in their lives, such as teachers, clergy, older friends at school.

Were you? Your gender is really very significant in the kind of attitude to politics that you have, and your sexual orientation is equally important. Lesbians and gay men live more closely to the political aspects and nuances of life than straight people do. Class and socioeconomic factors are obviously central, too, and so is ethnic, religious, and national background. In Western societies, the feeling of being oppressed by a domestic tyrant, whether male or female, or of seeing other family members as oppressed, can give rise to a sharp sense of injustice and embryonic revolutionary feelings.

Sometimes when I talk to people about what has formed their politics, they start to speak about an event or moment that they remember-their first political memory, the first time they became aware that there is a political system with power at its core, including disparities of wealth and influence. Did you explore these first political memories with your own analyst?

Another way to look at the notion of the inner politician is to imagine a political energy scale on which ten stands for political fanaticism, even martyrdom, and zero stands for absolute passivity, a total lack of interest in politics. Where would you place yourself right now in your life-what level of political energy do you have? Play around with the scale. When you're with people of the same sex, does the energy level go up or down or stay the same?

Is it higher at home or at work? Are there some issues

that send it skyrocketing and some that bring it down? Think of the last big interpersonal disagreement or fight with someone you love. Could it be that there was a different level of political energy at work in each of you?

Let's take this thinking right into the traditional heartland of psychotherapy. What was your mother's level of political energy compared with yours, or with your father's? What was your level compared with the typical level of those from the street or neighborhood where you grew up? Continuing to sketch the inner politician, I come to the question of political style. I have noticed in my conflict resolution work that those in conflict are often operating not only with very different levels of political energy, but also with very different political styles. Hence, in my work as a political consultant, I am using the idea of conflicting political styles in many settings.

My inspiration in overall terms was Jung's model of psychological types: extroversion, introversion, thinking, feeling, sensation, intuition. As in life generally, for a variety of reasons (some having to do with personal backgrounds, some with inborn political constitutions), people live out the political aspects of themselves in different ways. Some are violent terrorists; some are pacifists.

Some want empirical backup for their ideas; others prefer to fly by the seat of their pants. Some definitely enjoy cooperative political activity; others will suffer the nightmare of working in a group only because they passionately believe in the ends being pursued. As we begin to work out a psychologically driven transformative politics, let us not make the mistake of insisting that everyone do it in precisely the same way.

If we are to promote political creativity, we need to value and honour diverse political styles and types, and to think of ways of protecting such diversity. (I am indebted to Muriel Dimen [personal communication] for the observation that political style and self-state have something in common as approaches to the diversity of personality.)

As I mentioned, the notion of political style is useful when addressing conflict, whether interpersonal or within organizations or even between nations or parts of nations. Just as introverts and extroverts suffer from mutual incomprehension, persons who employ a particular political style often have very little understanding of how other persons or groups are actually doing their politics. This is not to say that political content per se is irrelevant, only that there may be more that divides opponents than their different views.

One might list words that evoke images of differing political types as follows, in a spectrum ranging from active styles to passive ones: warrior, terrorist, exhibitionist, leader, activist, parent, follower, child, martyr, victim, trickster, healer, analyst, negotiator, bridge builder, diplomat, philosopher, mystic, ostrich.

When working on questions of political style, it is not necessary to encourage anyone to stick to just one style. In fact, the opposite is true. The context in which the politics in question is taking place needs to be borne in mind. Some people will use one political style in one setting and quite another in a different one. A negotiator at work may be a terrorist at home. Some may have a superior political style, an inferior political style, and auxiliary styles, to borrow the words of Jimg's typological schema. Thus, a warrior may have neglected her philosopher or a diplomat his activist.

This approach was partially fashioned on the basis of my work with a mixed group of Israeli Arabs and Israelis of Jewish background in Jerusalem in the early 1990s. It became clear that, aside from the obvious irreconcilable differences in how the Middle East political scene was understood, there were individuals on both sides of the divide who were participating in the group in very similar or identical ways.

I pointed this out and reorganized the spatiality and seating plan of the group along style lines rather than content lines. There were discernible improvements in comprehension, and even, to a limited extent, in goodwill. The warring factions were presented not with an analysis of what they were saying (that came later), but with a panorama of the ways in which they were saying it-that is to say, with the style of politics they were using.

I have also found the same approach useful in addressing organizational and theoretical disputes in the psychotherapy field and, most recently, in work with senior administrators in Britain's beleaguered National Health Service.

Psychotherapy, Politics, and Spirituality

Attempts are constantly made to improve things in the political world, usually by redistributing wealth or changing legislative and constitutional structures or defusing warlike situations. It is not that nothing is being tried to make things better. Equally vigorous attempts are made to resist and to contest such changes, and most social systems have a gigantic, impersonal capacity to resist change anyway.

But projects of reform are valuable and necessary and generate their own psychological changes. For example, the consequences of fair and effective minimum wage legislation or devolving power to the regions of a country or amending the constitution would have effects that would show up on any national emotional audit.

But a materialist approach deriving exclusively from economics, or one that depends solely on altering the structures of the state, will not refresh those parts of the individual citizen that a psychological perspective can reach.

Our disappointment at liberal democracy's failure to deliver the spiritual goods and our growing realization that there are limits to what can be achieved by economic redistribution or altering constitutional structures strengthen my overall argument: something is missing in contemporary Western politics, something that involves a calamitous denial of the secret life at its core. We can change the clothes and shift the pieces around, but the specter that haunts materialist and constitutional moves in the political world is that they only ruffle the surface. They do not (because-alone-they cannot) bring about the transformations for which the political soul yearns.

The perspectives advocated here may never, ever be applied to our political culture. Everything psychotherapists and analysts have said or done may fail to make one iota of difference in the condition of the world. So I conclude with a few words about failure by Samuel Beckett, who lived and struggled as intensely as anyone with what it might mean to be a good-enough citizen, involving a profound acceptance of the need to go on in the face of not being able to go on: "No matter. Fail again. Fail better."

Chapter 5

Gestural Politics: Civil Society

The study of civil society in Singapore is an academic field attracting significant interest and analysis. It is commonly recognized as an important element in a vibrant and innovative society. Citizen participation in the policy process also plays a crucial role in a modern knowledge-based economy.

Authoritarianism under the PAP People's Action Party has never prevented social organization per se, including the conditional existence of autonomous groups not threatening to the PAP. In fact, at times the PAP has actively but selectively encouraged social organization as a way of embedding the regime.

In early 2005, E. Kay Gillis published a monograph entitled Singapore Civil Society and British Power, tracing the "history" of civil society by investigating "associational activity" in Singapore from 1819 to 1963, or during the era of British power and rule. Gillis found through her research that civil society in Singapore had been strong and effective throughout the period, despite the fact that the British regime was seen as authoritarian, demonstrating that civil society can exist outside a liberal democratic context.

In fact, Gillis argues that civil society, marked by open and autonomous citizen participation in the policy process, played a crucial role in the movement towards the nation's independence. (Others, however, question the existence of contemporary notions of civil society before the formation of the Singapore nation-state). According to Gillis, although civil society started to dismantle during the final period of British rule, it was the then newly elected PAP government's "introduction of domestic restrictive policies on the grounds that the survival of Singapore was at stake" that brought civil society to its lowest ebb.

Although Singapore has since not only survived but prospered economically under the control and rule of the PAP, many of these restrictive—and arguably, repressive—policies continue to affect the cultivation of civil society in contemporary Singapore. Singapore's brand of authoritarianism, one of the more dubious reasons for its remarkable success over the past four decades, has been characterized by both legal and "extra-legal" limits to independent social and political activities.

While legal limits would include somewhat repressive and political laws such as the Internal Security Act (ISA) and the Societies Act of 1968, the application of what I would call "extra-legal" strategies are far broader. These include, inter alia, "extensive mechanisms of political co-option to channel contention through state-controlled institutions", the creation of quasi-opposition in parliament via the Nominated Member of Parliament (NMP) scheme, as well as the ambiguously framed yet enduring discourse of out-of-bounds markers (or "OB markers"), an important element in our study of civil society in Singapore which will be deliberated in this paper.

The encroachment of the state into many facets of everyday life led to calls, particularly by the newly emerging middle-class Singaporeans, for greater liberalization of the cultural sphere. As a consequence, interests in civil society—both in socio-cultural and political terms—were rekindled from the mid-1980s onwards, though not much happened until the early 1990s. In November 1990, Singapore witnessed its first "changing of the guard" when Goh Chok Tong became the country's second Prime Minister. Upon taking up his new position, Prime Minister Goh declared his intention to embrace a more open, consultative, and consensual leadership style.

To many observers, this meant that Singapore was on course for a less authoritarian mode of rule, which translated to a more participatory form of democracy, and one that would appear to be more sympathetic and welcoming to civil society. The reality, however, was starker than envisaged. While the 1990s saw a revival of interest in the concept of civil society in Singapore, it was also the decade that led to the entrenchment of "OB markers", a golfing terminology that is intended to demarcate the parameters of political debate and thus render civil society meaningless, into Singapore's political lexicon.

Then in January 2004, shortly after then Deputy Prime Minister and Finance Minister Lee Hsien Loong was declared Singapore's next premier, he gave a major speech on the future of politics and society in Singapore at the 35th Anniversary Dinner of the Harvard Club of Singapore. In a speech intended as a preview to his style of rule, Lee laid down his protocol for government-people interaction, as well as the limits of political engagement, by declaring that Singapore "must open up further" by promoting "further civic participation".

Without quite explaining what he meant by "civic" or "opening up", Lee proffered five broad "suggestions"—better read as caveats—on how to promote "civic participation" and therefore build a more "civic society" in Singapore, namely: guidelines for public consultations on new policies or regulations, space for rigorous and robust debate, an emphasis on action or active citizenship, a constructive and "non-crusading" media, and a government that continues to lead the way even as it becomes more open to views. Taking a leaf from his predecessor's book, Lee was in fact pre-empting the "noise" of civil society and political criticism by declaring that he would become an open, inclusive, and consultative leader.

As this paper will go on to contend, the use of populist rhetoric like "openness" and "inclusiveness", as representations of a "civic" and/or "civil" society, must not be taken at face value, since they are often cryptic and ambiguous. Rather, these broad terms and loose concepts exemplify what I would present as "gestural politics", where, "by displaying the "liberal" gestures of the regime, Singaporean voters as well as foreign visitors and investors would be attracted to the new Singapore and its leadership one way or another". In other words, the "gesture" of civil society is more pertinent than its substance. After all, the rise of globalization, along with global (if Western) socio-political influences and rapid advances in media technologies, has meant that it was a matter of time before the government had to deal with the incursion of an increasingly politicized civil society that could threaten PAP rule.

Gestural politics thus helps to "nip the problem in the bud". Recognizing that the concept of civil society comes in various contours, forms, and content, and as such is always arbitrary and ill-defined, it is therefore up to the regime to define, and thus scope, civil society for its own ends and purposes. For better or worse, the equivocal but complex notion of civic and/or civil society makes it particularly amenable to wide (mis)appropriation, hence a "perfect" representation of gestural politics. As Kumar connotes, albeit in another context:

> "Civil society" sounds good; it has a good feel to it; it has the look of a fine old wine, full of depth and complexity. Who could possibly object to it, who will not wish for its fulfilment?

The discussion that follows provides a broad summary of how the term "civil society" has been employed in Singaporean public (and political) discourse: from its promulgation as "civic" society by George Yeo in the 1990s to its reassertion as a government vision statement calling for "active citizenship" and citizens' "feedback" at the turn of the millennium (especially in Singapore 21: Together, We Make the Difference) from 1999; to its current—and arguably, future—place in a supposedly "new" Singapore of the 21st century, creatively captured by the theme of an "open and inclusive Singapore", first articulated by Lee in January 2004 and followed up in his brief "swearing-in" speech on 12 August 2004. In essence, this paper considers how civil society exemplifies "gestural politics" in Singapore. It argues that while to some extent, engagement with the concept of civil society has become a political necessity, "new" rhetoric about politics and civil society in Singapore remains by and large gestural. Or as Chua puts it in his socio-political assessment of "Singapore in the next decade", the "new" Singapore of the

21st century is likely to be marked by greater liberalization, and not a democratization, of the social, cultural—and indeed public—sphere. The 1990s: Civic Society and Active Citizenship Citizenship is not a reality TV show.

You cannot just watch in the comfort of your home. You need to participate. Every time we participate, we reaffirm our membership and allegiance to our fellow citizens, our community and our country. [Participation] is critical in rooting Singaporeans to the country. (Raymond Lim, Singapore's Minister of State for Foreign Affairs and Trade and Industry)

In June 1991, while government administrators were implementing voter-friendly "consultative" strategies of the "new guard" led by newly installed Prime Minister Goh Chok Tong, the concept of civic society was promulgated in Singapore by a "new guard" minister, George Yeo, who was at the time acting in the portfolio of Information and the Arts] Widely regarded as one of contemporary Singapore's most eloquent politicians, Yeo made his—and indeed Singapore's—seminal speech on "civic society" to suggest a need for Singaporeans to be actively involved not so much in parliamentary, partisan, or lobbyist politics, but in creating a "Singapore soul", marked by a nationalistic and deep emotional attachment to Singapore. His intention was to urge Singaporeans to participate or play a part in enhancing the civic life in and of Singapore so that people will treat the country as home rather than a "soulless hotel" where one can come and go as one pleases.

As Yeo declared: If we are not to be only a hotel, we must have a soul. To develop that soul, we need a lively civic society. The State must pull back some so that the circle of public participation can grow.

The use of the term "soul" to refer to one's deep affiliation with the nation is a powerful metaphor. As Nikolas Rose elucidates in his Foucaultian analyses of contemporary governmentality, good government "operates through the delicate and minute infiltration of the ambitions of regulation" into the very interior—or soul—of human existence and experience. Thus, to equate a "lively civic society" with the "soul" of a nation is to effectively forge symmetry between the desires of the individual as citizen and the urge of governments to manage the individual as a participatory subject and cultural citizen.

In this way, the state would be able to, as Yeo puts it quite plainly, "pull back some" to provide "space" for citizens to perform their patriotic citizenship duties. In the case of Singapore during the 1990s, the intention of raising the stakes of civil society-cum-public participation was not so much to enable a thriving public sphere, but to advance and perfect the regulatory apparatuses-cum-technologies of government. Yeo's vision of a civic society is, after all, consistent with then Prime Minister Goh's professed commitment towards a more consultative style of government. The problem though is that the term "civic society" is not quite identical to that of a "civil society". As Singaporean sociologist Chua Beng Huat points out: The difference between the two terms, "civic society" and "civil society" is not some inconsequential play of words, but an indication of one's political stance on the appropriate balance in the relationship between state and society in Singapore.

In other words, when Singaporean politicians use the term "civic society", they are effectively talking about the "civic" responsibilities of citizens as opposed to that of the "rights" of citizenship espoused in the conventional and political understanding of the concept of "civil society". Likewise, Koh Tai Ann suggests that Singapore's model of "civic society" seeks primarily to forestall the potentially destabilizing "politicking" practices of civil society. By placing emphasis on the term "civic"—and the attendant discourses of courtesy, kindness, graciousness, and civility—which spells how citizens ought to behave and conduct themselves publicly, it is hoped that Singaporeans would be discouraged or distracted from real politicking activities.

The choice of the term "civic" by Yeo and other government officials is thus prudent and well-calculated, one that is "consistent with the PAP's language of politics". Even if "civic society" does become interpreted—or confused—as "civil society", the grounds are well covered. At an Institute of Policy Studies conference on civil society in May 1998, George Yeo—who was by then elevated to the full senior status of Minister of Information and the Arts—made a conceptual departure from his original "civic society" speech by declaring that a "civic" society was really Singapore's idea of "civil society".

Civil society to Yeo is not just about citizenship in the form of voting rights or the right to carry a Singapore passport, it is more veraciously about enhancing the relationship between state and the non-state for the sake of the nation and its citizens. In trying to depoliticize "civil society", Yeo was in effect attempting to engage—somewhat pre-emptively—the proponents of an autonomous civil society by defining the very terms and tenets of future political engagement. Far from being depoliticized or non-political, this move to carve out a "civic" mode of civil society for Singapore was motivated by political expedience.

Indeed, like most aspects of politics in Singapore, civic or civil society has its own "special meanings", explicable and interpretable only by the PAP. By "pre-defining" civil society, the government could thus go on to talk about various aspects of "civic-ness" and "civility" as captured in less problematic public discourses such as courtesy, kindness, and graciousness.

It could also go on to "proselytize" about the merits of citizen participation in the policy process or "active citizenship", the central theme of "Singapore 21" (the government's 1999 vision of Singapore in the 21st century), knowing full well that free and autonomous participation is mostly absent in a society that is notorious for being politically passive and apathetic. Ho Khai Leong alludes to this problem when he notes that:

> The extent to which Singapore citizens can influence policy making depends on the extent to which the PAP allows it to happen. The basic ground rules are set from above and citizenry is merely passively reacting to those regulations.

Although most Singaporeans perceive "Singapore 21" as

yet another motherhood statement by the self-proclaimed all-knowing government, the call for "active citizenship" was generally well-received by many people, including those affiliated with local interest groups. The possibility of forging a new "social contract" between the government and its people was sufficiently attractive to groups which had previously existed on the periphery.

Groups such as The Working Committee (TWC), a civil society advocate group, proclaimed in October 1999 that it would be going online to promote civil society. Even the well-known Internet-based association People Like Us (PLU), a group which aims to promote awareness of issues concerning gays and lesbians in society, decided in 2000 to "roll up their sleeves" to publicly discuss about their "active citizenship" roles in conservative Singapore.

That year, an application by the PLU to hold a public forum on "Gays and Lesbians within Singapore 21" was flatly rejected by the Police Public Entertainment Licensing Unit (PELU) on the grounds that mainstream moral values of Singaporeans are conservative, and that Singapore's Penal Code has clear provisions against certain homosexual practices. As Lee summarizes the episode:

> [A]ctive citizenship and participation in the Singapore context not only has legal, social and cultural limits, but comes with political and ideological boundaries that can and will be strictly enforced at the sole discretion of the authorities.

The PLU's brush with the law enforcers made it clear that while groups with socially "off-centre" or politically sensitive agendas may continue to exist, they should remain "closeted" from the public at all times. Although "Singapore 21" had been depicted as a large-scale consultative project involving some 6,000 ordinary Singaporeans from all walks of life (Singapore 21, "Preface"), it was never intended as a "bottom-up" mass participation exercise, nor was it designed, strictly speaking, to cultivate the growth of civil society.

On the contrary, it became more like a strategic attempt at addressing the long-standing "problem" of political apathy and passivity among Singaporeans, measured predominantly by their seeming disinterest in politics and reluctance to offer feedback via established channels. The concept of feedback, understood quite simply as the expression of one's views on public policy, is deemed one of the most evident and active signs of citizen participation in government. Yet, it has been—and remains—a vexed political issue in Singapore, with a sizeable number of Singaporeans politically apathetic, passively docile, or fearful of reprisal.

As Terence Chong explains with cogency: Past examples of alternative political activism have ingrained in Singaporeans the lessons of challenging the Government. The spectre of incarceration, bankruptcy and exile of political opponents, has, rightly or wrongly, penetrated the middle-class psyche. Apathy thus protects [Singaporeans] from personal distress and embarrassment.

Such apathetic condition is also understandable in view of the fact that the highest consultation channel in Singapore, the centrally controlled Feedback Unit, headed by PAP members of parliament (MPs) and civil servants, was created "out of political necessity" in March 1985:. The formation of the Feedback Unit was a result of the PAP government's frustration at losing two seats to the opposition and winning a smaller share of the popular vote than expected at the 1984 General Election.

As Birch explicates, one of the key words of the post-Lee Kuan Yew's "new guard" has been "feedback", designed not so much to replace a top-down mode of rule, but to manage dissenting voices or public dissonance. At the annual conference of Feedback Groups in Singapore in January 2004, the Minister of State for Foreign Affairs and Trade and Industry, Raymond Lim, reiterated the prime objectives of the Feedback Unit in a speech entitled "Feedback and the Public Purpose" by declaring that:

Feedback makes policy formulation in government a more informed process, ensuring above all that it is relevant. It also makes policy implementation a more effective process, as it enhances public receptiveness based on a better understanding and acceptance of the policy.

Minister Lim's statement makes it quite clear that prime intention of the Feedback Unit is to enhance" public receptiveness" to government policies. It is, in other words, highly functional and predominantly gestural. Any feedback on policies, especially impending and potentially unpopular ones, would thus facilitate the forging of" consensus politics" between the citizenry and the government.

In this way, the concept of feedback or consultation becomes another" gesture" of the government used to gauge political support or otherwise. As a result, those who do not support specific policies would never use established feedback channels to voice their thoughts. It is interesting to note from a 2003 survey that while 80 per cent of Singaporeans find the Feedback Unit's channels accessible and adequate, and 77 per cent acknowledge the Unit as an effective means for feedback, only about 6,800 feedback inputs--out of a total population numbering more than four million--were received that same year.

By contrast, however, the" Forum" page of the national and most widely read daily, the Straits Times, attracts more than 2,000 letters every month. The Straits Times Forum has become, virtually by default, the most popular site for public feedback and discussion in Singapore, serving to amplify public sentiments on a broad range of social, cultural, economic and, to a lesser extent, political issues. However, it is important to note that while the Forum page has been labelled the" most democratic space in Singapore" , the extent to which one can engage in political debate through this forum is almost solely determined by editorial decision and judgement. If the media in Singapore is, as Birch notes in Althusserian terms, an" ideological state apparatus" , then genuine or active participation in policy-making via the state-managed newspaper outlet is either futile or not possible, thus reinforcing Ooi Can Seng's (" State-Civil Society Relations and Tourism" , in this issue) claim that the Singapore government has been able to re-define civil spaces for its own interests. The corollary is that letters that are deemed politically offensive or destabilizing would not make the cut, thus making the Straits Times Forum a poor example of civil society as it is a socially and politically unproblematic space for the establishment.

The call by" Singapore 21" to embrace" active citizenship" needs to be examined against the backdrop of political hegemony and apathy in Singapore. Calls to participate are typically accompanied by important caveats, including unwritten rules about the limits of participation, exemplified most prominently by OB markers (which the next section of this paper will address). Riding on the context of the Forum, what is not being said tends to speak louder than what is or has been. In this regard," active citizenship" is at best a Machiavellian political gesture aimed at instructing Singaporeans on how to become good and obedient citizens by working with and alongside the state to minimize resistances to government policies. Contrary to the minister's comments in the opening quote to this section, active citizenship in Singapore is precisely a" reality TV show," where citizens who consciously choose to remain apathetic and" inactive" --that is, those who watch the unfolding drama of politics from the comfort of their homes--are the model" participants" in a society that values political compliance and acquiescence.

OB Markers and" New" Politics

Some groups would like [the government] to open faster--not just loosen restrictions but remove them altogether. But while we talk about OB markers and wider fairways, remember that most Singaporeans still do not play golf. Bread and butter issues are still uppermost on their minds. [...] The test of our policies is not how closely we approach an idealized model, but how well we move the majority forward so that we remake Singapore into a dynamic global city and the best home for Singaporeans.

The concept of the OB markers arose following an episode in 1994 dubbed "the Catherine Lim affair". On 20 November 1994, well-known Singaporean novelist and social commentator Catherine Lim's political commentary entitled

"One Government, Two Styles" was published in the Sunday edition of Singapore's Straits Times daily. In it, Lim opined that Prime Minister Goh Chok Tong's promise of a more open, consultative, and consensual leadership style had been abandoned in favour of the authoritarian style of his predecessor, referring specifically to the former premier Lee Kuan Yew. This was the gist of Lim's contention:

Over the years, a pattern of governance has emerged that is not exactly what was envisaged. Increasingly, the promised Goh style of people-orientation is being subsumed under the old style of top-down decisions.

Chapter 6

Model for the World Press

In the study of the global media, there is abundant literature about the dominance of the Western media. Much less prominent as a research subject is the dominance of Western perspectives in building media theories, such as the four theories of the press, which have been used as a universal guide to the understanding of the press systems around the world since they were created in 1956.

It is interesting to address the issue of the dominance of Western scholarship in media research in view of the ancient civilizations of the East, especially India, where several of the world's religions originated, and China, where paper and the printing press were first invented. Pi Sheng, a Chinese metalworker, invented the movable-type printing press in 1045, more than 400 years before Gutenberg did when the latter reinvented the printing press in Europe. But in some of the American media history textbooks, only the name of Gutenberg was introduced.

Since the fall of the Iron Curtain, the further opening-up of the economies in China and India, and the arrival of the Internet, the meeting of the minds of the East and West has been accelerated. More and more media researchers from both the East and the West have come to re-examine the four theories of the press as the dominant paradigm in studying world press systems. Jiafei Yin encountered major difficulties in using the theories as a guide in describing press systems in Asia because the four press theories were built primarily on Western perspectives. When theories fail to serve as an effective guide to the understanding of the subject of inquiry, it is time that new theories were developed, theories that would be based on cultural values not only from the West but also from the East.

The Asian civilization is as different from the Western civilization as any two civilizations can be. Moreover, Asia is a politically and culturally diverse continent, where reforming and developing communist countries are right next door to some of the most successful capitalist countries in the world. And no one or two religions dominate the continent.

It is hard to lump sum Asia together in any kind of description, and it is even harder to pigeonhole the vastly diverse Asian media systems into the four press categories developed by Western media scholars, who failed to include media experiences from the East in building their theories. This chapter debates the applicability of the four press theories in the Asian media context and the reliability of press freedom ratings of each country given by the Freedom House. The chapter starts with a review of the well-established press theories and continues with an analysis of representative media systems in Asia.

As Asia is a vast and diverse continent with dozens of countries, it is not feasible to analyse every media system in the region. Therefore, representative media systems were chosen in analyzing the applicability of the established press theories while more countries were included in brief discussions where common characteristics make the analysis also apply.

Discussions focus on comparisons of the theories with the media systems in Asia and on identifying the difficulties in trying to match the two. The second part of the chapter proposes an alternative press model based on an analysis of Eastern and Western philosophical thinking and cultural values relevant to the media.

THE DOMINANT FOUR THEORIES OF THE PRESS

The seminal work Four Theories of the Press established the dominant paradigm in analyzing global media systems and, in particular, in assessing levels of press freedom in countries and regions throughout the world. Other theories on press systems followed, such as development journalism in developing countries, revolutionary media, and democratic-participant media. However, the newer theories were mostly complementary to the established four theories of the press.

Of the four theories, "the authoritarian system has been most pervasive both historically and geographically," according to Siebert. The goal of the media under such a system was to support and advance the policies of the government so that it could achieve its objectives.

Werner J. Severin and James W. Tankard, Jr. in summarizing the major characteristics of the four theories wrote that the authoritarian concept was based on the sixteenth and seventeenth century English history and philosophy of the absolute power of the monarch.

Contrary to the authoritarian theory, libertarian theory held that man was rational and an end in himself. The happiness and the well-being of the individual was the goal of society.

The social responsibility theory was an outgrowth of the libertarian theory and was first developed in the twentieth century United States by the Commission on Freedom of the Press, which emphasized social responsibility of the press.

The last of the four theories was the Soviet communist theory, which was based on Marxist ideology and value of unity - unity of the working class and unity of the Party. For the sake of unity, there should be only one right position and only one truth, the absolute truth. Under the Soviet system, the government had a division of censorship.

CRITICISM OF THE FOUR THEORIES

Dominant as the four theories have been, there is no lack of criticism of them. Critical of the social responsibility theory, John C. Merrill, who strongly argued for the independence of individual journalists in his writings, asked his students: Who should be the authority in defining what responsible journalism is? Shouldn't journalists themselves be allowed to make that judgment?

The most comprehensive criticism of the four theories came almost forty years after the theories were first published. In "Last Rights: Revisiting Four Theories of the Press," published in 1995 and written by a group of media scholars from the same school where the four theories originated, the authors found the overall theoretical framework of the four theories flawed.

The book, edited by John C. Nerone, pointed out that the four theories were not value-free despite their valuefree appearance. The theories were based on a pro-capitalist bias and were the products of capitalism and of the Cold War era. Because of such bias, the authors contended that while the four theories were critical of the Soviet communist media, they ignored the concerns of the libertarian media, especially the concentration of media ownership.

The authors argued that the theories focused only on the political control of the media, state power, but were silent on other kinds of power and restraint on the media. For example, the theories only discussed media's political freedom, not economic freedom from the market forces and ownership ties. Another problem with the theories, the authors argued, was that it allowed only two media environments - libertarian and authoritarian - the other two being only the derivatives of the free and the controlled media environments. The book also listed "internal inconsistencies and inadequacies" among the four theories.

In a study examining the press systems in China and Japan, Betty H. Winfield et al. found that Western scholarship on press systems tended to disregard the cultures, philosophies, and traditions that distinguish Asian mass media. She said studies such as the four theories of the press keep a Western emphasis while ignoring political foundations and beliefs in Asian societies.

Shelton A. Gunaratne conducted research on West-centrism in communication theories. He believed that the four theories "ignored the dynamic diversity inherent in complex dissipative social systems" and found them "static" and "deontic".

WESTERN PRESS THEORIES VERSUS EASTERN PRESS SYSTEMS

In an attempt to research and categorize press systems in Asian countries, Jiafei Yin found major difficulties or misfits in trying to pigeonhole Asian media systems according to the four press theories, which were developed by Western media scholars and were based on Western philosophies and the analysis of Western history, politics, and culture. The following section discusses why the dominant press theories could not satisfactorily describe the realities of media in Asia.

THE "LIBERTARIAN PRESS" IN ASIA

SELF-CENSORSHIP IN THE ASIAN PRESS

The Japanese press is considered the liveliest in East Asia and was ranked the freest in Asia by the Freedom House for 2005. Reporters Without Borders gave Japan the second-highest ranking in Asia in press freedom after South Korea for its 2005 report.

Japan's press industry is the largest in the world. It has five national daily newspapers, each claiming a circulation in the millions. That compares with the top two dailies in the United States -USA Today and The Wall Street Journal - each of which has a circulation of around 2 million.

Yomiuri Shimbun, the paper with the largest circulation in the world, has a circulation of 14 million. Asahi Shimbun has a circulation of 12 million. These two Japanese national dailies are the only two newspapers in the world with a circulation surpassing 10 million. The circulations of the other three range from 2.7 million to 5.6 million.

Japanese journalists are well trained and well informed. They have to study for months to pass rigorous exams to even get hired. The exam includes a ninety-minute general intelligence test, a ninety-minute writing test, and a ninety-minute foreign language proficiency test, usually in English, Spanish, French, or Chinese.

Even if a candidate gets good scores, he or she has to pass three to four interviews. Special schools help prepare university students and graduates for the test. But Japanese journalists may find their training and skills wasted under a press club system.

To understand the nature of the Japanese press system, the economic system in Japan has to be examined first. Democracy describes Japan's political system, but freewheeling capitalism is out of the question in Japan although, theoretically speaking, Japan practices free market capitalism. The Japanese economy has thrived and become a dominant force in the global economy under state-guided capitalism.

Instead of regulating the industry, the government helps the industry to grow and compete on the global market. Government and big corporations in Japan are partners in nation building. Political freedom and rights do not translate into economic liberalism in Japan, which has much to do with the Japanese culture, or the Asian culture.

In Asian societies, especially those under the influence of Confucian thought, the strength of a country is regarded as more important than the profitability of a company, and the well-being of a family is more important than individual rights and freedom.

For a country like Japan with limited arable land and scarce resources, the survival and prosperity of the nation take priority in national life. The royal family and often the government are symbols of the nation, and they command respect.

Such a cultural tradition contradicts the Western concept of media as a watchdog and the ultimate goal of libertarian philosophies - man as an end in himself. In Japan, media keep cozy relations with the government and the big industries through the press club system, or "information cartels," which comprise press clubs, industry associations, and media conglomerates, which Freeman calls "the unholy trinity." The press clubs channel information from government offices to media organizations.

Such a club system discourages independent reporting and thoroughness in journalistic investigations and results in "uniformity of content" and "pro-establishment style of journalism". The information cartels ensure no competition among media outlets and no scoops. In Asian societies, the motto promoted is not Darwin's "survival of the fittest," but the survival of all, which may explain why in many Asian countries, such as Japan, China, and Singapore, comparative advertising is banned.

The club system works well for the Japanese press, which profits from large circulations, high advertising revenue, and exclusive information access from the government. But it is a system designed by the industry to serve media companies' economic interests, a system that has frequently led the press to support state goals.

It is in this sense that the media can be understood as collaborators with the state in the management of society, Freeman said. Such a system discourages investigative reporting and places a premium on relying on official sources rather than alternative information. It interferes with the public's right to receive relevant information in a timely manner.

As a result, all the high-profile political scandals that emerged in the first half of 2002 were not uncovered by the vernacular dailies, but by the non-mainstream weeklies. Because of its less than rigorous reporting, the Japanese press fails to act as a watchdog of the government and is called a lapdog, which was blamed for failing to keep the public informed of the irregularities within the financial industry and the corruption within the government. When the Asian financial crash hit Japan in 1997, the magnitude of the crisis took the public by surprise.

An in-depth analysis of the Japanese press system makes it clear that the ideas available at the "marketplace of ideas" are rather limited. Free competition that is at the very core of the libertarian theory is stifled under the press club system, which also bars reporters from foreign and non-mainstream media outlets from attending exclusive press briefings and getting official press releases.

While government control of the press in Japan is not a major issue, control by professional associations and the media organizations themselves is still very effective and produces the same result of a less informed public. The reason why the Freedom House rated the Japanese press as the freest in Asia may be because of the fact that the Japanese government seldom takes direct actions against the press or journalists. In Japan, there is hardly such need, as the press polices itself rather diligently.

Like Japan, South Korea is a newspaper-rich country. South Koreans get their news primarily from daily newspapers. The country has ten national dailies, which are in circulation wars in the millions. In addition, there are 100 free dailies, 314 specialized dailies, 1,999 weeklies, 2,319 monthlies, and 1,245 other periodicals. All newspapers print forty-eight to fifty-six pages for advertising space. In South Korea, each household subscribes to two or three national papers and one local paper, a dream for newspaper owners in any country.

For 2005, the Freedom House rated the press in South Korea "free." And the Reporters Without Borders described the South Korean press as opposite of that of North Korea: "diverse, privately owned and critical of the government". South Korea is a relatively new democracy. After decades of fighting for democracy, South Koreans started to enjoy their political rights in 1987 when a civilian government was sworn in after a general election.

But until Kim Dae Jung, a freedom fighter and folk hero, became president in 1998, the newly found press freedom in South Korea had been contained by its press club system like Japan's, by the common economic interests of the government and big business in South Korea, including the media, and by the influence of Confucian values.

South Korean industries, like those of Japan, used to be guided and supported by the government. The press in South

Korea has allied itself with the government and big businesses and is widely seen as "pro-business," "pro-government," and "conservative". Chong-Hyuk Kim, a reporter for the Joong Ang Ilbo in South Korea, told a Freedom Forum panel that South Korea's ostensibly democratic government barred publishing the size of foreign reserves and foreign debt. He said, "It has become traditional practice between government and media in South Korea not to report critical and important information.

The government insisted if that kind of information were revealed, it would be harmful to national security and the national reputation. The media accepted that kind of assertion". The result of such secrecy was the unexpected Asian financial crash in 1997, which hit the South Korean economy hard and caught its people unprepared.

A reader of the Chosun Ilbo, one of the largest papers in the country, wrote: "Korean journalism still is a superficial observer of the events and does not carry a torch for the righteous social and ethical standards in a rapidly transforming materialistic society. It still is timid and not impartial and indifferent to power politics".

The press system in South Korea had many similarities with that of Japan until Kim Dae Jung became president in 1998. Since then the South Korean press has started to develop in a new direction, and the press club system is being phased out. Press freedom in South Korea improved noticeably during the tenure of Kim, when the press became more aggressive in covering the government and more vocal in criticizing government policies. But the unprecedented press freedom in Korean history under Kirn's government was overshadowed by government's crackdown on the major papers with charges of tax evasion in 2001.

Press freedom is still fragile in South Korea, and its press system is in a transitional stage. It remains to be seen if the South Korean press is finally breaking away from self-censorship or if it still wants to maintain good relations with the government and big businesses by avoiding coverage of critical issues. Self-censorship is not only a major issue in Japan and South Korea but also a major concern in Hong Kong and Thailand. The media in Hong Kong and Thailand are in a category of their own. They are among the freest in Asia when they resort to sensationalism to survive the intense competition.

In Hong Kong, tabloids represent the mainstream press. Practice of yellow journalism, including sensationalized reporting, price wars, and stealing talent from competitors, reached its climax in 1995 and again in 1997. In both Hong Kong and Thailand, the press exercises a high degree of freedom when it is dealing with non-political topics, but starts to be cautious when news stories concern politics, the government, or the royal family.

Before Hong Kong was returned to China, many of the newspapers in the former British colony were pro-British. Since the sovereignty changed hands, more papers are now pro-Beijing. Self-censorship is considered a major concern and the main threat to an independent and free press in Hong Kong despite a great deal of aggressive reporting.

Part of the problem of press self-censorship was due to the fact that after Hong Kong was returned to China, the ownership of some of the major newspapers changed hands, including the South China Morning Post. The new press owners have investments on the Chinese mainland and do not want to offend the officials in Beijing.

BBC News introduced the media in Hong Kong as editorially dynamic, free, and diverse, but it cited increasing self-censorship and pressures on editorial policies. In Hong Kong, direct government intervention of the press is minimal. However, pressure from the central government in Beijing and new owners of the press makes many editors and reporters wary of how to handle sensitive information or topics.

A public opinion poll found that 48% of the people in Hong Kong believed the local news media practiced self-censorship. The study showed that 62% believed the local news media had qualms when criticizing the central government, while only 34% believed it had concerns in criticizing the local government. "The number of respondents who said the media practices self-censorship has significantly increased, mainly because they think the media has become apprehensive when criticizing the central government," a survey organizer said.

Newspapers in Hong Kong adopted specific strategies in the politics of self-censorship. Francis L. F. Lee and Angel M. Y. Lin argued that in transitional societies such as Hong Kong when political pressure on the press is added to a commercial media system and a professional journalistic culture, the politics of self-censorship often becomes a strategic contest between the media and political actors.

The Ming Pao daily constructed the debate as a factional rivalry in order to position itself as an arbitrator, according to Lee and Lin. In contrast, the popular Apple Daily presented the story as a sovereign people's fight against a powerful entity, which was much more critical toward the central government. "Nevertheless, it also appropriated the dominant discourse, constructed internal contradictions, and decentralized the Chinese central government to smooth out the radicalism of its criticisms".

Jasper Decker, a former staff member at the South China Morning Post, also observed less obvious characteristics of self-censorship, such as the tone and attitude in news stories concerning China. Reporting became less aggressive. Management emphasized the virtues of writing to allow readers to read between the lines. In 1997, the New York Times noted that Ming Pao had "reduced the space given to columnists critical of China and has toned down its previously aggressive reporting of China".

Other newspapers avoided devoting space to politically sensitive topics by assigning their reporters to cover other, non-controversial topics. A content analysis of 1997 editorials of major newspapers in Hong Kong found that 56.2% of the editorials addressed local issues in Hong Kong, while only 8% of the editorials discussed issues in China and 7.6% dealt with topics related to the ties between Hong Kong and China.

Self-censorship was an issue even before 1997. Jim Sciutto, a former Hong Kong journalist, claimed, "Self-censorship is nearly epidemic in Hong Kong, affecting the entire media hierarchy from publishers to beat reporters. A free Hong Kong press is already eroding."

In a 1990 survey of Hong Kong journalists, 5% admitted fear of criticizing China in their work, and 54% believed that their fellow journalists felt the same way. The anxiety was not alleviated in the following six years as a similar survey in 1996 found that one in every four journalists expressed concerns over criticizing China.

As much of the self-censorship in Hong Kong was the result of pressure from newspaper editors and owners, some local journalists and researchers argued that it was censorship, not self-censorship on the part of the reporters. Carol Lai, a former chairwoman of the Hong Kong Journalist Association, believed that the influence of editors might have impacted journalists' writing more than any threats from the government.

She believed most of the reporters wanted integrity in their reporting, tried to report accurately and objectively and seldom censored themselves. Some editors, however, watered down criticism or killed stories they deemed offensive. Media owners and editors censored their reporters in the hope of preventing interference from the central government so they could keep their papers in business.

Others might wish to expand their investment on the mainland. The Hong Kong Journalist Association noted that the South Chin Morning Post had reduced and diluted its coverage of China since Robert Kuok became an owner in 1993. "In Hong Kong, pro-Beijing forces don't fight the media, they buy it".

In order to be successful, the media in Hong Kong have learned to remain apolitical. Since the late 1960s, major newspapers in Hong Kong have become increasingly less partisan and have avoided taking less popular stand on issues, and instead, have focused more on the market and middle-class liberalism in order to increase profits.

Self-censorship in Hong Kong prompted one Hong Kong journalist to compare Hong Kong tycoons, who toned down their coverage of China, with mainland media outlets, which became more aggressive in their reporting as they sought market share. In the near future, Hong Kong may have to learn a thing or two from the mainland press when it comes to press freedom, according to Mark Simon of the Apple Daily.

In Southeast Asia, the Thai press enjoys a considerable degree of freedom. Its 1997 constitution protects media freedom, freedom of expression, and access to information. Even under the media-unfriendly prime minister Thaksin Shinawatra the media were free to criticize government policies and cover cases of corruption and human rights abuses, but journalists tended to exercise self-censorship regarding the military, the monarchy, the judiciary, and other sensitive issues.

Press freedom is deep-rooted in the Thai culture. However, the tradition of self-censorship in Thailand is as long as its history of a free press. Despite the freedom they enjoyed in the 1980s, Thai editorial writers and reporters censored themselves, mindful that there were unwritten government rules regarding the coverage of the monarchy, government affairs, internal security matters, and Thailand's international image.

"Self-censorship is probably a perfect form of political control. Politicians in power don't have to risk creating public ire by openly bullying the media. Media proprietors and journalists know exactly what the 'invisible rules' are". The degree of press freedom and selfcensorship in Thailand is often dependent on the kind of government that is in power. The Thai government under Prime Minister Thaksin provided a telling example.

Since Thaksin came to power, the majority of media outlets were forced into submission. Some journalists lamented that truly independent journalists were now "a rare and endangered species" as too many members of the media were influenced by the lure of political favour, or in fear of political power. The government rewarded media outlets supportive of its policies through the allocation of advertising by telecommunications firms and state enterprises, which resulted in an increasing level of self-censorship. More sophisticated media outlets included mild criticism of the government in their coverage but avoided more serious issues or pursuing issues further.

In such a media environment, anyone in the broadcast media speaking more than "30% of the truth" could get into trouble. The media were thus forced into three categories - government partisans, government mouthpieces, and those that engage in self-censorship.

Most mainstream newspapers were won over by the government either through friendly persuasions sweetened with advertising deals or through political pressure, and all television stations were pressured into practicing self-censorship in covering the government.

Using sharper words, The Nation wrote, "...the majority of those who own media outlets sense Thaksin's political invincibility and are prostituting themselves voluntarily. The broadcast media are the most obvious, acting in collusion with the government.... Nowadays, broadcasters are considered strategic partners with the government. Lump-sum financial rewards have made parts of the media into circus dogs that are ready to do summersaults."

The print media were no exception, the article said. Publishers were more willing to follow the government line to ensure their business future. Self-censorship was increasingly becoming the normal code of conduct for editors and journalists under Thaksin.

Under a climate of fear and self-censorship within the media community, the Thai media have morphed into the "custodian of the government". In one particular case, the owner of the newsmagazine, Siamrath, exercised self-censorship by canceling the distribution of 30,000 copies of an issue that contained reports critical of the government. In another case, the management of the Bangkok Post removed its editor Veera Prateepchaikul for "irritating" the prime minister by using the word "arrogance".

Concerned over the retreat of press freedom, The Nation argued, "The professional integrity of the media should never be conditional on the political power or popularity of a leader, much less his power of patronage to throw financial benefits their way".

Two recent court rulings upheld the constitutional rights to freedom of expression in the country, one vindicating former iTV journalists, who were dismissed for refusing to compromise their professional integrity, and the other in favour of media-freedom advocate Supinya Klangnarong and the Thai Post, who were sued for defamation.

Also in 2006, all the free TV channels covered the anti-Thaksin activities, with the exception of only one channel. That was unprecedented under the government of Thaksin. The Freedom House can rate the Thai press as "free," such as in 2002, or "partly free" since 2003. But it is certainly a different kind of free press even though its self-censorship practices are much less systematic than Japan's.

SELF-CENSORSHIP VERSUS SOCIAL RESPONSIBILITY THEORY

There are fundamental differences between press self-censorship in Asia and the Western social responsibility press theory. First, as discussed earlier, the social responsibility theory derived from the libertarian theory, which emphasizes the freedom of the press and pluralism in the marketplace of ideas. Therefore, the basis of the social responsibility theory is still press freedom, even when the press is urged to use that freedom responsibly.

Press self-censorship in Asia, however, is based either on control by the press clubs in the case of Japan and, formerly, South Korea or on fear of government retribution in the case of Hong Kong and Thailand. In either case, freedom of the press is being severely curtailed. Second, the goal of the Hutchins report, A Free and Responsible Press, is to recommend ways in which a free press can better serve the society at large.

The report proposed five standards in improving the quality of news reporting, including the comprehensive coverage of news events to ensure its accuracy, representation of different demographic groups in society in news reports, and the provision of service to all the constituencies of society. But the primary goal of press self-censorship in Asia is for self-preservation. It is to protect the business interests of the press rather than to better serve the public. Newspapers in these Asian countries are highly profitable; thus, the management does not want to offend the government or big business.

Third, ideally speaking, if the social responsibility press theory is implemented in the newsroom, the result will be a better-informed public and a more ethical and responsible press, whereas press self-censorship in Asia can only result in uniform content, suppressed information, and a poorly informed public. If the ultimate goal of the press in these Asian societies is the pursuit of profits, it will be difficult for the press to be socially responsible or professionally ethical.

Chapter 7

Archism in the Asian Press

Although Asia is rarely known for press freedom, there are some rather free press systems in the region, particularly transitional press systems such as the ones in Taiwan, the Philippines, and Indonesia, where the whole control system was torn down when martial law was ended or strongmen overthrown and where there was tremendous backlash against press control. But often the enthusiasm for newfound press freedom in these countries leaves the press bordering on a state of anarchy.

After decades of government suppression, the press in Taiwan, the Philippines, and Indonesia was enjoying unprecedented freedom and explosive growth when the rules, regulations, and bans were lifted, licenses for starting up newspapers became easier to obtain, and the enthusiasm for starting up newspapers was high. Such outpouring energy overwhelmed the governments in these societies after decades of authoritarian or military rule.

These governments had yet to establish trust and credibility among the people and construct new frameworks in regulating the press without the suspicion that democratically elected governments were reintroducing government control over the press. The booming press industry tipped the balance between supply and demand. Intensified competition combined with new press freedom drove many of the papers in these countries to" freakdom" of the press, meaning sensationalism in news coverage.

In Indonesia, now that the press is finally free, the main problem is a lack of professional standards and ethics among journalists. More and more journalists are violating the most sacred principle of the profession: tell the truth. Journalists today are accountable to no one but themselves and their proprietors because of the sweeping deregulation of the media. The ministry of information was abolished, and gone also was the licensing system. In 1999, a new press law was passed to guarantee freedom. But excesses and abuses of press freedom have ironically prompted calls from the public for the government to restore some control of the press.

Freedom of the press is a double-sided sword, which can expose corruption and injustice but can also hurt the freedom and media if the freedom is abused. Media in Indonesia has changed its role from being a mouthpiece of the government under Suharto to being a critical watchdog today. " Barking headlines, hard-biting editorials, sharp commentaries, satirical cartoons and investigative exposés are now common features of our media".But the media in general failed to promote the basic principles of journalism, such as accuracy and balanced reporting.

Syamsul Muarif, the state minister for information and communication, a new government agency, listed five diseases of the press: pornography, character assassination, false and provocative news, misleading advertisements, and unprofessional journalists.

Media hold up a mirror to the society they cover; in the case of Indonesia, what is reflected is pervasive corruption, which poisons the soul of journalism. Indonesia was rated as the fifth most corrupt country in the world, where corruption spread from the central government to local governments. This culture of corruption gave rise to" envelope journalism" and" bogus journalism".With" envelope journalism," journalists receive cash from news sources to compensate for their low salaries, compromising the integrity of the press.

" Many people are willing to provide bribes for journalists to ensure that the press will cover or blow up good stories about them or stop publishing bad news about them." And this is a common practice for almost all private and state organizations. Every day no fewer than 2,000 journalists make their fortune by asking the members of the parliament for money.

The amount offered was so enticing that it attracted fake journalists to news conferences for the enveloped cash, resulting in" bogus journalists," who reached hundreds in Jakarta alone. Some of these bogus journalists were laid-off journalists, while others had no previous connections with the media.

" Envelope journalism" brought about public complaints that news stories were inaccurate and failed to cover both sides of a story. Ulin Ni'am Yusron, chairman of the Jakarta Independent Journalists Alliance (AJI), said," It is too much to ask them to make impartial, quality news if they are underpaid".

In Indonesia, only 30% of about 1,200 publishers in the print media were financially healthy. Therefore, not only journalists can be bought, media organizations can be bought as well. A 2005 survey published by the Alliance for Reform and Democracy in Asia found that 40% of the respondents in Indonesia did not perceive the media to be free and independent of the government and" other sources".

Respondents cited widespread bribery of journalists, the buying of air time on talk shows and other forms of advertisements by public figures, and the efforts of both political parties and big business in establishing their own media or buying into media in order to influence public opinion.

Blame was laid on the lack of professionalism and increasing competition from both the local and foreign media. Nurbaiti contended that the immediate future did not look bright either. The outlook for 2006 was that" the Indonesian media will continue to compromise in the search for balance between profit and quality journalism".

Advocacy journalism sells papers too. During the height of the brutal communal conflict in Maluku province, the Jawa Pos media group was accused of profiting immensely from the conflict, which split up the community along ethnic and religious lines. The group's new paper launched during the middle of the conflict, the Ambon Express, was labeled a" Muslim" daily, and the group's established paper, Suara Maluku, was considered a" Christian" paper. Almost all media outlets in Maluku at that time were accused of taking sides.

The same kind of" provocative reporting" was used during the tension between Indonesia and Malaysia over the disputed Ambalat offshore oil block in the Sulawesi Sea.

In their coverage, the Indonesian media failed to promote peace; instead, it contributed to the tension. The national media focused on the possibility of war rather than advocating a peaceful settlement, and the local media preferred to cover the deployment of soldiers or the recruitment of volunteers to attack Malaysia.

In the Philippines, the press claims to be the freest in Asia even though broadcasting is still subject to regulation. Sheila S. Coronel described the Philippine press as" rowdy," " vibrant," " pluralistic," and" anarchistic." She said Filipino journalists are noisy and powerful. Media exposes have caused the resignation of officials and raised public awareness about important issues. Because of their recent history, Filipino journalists protect their freedom fiercely and are firm believers in the watchdog role of the press.

In post-Marcos days, the Philippine media were able to publish information with few restraints. But with few principles of ethics or responsibility to guide them, journalists followed their own set of rules.

As a result, accuracy and truth were compromised. Many Philippine journalists believed that journalism was mostly instinctive, and that theories and principles were not much more help than as mere guidesthat there existed no rules specific enough to constitute applicable and reliable standards.

" Never has the profession been so cheapened-and cheapened yet by its own practitioners". This belief led to the general deterioration in the quality of the profession. Part of the problem was due to the mushrooming of news media outlets and the growing demand for journalists.

The proliferation of news media outlets depleted the supply of qualified journalists and" opened the profession to invasion by pseudo-journalists, resulting in widespread malpractice".

The news media were criticized for irresponsible and sloppy reporting, for checkbook journalism, and for using its freedom to commercially exploit the public's taste for the sensational. Television bore the brunt of criticism. In the words of a print journalist-turned TV journalist," Philippine TV has not reached the point of maturity, where we can say that it is really doing things in the service of Filipinos.

At this point, it is more of the service of business, making money, fighting the ratings game, and being No. 1". Journalists were eager to present to the public every possible news source without checking his or her credibility." Anything that would raise the decibel of noise (was deemed to be) good".

A TV reporter who covered the police beat wrote an article in the Philippine Journalism Review, introducing his work. It seemed the most important story to him that day was an action-packed exclusive. The kind of exclusive he was referring to was stories like a fight in a bar between two groups of men.

He described that as his" most memorable" story -" The protagonists hurled chairs and exchanged fierce blows (one had his nose bridge badly broken; the other had his face bloodied) until police on patrol intervened. We had everything caught on tape, and my crew and I went home happy with an action-packed exclusive".

Other scoops the reporter and his crew chased included a fire that gutted a car after it crashed into a ten-wheeler, a holdup incident, carjacking in a tunnel, and a fake kidn-apping case. Such stories were the focus of his news coverage and the theme of his article. Given the rampant corruption, the high profile problem of murdering journalists and other challenges the country is facing, can the freedom and the power of the media be put to better use?

The news media have also used their freedom to outdo rivals in the race to peddle newspapers and television programs. When members of the First Philippine Mount Everest Expedition scaled the world's tallest mountain, crews from both ABS-CBN and GMA-7, two TV networks, followed the team to cover the event. Both were exclusive broadcast partners, each network sponsoring its own climbers. Both networks wanted to break the news first and have better videos. And both networks denied that they tried to dictate the pace of the ascent. The competition was viewed as a" ratings war," or" a network war," which the networks denied.

The race in ratings sometimes resulted in tragedy. More than seventy people died in a rush to get inside a sports stadium, where a TV extravaganza sponsored by ABS-CBN was to take place, and the network found itself the subject of news. The motivation for staging the event was again fierce competition between ABS-CBN and GMA-7.

Media ownership pattern, on the other hand, is hardly representative of the interests of different sectors of the society when anybody can buy into the media as long as he or she has money.

Media in the Philippines remain an elite enterprise, and newspapers operate in the vested interests of their owners. Media owners sometimes use their newspapers to defend and advance their businesses and political interests. And political patronage in the press is not unusual.

Similar to the situation in Indonesia, money corrupts individual journalists as bribery gets in the way of reporting the truth." There are many journalists who allow themselves to be used as tools of the government".

One reporter wrote about a typical case where a highranking government official was trying to buy her silence with a thick envelope of cash.

The reporter was investigating bribery charges against the official and his wife. The reporter was" stunned" and" humiliated" by the matter-of-fact manner in which the bribes were delivered. The case showed the prevalence of corruption in Philippine journalism.

The chase after profits and mounting libel suits against the media prompted growing criticism against the media and calls for improving professionalism. The establishment of Citizen Press Councils and calls for appointing media ombudsmen to keep down libel suits were part of the efforts by the media industry to use the power of a free press more responsibly.

In Taiwan, the press started to enjoy press freedom after martial law was lifted in 1987, and political discussions are much more open in the press since. According to the 2005 Freedom House report, Taiwan is well known for having one of the freest media environments in East Asia because of its firm commitment to judicial independence and economic freedom. Today's media in Taiwan are among the freest and most competitive in Asia.

The media in Taiwan are free and powerful." For all its shortcomings, the press is free, bold and aggressive". Like their counterpart in the Philippines, the news media in Taiwan play a critical role in exposing government corruption, which would have remained hidden from public view without investigations by the media. Media exposés of corruption cases and scandals involving high-ranking officials resulted in devastating defeats in local elections and resignations of high officials.

However, the media in Taiwan are often criticized for abusing that power and freedom. They are often regarded as a source of social chaos and accused of stirring up disorder by making" unfounded reports" and spreading stories that were not true. Some media organizations tend to be biased or sensationalize their reports.

As Taiwan's democracy is sometimes ridiculed as" rambunctious," its media are also considered as lacking accuracy and accountability. To win sympathy and support, the island's embattled president Chen Shui-bian trumped up his family troubles, and the media dutifully sensationalized the story as soap operas.

For circulations and ratings, the media spent too much energy on sensationalizing crime stories and the private lives of public figures. One recent example involved a police investigation of a death. For two weeks, the media provided excessive coverage of the case on a daily basis, including the daily activities of the suspect and the police's pursuit.

In another extreme case, the Scoop Weekly, a tabloid

magazine, enclosed a VCD of an alleged sexual encounter of a female legislative candidate in one of its issues. The magazine defended itself by saying that the VCDs were enclosed in the magazine as" evidence" supporting the veracity of its investigative reporting.

Some reporters, in the rush to be the first to get the story out, sacrificed accuracy in their reporting rather than tried to find credible sources to check out the facts. And sometimes police complained that newsgathering and reporting got in the way of solving criminal cases." The freedoms that were so hard to obtain, ironically, now threaten some parts of a society that considers the press the enemy because of its influence and power".

The excesses of press freedom in Taiwan, the Philippines, and Indonesia are typical of press systems in transition from being tightly controlled to almost completely free. The new democracies in Eastern Europe have encountered similar problems, such as the boom of tabloid journalism, the withering of quality press, bribery, and corruption.

The media systems in transition reflect the problems of those societies undergoing major transformations - rough politics in the fight for the power vacuum, partisan press, intense competition because of the new freedom, corruption for lack of a strong and independent judiciary system, weak financial foundation for the media, and lack of training of the journalists.

Democracy is still young in these societies; it will take time for a democratic system to mature. Because of traditions and culture, press freedom in these countries will still have its ups and downs. The newfound press freedom in Asian societies has its own distinctive social and cultural contexts.

THE "AUTHORITARIAN PRESS" IN ASIA - THE INFLUENCE OF CONFUCIANISM

The press in Singapore and Malaysia is often regarded as the prototype of authoritarian press in Asia. In both countries, the means to control the press are very similar to those used in sixteenth or seventeenth century England, including government censorship, suspension of license, legal actions against the press, and even shutdown of the offending publications.

But that is where similarities with Western authoritarianism end. The authoritarian press theory was based on the historical analysis of sixteenth and seventeenth century England while the authoritarian press in Singapore and Malaysia is shaped more by the Asian cultural tradition and the practical needs of the countries' geo-political realities.

While government authority came more from the absolute power of the monarchy in sixteenth and seventeenth century England, in Asian societies, especially in Singapore, which is under the heavy influence of Confucius's teachings, governments regard themselves both as parents and as rulers, which helps explain why even gum chewing and flushing toilets are regulated. According to the Confucian hierarchical order of political system, government is the paternalistic figure of the land.

"The ruler is the wind. People are the grass. When the wind blows, the grass is sure to bend," Confucius said. But Confucius was also a philosopher. He said, "Authority springs from morality, not force". He believed that people should accept authority, but authority must be just. Confucius asked: "When government leads by the right example, who dares to go astray?" In contrast, authoritarian theory does not address the quality of a government or the morality of the rulers.

Singapore is a society where a no-nonsense government promotes Confucian values of education, hard work and clear moral principles. The Singaporean government is one of the very few in Asia where corruption is rare. The government is as clean as the streets in Singapore, which is often considered the cleanest city in the world. The government in Singapore prides itself on its system of meritocracy and efficiency.

Different views are tolerated to a certain extent, but if the press publishes articles the government takes offense to, the government pursues the press relentlessly all the way to the court, which often has a chilling effect on the press. Confucianism extols cooperative and harmonious relations, which are what the Singaporean government hopes to cultivate both at home and abroad.

The government keeps a watchful eye on the press for any stories that address race relations, religion, or problems in neighboring countries. Such stories are banned in the Singaporean press because of the mixed racial and religious makeup of its population and its often-sensitive relations with its neighbors.

Violence and chaos caused by racial and religious differences in neighboring countries put the Singaporean government on high alert. Former Prime Minister Lee Kuan Yew said that any journalist who did not support Singapore-Malaysia relations would be sent to jail.

Malaysia has many similarities with its neighbour, Singapore, in its treatment of the press, as the two countries were once merged into one for a brief period in their history. Both governments are unequivocal promoters of" Asian values" and loud critics of Western culture.

Asian values in Malaysia include emphasis on the social role of the press, which is for development, and on morality, which in part might have resulted from the Islamic influence in the country.

Confucian influences are not as heavy in Malaysia as in Singapore, where Chinese account for about 75% of the population. In Malaysia, Muslims make up about half of the population. Malaysian leaders, especially former Prime Minister Mahathir, have the government-knows-best attitude.

The government has set the goal of making Malaysia a developed country by the year 2020, and it wants the press to help in that endeavor, which means highlighting government development plans, promoting racial and religious harmony by suppressing coverage of racial and religious issues, and controlling Western influences by limiting overseas TV programming to 30%. While the Singaporean government is often criticized for trying to silence dissent and punish the press for negative coverage, the government in Malaysia has promoted positive press coverage on such topics as" Asian values" and national development.

In some aspects, Malaysian media seem to border on the communist system not only in promoting positive news coverage, but also in media ownership. Party press sets the trend in Malaysia, where political parties own major stocks in media agencies. The ruling political party UMNO owns media giants the New Straits Times and Utusan Malaysia.

The Chinese and Indian parties in the country also have acquired major stocks in media agencies that cater to their ethnic groups.

The government has a direct stake in the media too by owning the national news agency, Bernama, which has the right to distribute foreign news reports. Under authoritarian rule, governments do not own the media; they punish the media when they are not happy with the coverage. One salient feature of the authoritarian press system is government's various ways of punishing and controlling the press when the press is defiant.

Even though the Malaysian government punishes occasional rebellious papers, the Malaysian press, especially the mainstream press, mostly saves the government's wrath through compliance with very restrictive press laws.

The Printing Presses and Publications Act of 1984 gives the minister of home affairs the power to revoke publishing licenses without judicial review. As a result, the Malaysian mainstream press has become so tame that its credibility has been questioned.

Zaharom Nain wrote,"... The Malaysian mainstream media - the press and broadcasting - have never aspired to be the guardians of the freedom of speech." "... The mainstream newspapers'failure to be a credible source of information is a reflection of a journalist's failure in performing her duties professionally," a member of the National Union of Journalists said. The inaction of the press against government suppression of press freedom came under fire too." The credibility of Malaysian journalists has been damaged as much by dilution of professional standards and ethics as by passivity in tackling legal and administrative restrictions".

Chapter 8

Communist Press in Asia

Today's Asia hosts the majority of the world's remaining communist countries - China, Vietnam, Laos, and North Korea. Trying to understand the press systems in these countries using the Soviet communist press theory as a guide would be misleading.

The communist press theory was based on the model of the Soviet press system, which can't satisfactorily describe the varied press systems in these remaining communist countries today, especially the Chinese press system after more than twenty years of sweeping economic liberalization and opening to the outside world.

The Freedom House rated China 7 for political rights and 7 for civil liberties, not free for 1997-98 (on a scale of one to seven with one being most free and 5.5+ being not free), the same ratings for 1972-73, which meant that for the twenty-five years in between, political rights and civil liberties in the Chinese society remained the same. For its 2005 survey on press freedom, it ranked China the 177th out of a total of 197 countries studied.

The Freedom House rating was in sharp contrast to the 1998 U.S. State Department report, which stated that Chinese citizens benefited from" higher disposable income, looser economic control, greater freedom of movement, increased access to outside sources of information, greater room for individual choice, and more diversity in cultural life". Emmons wrote that," There are those who believe that the media and freedom of speech, in general, never have been as uninhibited as they are today...". Emmons cited in his paper," Surprisingly, the average Chinese citizen enjoys significantly more personal freedom today than ever before".

When China is undergoing economic reforms, what exactly does" media reform" mean? It meant the public's right to know according to late premier Zhao Ziyang; it meant commercializing Chinese media and building a stronger media industry according to late reform architect Deng Xiaoping; and it means the relevance of the media to the people according to current Chinese leader Hu Jintao.

Reforms bring choices, and freedom means having choices. Since the reform started, China's media outlets proliferated. Today China has around 2,000 newspapers, more than 9,000 magazines, 1,000 radio stations, and 200 TV stations broadcasting 2,900 channels. The choices and competition on the media market today stand in sharp contrast to the one voice on the media scene in the past when every city had only one Party paper. Choices, instead of one voice, symbolize the major changes Chinese media consumers have experienced.

Introducing the profit motive, which is absent from the Soviet press model, into the media sector was another reform measure that caused sweeping changes to the industry-it changed the nature of the media in China. Economic reform of the media in China began almost as early as the overall economic reform. And media commercialization becomes an important part of the development of the market economy as the government has adopted a policy of gradually cutting subsidies and encouraging commercialized financing.

Advertising, the capitalist genie, has returned to the world of communist media. To meet the new challenge, the press, including the ones directly under the control of the Party, is becoming increasingly commercialized. Even the official Xinhua news agency and the Party paper, People's Daily, are diversifying their product line to increase profits.

To be competitive on a booming media market, where the number of journalists has doubled in twenty years, media in China have to appeal to the readers, some of them by resorting to sensationalism. To speed up the reform, the government announced in June 2003 that it would end subsidies to all the newspapers in China except three papers and one journal, and all the publications in China had to sever their ties to government departments and stop mandatory subscriptions.

Those titles earning less than 50% of their revenues through voluntarily paid subscriptions had to be shut down. By November that year, a total of 1,452 Party and government newspapers had been affected, 673 of which had been suspended from publication.

The overhaul of the Chinese press system has substantially changed the economic and administrative relationships between the government and the press. From then on, the press has been financially independent of the government, even though the state remains the owner of the press. The biggest challenge facing Chinese editors today is to strike the right balance between being politically correct and economically viable.

In fact, one of the major problems hampering the development of the Chinese press today is the low ethical standards held by some local and commercial papers. Hunan TV, a challenging rival of China Central TV (CCTV), developed a huge following with a series on an orphaned woman looking for her biological parents. In its reporting, the network turned an old rape case into a love story, resulting in being sued. Some media outlets were given warnings and reporters detained for extorting large sums of money from people allegedly involved in wrongdoing.

It is no longer rare in China today that newspapers are exposed for their sensationalism, fabrications, or staged news, which are commonplace in a free press environment but seldom occur under a tightly controlled communist media system. Orthodox communist papers are serious and" clean."

The Soviet press model mostly prescribes a promotional role for the press - the press should be an agitator, an organizer, and propagandist for the socialist cause, but never a watchdog. In the Chinese press today, there is no lack of exposés or negative news, which is a taboo in the rigid communist media model, as bad news is perceived as demoralizing.

Given the rampant corruption among government

officials in China, some high-level government officials encouraged the press to play the watchdog role by engaging in more investigations. Zhang Baoming, head of the State Administration for Production Safety, called on the media for more active participation in the investigation of major industrial accidents, almost every one of which, he said, was connected with corruption.

Caijing, a financial magazine, made a name for itself for its investigative reporting of the financial sector. Who would have imagined that the communist press would engage in investigative reporting? Former Chinese Premier Zhu Rongji tried to promote the watchdog role of the media.

Commenting on a popular talk show on China Central Television," Focal Point" (Jiaodian Fangtan), which routinely exposes official corruption and mismanagement, Zhu praised the programme as" a mirror and watchdog of the government and a supervisor of the government through public opinion". Wu Guanzheng, secretary of the Central Commission for Disciplinary Inspection, also urged the media to play the watchdog role in the national campaign against corruption. He said media publicity was vital to the campaign, and the authorities should listen to" the voice of the media."

The Zhejiang provincial government encouraged the news media to provide tips directly to its inspection department as the government found it effective to follow and prosecute corruption cases exposed in the media. The government even offered rewards of up to 20,000 yuan ($2,500) if the tips were verified and led to prosecution. In contrast, the municipal government of Nanjing was widely criticized for stipulating that all corruption exposés be signed off by the person exposed in the story.

In Qijiang County, Chongqing municipality, hidden cameras were installed to monitor the performance of government officials. The Southern Metropolis Daily and the Beijing News both carried editorials, arguing that the watchdog role of the media would be much more powerful and effective than the hidden cameras, as it is a bottom-up rather than a top-down approach.

In many cases, the news media are playing such a vigorous watchdog role that a" Witness Protection Law" is being proposed as investigative reporting invites reprisals. Some news sources were detained, jailed, or sent to labour camps. In one case, an editor was beaten to death by Taizhou city police for an embarrassing exposé.

Attacks against journalists have increased in China in recent years as reporters have become more aggressive in reporting sensitive social issues. At least 100 journalists were physically attacked in 2003. In 2002, the central government was investigating provincial government officials in Jiangxi and Zhejiang provinces for punishing journalists who exposed problems in their jurisdictions.

The Soviet communist media did not carry exposés. In China, exposés of high-ranking officials, though allowed, still have to be approved by the government however. One other important feature of the communist press system is the state ownership of the media. The majority of the media outlets in China today are still owned by the state.

However, foreign investment is entering the Chinese media sector, and such investment as mandated by the rules of the World Trade Organization is increasing with the deepening of press reforms. Interest in China among international media groups surged in 2005 after the Chinese government issued rules allowing foreign investment in joint-venture television, radio, and film production companies. News Corporation, Viacom, and Sony Pictures were among the big names involved in joint ventures with Chinese media companies.

The current policy stipulates that investors are denied decision-making power in the media outlets'editorial content. But in practice, the situation is getting murky. The editorial staff of the China International Business, a monthly economic review, gets its salaries from Ringier AG of Switzerland. Such business arrangements are not rare. Many foreign publishers sign deals in media advertising or consulting but actually help produce content.

Under the Soviet press system, there was tight control of

information and very limited access to government information, resulting in more propaganda than information in the news media. In China today despite government control, access to information has gained substantial progress in recent years.

In 2000, the government of Anhui Province took the unprecedented step of issuing a regulation banning its officials from refusing interviews to the press. Other provinces and cities followed suit. Such regulations were unimaginable before the reforms or under the Soviet media model. The central government now has also installed a spokesman system to meet the needs of the press, both national and international.

In Shanghai, a reporter, based on a city ordinance mandating the disclosure of public information, sued the city planning department for repeatedly declining interviews. This was the first such case in China where a reporter sued a government department for violating his rights to reporting.

The reporter complained that city government departments often denied interviews to him. The city ordinance required city departments to disclose information concerning the economy, city management, and public services. Such ordinance was listed as top priority in the legislative plan of the State Council.

It would make disclosure as the principle and non-disclosure as the exception rather than the other way around as in the past. China is opening up. It has opened up its market to the world, including the media market, even though it is only the entertainment media for now. It is not difficult today to find popular foreign consumer magazines on the newsstands in China.

International Data Group, a Boston publisher, alone has invested $20 million in China, publishing twenty-eight titles and planning another four. These operations are either in the form of joint ventures or through licensing the titles and content for publication in China.

China is also working on an international media centre with a total floor space of 130,000 square meters, which will serve as an office building for more than 100 foreign media organizations in Beijing. And in 2001, Reuters's Qing Niao website, a site for trade information and e-business, made a low-key entry into China.

The Soviet communist media model was a closed system. But China has opened up, and it wants to reintegrate itself into the world community. The one medium that provides a public forum for the ordinary Chinese and connects the Chinese people directly with the rest of the world is the Internet, which claims about 137 million users in China by the end of 2006, the second largest in the world after the United States.

China has witnessed the fastest growth of Internet use among countries whose annual per-capita is less than $2,000, and the number of net users is expected to increase by at least 15% annually before 2010. The Internet is breaking through the silence of traditional media by posting stories rejected by official newspapers.

With its power of reaching millions of people at the same time, the Internet has directly helped in effecting legislative changes in the country by exposing police brutality, which brought about public outrage on an unprecedented scale and caught the attention of legislators and the government.

The Internet, with its public forums where people can discuss topics shunned by the traditional media, is producing a better informed, more vocal public and a more open society. Inadvertently, it has ushered in a public discourse that has been absent for almost half a century.

It also enabled direct communication between ordinary citizens and government officials. The acceptance of the Internet in China itself is one important indicator of the passing of the rigid communist media system in China, as Internet, a revolutionary medium, defies total control. Some media researchers argue that as long as there is government control, the media in China should be categorized as communist media.

It is true that there is still government control of the media in China - there are news topics on which diversity of opinion is not allowed, there are websites that are blocked, and there are newspaper editors that have been fired. However, since the start of the reforms, the changes that are occurring in China have substantially reduced government controls.

These changes are happening because of the intention of the government to open up, the new financial independence of the press, the proliferation of media outlets, and the availability of the Internet. Sometimes the sheer size of the country poses a challenge to effective control. For example, when the government could not effectively implement a ban on satellite dishes in 1994, it changed its policy by licensing them instead.

A year later the government also specified permissible programs and viewing hours. Foreign affairs used to be an area off limits for public discussions in the media. The advent of the Internet with its convenient online forums has made it a hot topic for public debate. Government control of the press is a universal phenomenon. The issue is the degree of control.

In the age of the Internet, total control is out of the question. And in the case of China, that control is being relaxed and challenged from all sides. More recent examples include the suspension and the return of the supplement of a major newspaper in Beijing and the debate over a section of a draft law on managing disasters and accidents.

The weekly" Freezing Point" published by the popular China Youth Daily, which stands out from other newspapers in China for its aggressive reporting and biting commentary, was shut down in late January 2006, and its editors removed to its research department because some government officials were not happy with one article.

The case was widely publicized by the media worldwide. The supplement resumed publication one month later following public outcry against such heavy-handedness against the press, including staff letters protesting the actions and an open letter to top Party officials signed by thirteen prominent scholars and former officials who were contributors to the supplement.

The writers of the open letter included Zhu Houze, a former Central Propaganda Department official; Hu Jiwei, a former editor-in-chief of the People's Daily, and He Weifang, a law professor from Peking University, who said," The purpose (of the letter) is to change the current incorrect policies on freedom of speech" , The letter said although not all signatories approved of the article, they all supported Freezing Point's right to publish it.

They quoted Chinese leader Hu Jintao as saying no organization in China has special legal privileges. The letter said that the newspaper suspension was neither legal nor sensible and it violated citizens'basic rights to speech and freedom of information, which are their constitutional rights.

Another controversy arose over a draft law on emergency management, which included industrial accidents, natural disasters, and health and public security crises. Part of the draft law addressed the news coverage of emergency situations by the media, stipulating that media outlets could face fines between 50,000 yuan (U.S.$6,250) and 100,000 yuan (U.S.$12,500) if they reported the emergency situations without authorization or released fraudulent reports and if such reports led to serious consequences.

The law was drafted following the aftermath of the outbreak of SARS, when health department officials hid the facts from the public, resulting in rampant rumors in the press and in the streets. Government officials said the purpose of the law was to ensure timely release of accurate information by local officials.

Opposition to the draft law was loud and clear. A legislator, He Keng, said journalism had its own rules and argued that the watchdog role of the media was not strong enough in China. The New Express, a commercial newspaper published by the Yangcheng Evening News, carried an editorial arguing that the law would diminish the watchdog role of the media, that there was no guarantee that the information released by government departments was accurate and that some" natural disasters" were man-made.

In a column in the outspoken Southern Metropolis Daily, Changping pointed out that in the case of coal mine disasters, often local officials and mine owners colluded with each other in covering up the facts of accidents as both profited from the mines. In such situations, how could the media wait for the local government to release accurate information? Changping argued.

One often ignored issue is the self-censorship in the newsrooms in China, which sometimes applies tighter control than the government does for the interests of the media organization or the management. For a lack of laws and regulations, the new media are trying to police themselves.

Nineteen websites jointly issued a set of self-disciplinary rules against bloggers'personal attacks, fabricated stories, plagiarism, and pornographic and violent content. Hosts of the sites said they were ready to delete such materials once they appear on their sites. Min Dahong, a journalism professor said that many big websites in the world have explicit written rules on deleting or editing users'messages that they regard as abusive, defamatory, offensive, obscene, or in violation of a specific law.

Ultimately how much freedom or control the Chinese media will experience is not only up to the government; it is also up to the editors and reporters of the media, especially those leading media organizations in Beijing, as to how far they will push. So far the most vigorous push comes mainly from local media outside of Beijing.

Following China's example, Vietnam started its own economic reforms in 1986 and" remains wedded to the Chinese model of reform". Its press system is also undergoing similar changes. The liberal economic reforms eroded the pervasive authority of the Party. As a result," Vietnam is no longer as tightly controlled as it used to be although it does remain an authoritarian one-party system". Facing a rise in corruption like China, the government encouraged the press to expose corruption, made new laws to facilitate news gathering, and warned against officials trying to obstruct journalists.

Even though strict censorship still exists in Vietnam today, meaningful independent journalism is possible on certain occasions. There are instances where journalists successfully challenged the police and the court in violating reporters'rights in newsgathering and forced the police and the court to back down.

" In terms of freedom, the press here in Vietnam has been getting better and more aggressive". One editor at Lao Dong (Labour), Nguyen Due Tuan, said," There is no question we have more freedom today.... Now, reporters like to see how far they can push and still get their stories published".

Similar to the situation in China, editors in Vietnam now have more discretion in deciding the content of their publications. The press in Vietnam is surprisingly lively in terms of the types of newspapers and magazines. Since the reforms, both the quantity and quality of the press have improved.

The press today is becoming more information oriented than ideology dependent, as the importance of information is generally recognized in a more market-oriented economy. The Internet entered Vietnam in 1997. By the end of 2006, the number of Internet users had reached 14.5 million.

Despite government announcement that access to the Internet would be unrestricted, the Freedom House reported that in 2004 the Vietnamese government suppressed dissent on the Internet with new guidelines of government control and censorship, including a permanent monitoring system aimed at the country's privately run Internet cafes.

Despite the reforms, the majority of the media outlets in Vietnam are still state-owned. But the government has permitted some form of private ownership of periodicals, a bolder step than China's. The condition for ownership is that the publication should be a joint undertaking between the owners and the relevant state agency. An example is the Vietnam Investment Review, the first foreign-owned, Western-style periodical in the country. The government also abolished direct subsidies to the press even though some form of state funding is still continuing.

As a result, the press is forced to become more commercialized, and the survival of the press is subject to market forces, which seems to dictate a success formula of tabloid journalism. Some papers publish uncommon crime stories gathered from police records, all in the name of exposing social problems. In the pursuit of profits, newspapers in Vietnam start to face criticisms about their low ethical standards. Some journalists in Vietnam now claim that they are having more debates on" responsibilities and morals of journalists" than on press freedom.

Early in the reform, the sensationalism and the increasingly aggressive investigative reporting alarmed the Party leaders, who worried that the state was losing control of information flow and wanted to rein in this threatening trend. The government began clamping down on the press in 1989 and tightened control of the media by establishing a new press department aimed at monitoring and controlling press coverage about security matters, issuing new rules regarding passing information to foreign news organizations, amending the 1990 press law, requiring compensation if news coverage leads to losses to the business interests of organizations or individuals.

The government also reminded the press to champion the fight against corruption and other social evils instead of seeking profits alone, but questioning Party rule remains expressly prohibited. The Vietnamese leaders are still ambivalent about the degree of control and the liberal reforms, which help with the country's economic development but threaten the power and control of the Party. North Korea may be the only communist country in Asia left with a press that could still fit the Soviet media model. There has been very little change in the country despite the fact that other remaining communist countries in Asia are undergoing major reforms to open up and revive their economies. Perhaps because of the poor performance of its economy, the widespread and chronic famine, and tremendous external pressure to change, the government is exercising strict control of information flow across its borders.

As a result, information about the country is scarce even with CNN's 2006 documentary, which was shot inside the country with a hidden cell-phone camera. North Korea is the most censored country in the world. Its people experience the world's deepest information void, and the country has no independent journalists.

The main role ascribed to the press is that of spreading the viewpoint of the government. All newspapers and broadcasting stations are under direct government control, and all news is positive. According to the 2003 annual report by Reporters Without Borders, all the news media in the country focused on the personality cult of Kim Jong Il.

The report said three subjects dominated the coverage in the print media: the personality of Kim Jong II, praise of the army, and criticism of the country's foes, especially South Korea, the United States, and Japan. In a story, the official Korean Central News Agency reported that Kim Jong Il was so beloved that after a deadly munitions train explosion in a populated area, people ran into buildings to save the ubiquitous portraits of the" Dear Leader" before they rescued their own family members.

Nothing was mentioned in the news media about the malnutrition among children and urban populations or the failure of the government's" self-reliance" policy. In the leading Party paper, the Rodong Shinmun, commentaries carry greater weight than news stories, and reporters do not compete for scoops among themselves, who are given instructions from the Central Party Committee's propaganda and agitation department on what to cover and in how many pages. Anyone disobeying the instructions is severely punished. Reporters may be jailed for a commentary that deviates from the Party line. Harassment, psychological pressure, intimidation, and round-the-clock surveillance are routine.

The North Korean newspapers do not carry any advertisements except a handful of government notices. For the mass media in North Korea, there is neither private ownership nor market competition. North Korea's revised 1998 constitution guarantees citizens'rights of freedom of speech, of the press, of assembly, demonstration, and association.

But the government prohibits the exercise of these rights in practice. There are strict controls to prevent access to any kind of news coming from abroad. Radios sold in North Korea can receive only domestic programming. Radios obtained from abroad must be altered to work in a similar manner. The national news agency has Internet sites hosted in Japan. Direct access to the web is limited to the privileged few. And to prevent Western influence, very few journalists in North Korea receive training in the West.

It is also hard for the foreign media to do reporting inside the country as they are all portrayed by the regime as liars seeking to destabilize the government. Foreign journalists visiting North Korea have to be on guided tours.

However, in 2006, the Associated Press became the first Western news organization to have a permanent bureau in the country. AP Television News's full-time office in Pyongyang operates in association with the country's state-run broadcaster and is staffed mainly by local reporters. With the increase in international trade, even North Koreans have started to have greater contact with foreigners, which might result in greater access to information from the outside world.

The press in North Korea seems to be the prototype of the communist press, but it does not represent the trend where the press in other communist countries is heading. It is misleading to put the press systems in China, Vietnam, and North Korea in the same category. To do so, media researchers have to disregard the sweeping changes in the Chinese and Vietnamese press.

THE" DEVELOPMENT MEDIA" IN ASIA

Neglected by the authors of the four press theories were media in the poorer countries of the world-development media. The press in South Asia may best be described by the concept of development journalism, a concept developed later to supplement the four theories, as the development of communities and giving voice to the underprivileged are major goals of many of the local media in the region.

The development press is popular in the region perhaps because South Asia is the least economically developed region on the continent. More than half of the world's underweight children lived in India, Bangladesh, and Pakistan, said a recent UNICEF report on the global progress on children's issues.

In India, approximately 47% of the under-five population

was underweight. The report found that South Asia was the only region that showed a gender bias with regard to child nourishment, with girls more likely to be underweight than boys. The issue of undernourishment points to the problems of poverty, lack of education, and inequality in the region.

In India, communication not only means the transfer of information, but also includes the participation in the society and in the community. The Indian brand of development journalism" focuses on the needs of the poor, the deprived, and the marginalized and emphasizes their effective participation in developmental planning". It motivates the participation of the people and advocates for their interests instead of the views of the policy makers and the planners. And it promotes social justice for all.

Journalists in the country believe that the media should not only carry stories about health campaigns like the one against AIDS but also discuss issues that are important for a civil society because only the mass media can reach the vast rural population and give them a voice in debates affecting their lives.

The mass media can also play a crucial role in social progress, as any transitional society will encounter new attitudes, a new mindset, and a new value system. Development journalism enthusiasts in India conducted workshops for social activists to train them to write stories about development issues and workshops for local editors and journalists to familiarize them with realities and issues in local communities. Commercial newspapers also play a role in development journalism.

The Jharkhand-based Prabhat Khabar had been doing development journalism by giving people information on science, information technology, economics, and the comparative financial progress of different states. The paper also conducted" readers'courts," where readers could interact with journalists and discuss ways of improving the quality of the paper, much like the role of the focus groups in civic or public journalism in the United States.

Radio plays a special role in development journalism in

South Asia because of its easy and wide reach in the vast rural areas, where literacy rate is still relatively low. The Indian communications NGO (non-government organi-zation) had been highlighting the importance of community radio in India for over half a decade and called for the extension of community broadcasting.

In India, awards are given to mentors of development journalism for encouraging and nurturing journalists to investigate and write on development issues and for supporting journalism initiatives towards" a common social good". Journalists and media researchers in India and Pakistan criticized some of the mainstream media for their elitist approach, focusing on the prominent while ignoring the plight of the underprivileged in rural communities by following Western news values.

The degree of press freedom in South Asia, however, varies considerably from country to country. Once the largest colony in the world, India is the largest democracy in the world today. Only under Prime Minister Indira Gandhi was an attempt made to curtail press freedom by declaring a political emergency to suspend civil rights. The government of Narasimha Rao tried to prevent exposés of government corruption under the pretext of protection of privacy. Despite such government attempts at control, the press in India has largely remained private, free, and vibrant. Cushrow R. Irani, editor-in-chief and managing director of The Statesman, said that India's press today is as free as it chooses to be. N. P. Chekkutty, editor of Media Focus, wrote," The Indian media works in an atmosphere of freedom. We are the purveyors of free thoughts and opinions. We do reflect the freedom of expression the Constitution guarantees to our citizens, and we, therefore, are the epitome of a free, liberal society".

With the freedom it enjoys, the press in India often plays its watchdog role seriously." Newspapers in India are completely free, as free as the newspapers in the United States, as they are privately owned and free of censorship". It is the newspapers that have exposed corruption in India, though some journalists are attacked for their investigative reporting.

The Indian press has always been vigilant about protecting its freedom and aggressive in reporting.

Free as it may be as the press in the United States, the Indian press clearly differs from the Western libertarian press system in the perception of its mission. For its social role, the Indian press may be closer to the civic or public journalism in America, which also prescribes an advocacy role for the press. However, in India development journalism represents the aspirations of many journalists, while in America the ethical implications of civic and public journalism are still being debated.

In India, press freedom is guaranteed by the Constitution and the independent court system, which is very similar to the situation in neighboring Pakistan, formerly a part of India before its independence. Behind India, which has a relatively low literacy rate of 65%, Pakistan's literacy rate is even lower at 38%, which limits the growth of its press industry.

There are about 1,330 newspapers in print in Pakistan, but only 1% of the population buys a newspaper. The press in Pakistan is independent of the government and mostly privately owned.

Major public issues are debated in the press, which has become an instrument for change. In Pakistan no law governs the registration of publications. In recent years, Pakistan has been moving toward greater press freedom, and its press is among the most outspoken in South Asia. In both India and Pakistan when the government tries to crack down on critical press coverage of the government, the courts often strike down government charges in support of press freedom.

There are exceptions to the constitutional guarantees of the freedom of speech and of the press in Pakistan, the most important of which is the" reasonable restrictions imposed by law in the interest of the glory of Islam". The Constitution prohibits the ridicule of Islam, of the armed forces, or of the judiciary.

Development journalism is perhaps less developed in Pakistan than in India. Circulation of newspapers in the rural areas of the country is one of the lowest in the world because of the urban orientation of the papers and the cost of subscription in addition to a low literacy rate. The rural market is largely untapped.

The dramatic increase in the number of publications in recent years is not supported with trained staff. Many journalists, especially rural ones, lack the basic skills to cover the complex issues important to their communities. However, electoral politics has increased the importance of rural centres in the emerging democracy of Pakistan.

Supporting development journalism, the Pakistan Press Foundation (PPF) was established to help raise the standards of journalism, particularly of the vernacular and regional press, and to promote greater awareness of social and development issues through the media. In 1999, PPF restarted the rural journalists'skills development project.

By 2002 hundreds of Pakistani rural journalists have attended the workshops. The emphasis of the workshops is on improving basic skills of newsgathering and news writing, as participants are given exercises using actual issues, such as violence against women, environmental issues, child labour, bonded labour, and crime rates. The end of monopoly of the electronic media in Pakistan provides new hopes of reaching a rural audience as radio is acknowledged to be a more suitable and affordable means of providing local communities with a voice of their own. It is more interactive and more suitable for community development. In less than six years, between 2000 and 2006, the broadcast sector completely changed the monolithic landscape that existed for about fifty-three years.

But the proliferation of radio stations has created the co-existence of robust liberty and open lawlessness, and commercial interests dominate the airwaves while development journalism still needs time to take hold. Research on the topic, however, is several steps ahead of the media industry.

Development journalism is regarded as an Asian model of journalism, stemming from the dissatisfaction with the Western news values that do not serve the cause of national development. Western news values of timeliness, prominence, proximity, conflict, and the bizarre exclude the ordinary people in the news unless they are involved in accidents, violence, or catastrophes.

Development journalism, on the other hand, should focus on the educational function of the news, stories about social needs, self-help projects, and obstacles to development. In the exploration of the development journalism model by Asian media researchers, the watchdog role of the media was emphasized, and the media were urged to remain vigilant against government involvement.

In Sri Lanka, three newspaper groups dominate the island's newspaper scene - the ANCL, the Upali Newspapers Ltd. and the Wijeya Newspapers Ltd. The ANCL has been under government control since 1973, while the other two are privately owned but have close family connections to political parties. In the broadcasting sector, Sri Lanka was perhaps the first British colony to introduce radio broadcasting a few years after its inauguration in Europe in 1920s. The country liberalized its radio and TV sectors ahead of the rest of Asia. It permitted the establishment of more commercial radio stations than any other country in the region and put the state-controlled Sri Lanka Broadcasting Corporation under considerable competitive pressure. It also allowed private radio stations to broadcast news and current affairs, unlike some of its neighboring countries.

Efforts at setting up community radio have never stopped in Sri Lanka. Universities in Sri Lanka and UNESCO played host to regional workshops on community radio for participants from South Asian countries. The goal of such workshops was to make community radio a reality in South Asia and encourage- cooperation among community radio advocates in the region. Radio still is a popular medium in South Asia, particularly in rural areas. In Sri Lanka telephone boxes, where a radio station button is installed, allow listeners to contact a station without paying a fee. The system makes it easier for listeners to participate in the programs and solve problems in the communities.

The mass media in Sri Lanka also play a role in

environmental education. Most people in both urban and rural areas use different media outlets as their primary source of environmental education, especially the print media. Television is the next major source of information for the urban population, while radio for the rural population. The media cover environmental issues in the form of news, editorials, investigative stories, entertainment, and educational programs.

Development journalism in the country can have a bigger potential if the government allows even greater participation by the public in media discussions, which is often limited when there is an increase in guerrilla warfare in the country. It is evident from the above discussions that the degree of press freedom under the development concept varies from country to country, and that is where the controversy with the concept lies. While one scholar describes it as" the pursuit of cultural and informational autonomy" and" support for democracy" among other goals, another scholar criticizes it as" a rationale for autocratic press control" and" guided press".

Where do all the discussions about the press systems in Asia leave us theoretically? When theories encounter major difficulties in serving as a guide to the understanding of the realities they are supposed to describe, new paradigms are needed. So are the criteria of the Freedom House for assessing global press freedom and civil liberties when their rankings fail to reflect changing realities. Obviously, more factors should be taken into consideration than the current criteria.

The Last Rights concluded that the four theories were a" durable" but now" questionable" map and that a" more adequate" map is needed. The book presented inspiring criticism of the four press theories but stopped short of proposing a new paradigm.

Chapter 9

Constructing Alternative Press Theories

Both Eastern and Western media researchers have tried to redress the deficiencies of the four-theory model by creating their own models. Three more theoretical concepts-development journalism, democratic-participant media, and the revolutionary media-were developed to accommodate the progress and changes in press systems and to supplement the dominant paradigm's four press categories.

Of the new theoretical concepts, development journalism has caused more controversies because the degree of press freedom varies greatly from society to society, and the very concept may imply a role for the government. The controversy also seems to stem from the fact that the deciding factor in creating the four press theories was the presence or absence of press freedom, which was defined mainly in terms of government control.

Based on such a criterion, how can one type of press system allow vastly different degrees of press freedom in different societies? When a new concept cannot be fit into the established paradigm, it becomes" controversial." Progressive, insightful, and creative as these new theories are, they are mostly supplementary to the established four press theories.

More ambitious efforts were made by Ralph Lowenstein, J. Henry Altschull, John C. Merrill, and Shelton A. Gunaratne, who constructed alternative models reclassifying press systems. Ralph Lowenstein developed a" progressive typology," according to which," press systems evolved from authoritarian to libertarian, to social libertarian or social centralist, and then to a big futuristic question mark".

This typology seems to have the same tendency as the established four theories of basing its discussions mainly on the development paths of Western press systems, which makes it less relevant to the evolution of press systems elsewhere in the world. J. Henry Altschull proposed three basic media models - market, Marxist, and developing. To make the concepts value free, Altschull described them as market, communitarian, and advancing. In trying to reclassify media systems, Altschull brought in the element of culture and belief systems.

He explained that the market system emphasized the" individual" while the communitarian system focused on the" communal life" or the" collective." Altschull also analysed the role of the media - preserving status quo under both market and communitarian models and advocating change under the advancing model.

He explained that there were variations within each model, giving the classification much flexibility. With the exception of the advancing model describing press systems in the South, Altschull's models were also based mainly on the analysis of Western media systems even though he classified his models also as East, West, and South, where East refers to Marxism and the former Soviet communist bloc in Eastern Europe rather than to Asia.

The only Eastern society mentioned in the analysis was Japan. Altschull explained that despite the variations within the market model, the basic belief systems - hostility to a communitarian belief system - remain intact." Discord notwithstanding, the broad sweep of the first movement of the symphony is heard throughout the industrialized capitalist world, in Japan as in Denmark and Canada".

Despite Western influence, the Japanese society, steeped in Asian culture and Confucian traditions, has no such hostility. As discussed earlier in this chapter, the press club system in Japan dictates communal behaviour within the industry by discouraging competition and scoops and encouraging collective reporting. A mixture of the East and the West, Japan proves to be a difficult case to be classified.

John C. Merrill's circular model shows that individualistic press systems gravitate toward libertarianism and more collectivistic systems are at the authoritarian end. Merrill said,"... the basic model is a simple spectrum, with authoritarianism at one end and libertarianism at the other. All press systems fall somewhere along this continuum".

Merrill's model resembles Altschull's models without the" advancing" or" South" element. Men-ill's model has the merit of built-in flexibility. The classification of a press system depends on in which direction the system gravitates. But it is still difficult to place Japan on Merrill's model. The Japanese press is mostly free from government control, but it is not individualistic. The press club system emphasizes collective action, but it cannot be described as authoritarian.

The models proposed by Altschull and Merrill represented major improvements over the four-theory model - AltschulPs model moved away from the exclusive emphasis on government control, and Men-ill's model had the merit of built-in flexibility to accommodate different types of press systems and changes within those systems.

Despite Men-ill's inclusion of the communitarian factor, the two models still seem to largely rely on Western philosophies, scholarship, and examples of Western media performances. Jiafei Yin called for the construction of a new model, which would be based on a broader foundation of both Western and Eastern philosophies and cultural influences, but did not produce an actual model.

Shelton A. Gunaratne brought in both Eastern and Western philosophical, religious, and cultural traditions in building his model-The Dao of the Press. There are two parts to Gunaratne's model: one part is the libertarian-authoritarian (L-A) continuum with varying shades of social responsibility across the continuum, and the other part is a centre-semiperiphery-periphery world system with individuals and groups, nation-states, and the world system at different levels. And all the three levels" autopoietically adjust the degree of free expression" along the L-A continuum. Gunaratne's model emphasizes both Eastern and Western cultural values in the definitions and interpretations of the term" social responsibility," giving the model much needed flexibility in accommodating different shades of social responsibility found in world cultures.

Merrill also addressed the relativity of the concept of responsibility among societies and even within a society. Similar to many of the previous press theories and models, Gunaratne's L-A continuum also focuses on the libertarian-authoritarian dichotomy, reflecting Western emphasis on freedom and liberty.

With the rich heritage of Asian philosophies and cultures, can a new model reflect diverse global cultural values and describe and explain press systems around the world without bias either from the West or the East?

After all, different cultures prioritize values differently. Therefore, press theories that are supposed to address global press systems should have a wider base to reflect a broader, more balanced global view. With adequate attention to factors such as world history, global cultures, and economic pressure, the problems inherent in the four established theories because of the authors'Western bias and their sole focus on governmental influences can be addressed.

For a new paradigm of press theories, the optimal balance between specificity and universality should also be considered. The four theories of the press have the beauty and elegance of a very simple but clear structure - four categories under a dichotomy, which aimed to describe and explain press systems in the whole world.

Conveniently general as they are, the four or five theories have difficulties in providing a reliable guide to the global press systems. The universality of the theories is limited. However, if categories are too specific and accurate in describing particular press systems, there may be too many categories for the model to be an effective guide. One other important factor that needs to be paid attention to in building a more reliable press model is that the model should be dynamic so that it can accommodate the changes in the press systems around the world. Obviously, press systems in the new democracies in Eastern Europe are very different from the press systems in the West even though they all operate under democratic systems now.

The press systems in the new democracies in Asia, such as Indonesia, Cambodia, the Philippines, Taiwan, and South Korea, vary from those in Eastern Europe despite the fact that they are all new democracies and share some similarities. And the press system in China today cannot be compared with the Chinese press system two decades ago, or the press system in North Korea. It would defeat the purpose of having models if every time any changes occur, new models have to be created.

A DICHOTOMY OF VALUES, EAST AND WEST

A new paradigm of press theories requires new ways of thinking in order to broaden the foundation. In this section, an examination is conducted of the dominant Eastern and Western cultural values, which are by no means exclusive to either the East or the West but rather reflect the quintessence of each.

To summarize Asian, or more particularly the Confucian, culture, leading Confucian scholar Tu Wei-ming said: "Industrial East Asia, under the influence of Confucian culture, seems to have developed a different kind of modern civilization, less adversarial, less individualistic, and less self-interested. One sees there the coexistence of market economy and government leadership, democratic parity with meritocracy and individual initiatives with group orientation."

THE INDIVIDUAL VERSUS THE STATE AND FAMILY (THE GROUP)

Western libertarian philosophy values the independence and rights of each individual. John Stuart Mill's On Liberty spelled out classic liberal individualism-it "set out the limits to the legitimate interference of collective opinion with individual independence". Mill wrote that the only warranted interference with the liberty of an individual is for mankind's self-protection, that is, to prevent harm to others, and that no power should be exercised over an individual for his own good. "Over himself, over his own body and mind, the individual is sovereign."

The Confucian thought, however, focuses on the state and the family. Confucius believed that only when the state and families are strong can the well-being of individuals be guaranteed. In the equation of the state, family, and individuals in Confucian societies, individuals are often encouraged and expected to sacrifice their own rights and interests for the sake of the state and family if contradictions should arise, which is in sharp contrast to Mill's belief that the individual is sovereign.

In Confucian societies, the state is sovereign. In Western culture, individualism is extolled, but in Eastern culture, people are taught to think about "us." In the West, ideal societies are composed of free individuals while in Confucian societies the individual "is not viewed as an isolated individual but as a centre of relationships".

The Chinese tradition has largely been influenced by a Confucian-based relational and social definition of person instead of by any concept of discrete individuality. "Under the sway of this relational understanding of human being, the mutuality and interdependence of personal, familial, societal, and political realization in the classical Chinese model can and has been generally conceded."

FREEDOM AND RIGHTS VERSUS RESPONSIBILITY

John Locke, an early libertarian, believes that freedom is essential to the full development of a human being. Merrill summarized Locke's philosophy as "Each person has a natural right to be free and not to be subjected to the will of another." Freedom, for Locke, is a "natural" right.

"Besides being bound by natural law, humans possess natural rights, in particular the right to life, self-defence, and freedom. They have also duties; in particular, the duty not to give away their rights".

The Enlightenment in eighteenth century Europe led to the rise of classical liberalism and capitalism. It also led to the French and American revolutions, which uprooted the power of religion and the aristocracy in France and heavily influenced the most distinguished leaders of the American Revolution-Jefferson, Washington, Franklin, and Paine.

"The language of natural law, of inherent freedoms, of self-determination, which seeped so deeply into the American grain, was the language of the Enlightenment..". "Give me liberty or give me death." Patrick Henry's rallying call meant that there was no compromise over liberty-to be free is the precondition to live.

In the East, the emphasis is on being responsible and loyal rather than on being free. Western libertarian philosophers' focus of attention falls on the welfare of the individual, so it is only logical that these philosophers advocate that these individuals should be equal and free to pursue what they want.

Confucian thought lays emphasis on the group; hence, there is the concern of being responsible and loyal to the group. In his research, Tu pointed out the Asian focus on the ethic of service and obligation.

INDIVIDUAL FREEDOM AND HAPPINESS VERSUS PUBLIC GOOD AND RESPONSIBILITY

Mill, a defender of personal and political liberty, said in his On Liberty: "The only freedom which deserves the name, is that of pursuing our own good in our own way, so long as we do not attempt to deprive others of theirs, or impede their efforts to obtain it".

Mill's "sovereign self" echoed the U.S. Bill of Rights and the Declaration of Independence in upholding individual freedom and rights and the pursuit of happiness, not individual or collective responsibility.

So when President Kennedy demanded, "Ask not what your country can do for you; ask what you can do for your country," it was refreshing to the American youth as their civic education focused mostly on the value of equality, freedom, and rights embedded in the Constitution when they grew up.

Confucius teachings emphasize a strong commitment to the world and encourage sacrifice of self-interest to be ethical. The Confucian concept of the ethical links up directly with the public good.

And Confucius believes "self-realization is fundamentally a social undertaking, therefore, 'selfish' concerns are to be rejected as an impediment to one's own growth and self-realization".

LEGAL VERSUS MORAL

In Western democratic societies, the legal system is very well developed as the law embodies the ideal that everyone is equal before the law. And citizens have a strong sense of the law, which sets the boundary of people's behaviour, including what parents legally can or cannot do in disciplining their children. In Asian societies, especially more traditional and less developed societies such as China, the legal system is much less well developed.

With the opening up of the country's economy, China's legislative body, the National People's Congress, has been busy making laws as conflicts in the past were resolved mostly through mediation based on judgments of who was right and who was wrong.

And a major part of Confucius's teachings comprises moral guidelines, which is why he was also considered a moralist. Confucius firmly believes that children are the responsibility of their parents and that aging parents are the responsibility of their grown-up children whether it is legally required or not. As a result, Chinese press occasionally exposes cases of mistreating aging parents by their grown-up children even though it is a private matter.

Likewise, Confucius believes that it is parents' fault if a child goes astray. Even today some immigrant Asian parents are surprised by the child abuse laws of the United States, where children are encouraged to call the police if they are spanked by their parents.

Such laws would shock Confucius. Confucius's teachings also place emphasis on being just and public minded. It would be unimaginable to Confucius that one country could have billionaires the same time it had a trillion dollars of national debt.

According to the moral teachings of Confucius, those who pursue only personal interests (Ii) are the "little men" (xiaoren), people of no character; only those who think about what is appropriate and beneficial to all concerned (yi) are the "gentlemen" (junzi), people of noble character.

TO BE FREE TO EXPLORE VERSUS TO KNOW RIGHT FROM WRONG

Western libertarians advocate for a free marketplace of ideas, where the public should be left free to explore and discover the truth on their own. In his pamphlet, Areopagitica, John Milton argues that truth would emerge victorious over falsehood should the two be locked in a grapple. John Milton also wrote about the importance of diversity of opinions and perspectives. In Asian societies influenced by Confucian thinking, especially in the case of China after almost 5,000 years of civilization, truth seems to be self-evident. In such cases, the focus is on teaching the people what is right and what is wrong rather than the freedom to explore what is right and what is wrong.

The real challenge becomes the task of convincing the people, or in an ideal Confucian way, for people to convince themselves, to always make the right choice. Confucian scholar Tu Wei-ming phrased the contrast as "the right to think" versus "right thinking."

In Western democracies, the emphasis is on the process-if decisions are made with public input. In Confucian societies, the emphasis is on the result-if the right decision is made. The process often is deemed less relevant.

DEMOCRACY VERSUS MERITOCRACY

The U.S. Declaration of Independence states unequivocally at the very beginning, "all men are created equal." The conviction in the equality among men forms the basis of Western democratic governments-government of the people, by the people, and for the people. Such libertarian thinking has deep roots in the history of Western philosophy. In Two Treatises of Civil Government, Locke maintains that before there were any states to make statutes, men were aware of a natural law, which taught that all men were equal and independent.

"These men, with no earthly superior above them, are in a state of liberty, but not a state of licence."In his book, A Theory of Justice, John Rawls promotes the adoption of a "veil of ignorance," which would ideally eliminate all the personal identifiers of each individual-male or female, black or white, rich or poor, intelligent or not-and return everyone to his or her original position of being equal with everyone else. "Rawls believes that justice will come forth from a discussion by rational and equal people concerned with their own interests but without anyone being advantaged or disadvantaged". Western societies are democratic and horizontal, emphasizing public participation in the government, while Confucian societies are hierarchical and vertical, believing in meritocracy instead of democracy.

For more than a thousand years in the history of China, only top scholars after rigorous national exams became government officials. In Singapore today, the brightest young people are selected for education in world's top universities supported with government funding so they will become the next generation of worthy leaders. "Statecraft is an integral part of Confucian learning". The ideal Confucian officials are people with "inner sagehood and outer kingliness."

Equality in human relations is a foreign concept in Confucian thinking as he decreed three sets of subservient relationships: subjects should obey their kings, sons should obey their fathers, and wives should obey their husbands. Confucius was not a democrat as some Confucian scholars tend to believe.

CIVIL LIBERTIES VERSUS SOCIAL ORDER AND STABILITY

The concept of human rights was developed during the

Enlightenment. The Bill of Rights as amendments to the U.S. Constitution marked a milestone in mankind's fight for civil liberties. Western democratic societies keep a watchful eye on the government to prevent it from encroaching upon those rights. The most recent example was the heated U.S. Congressional debate on the Bush administration's domestic spying programme.

In contrast, a salient feature of Confucian thinking in government is the primacy of political order. In China, the traditional assumption has been that personal order and the order of a society entail each other. Thus, in Confucian societies, governments expect respect and obedience to keep social order.

Social stability often takes precedence over civil liberties and is regarded as vital to the strength of a country and the welfare of its people. The Confucian order was built on traditional values and norms. Confucius's unwavering focus on social order and stability might have been the result of the endless wars China was embroiled in during his lifetime.

Thousands of years later, some Asian leaders could not agree more with the ancient Chinese philosopher. Fighting back criticism about too much control in his country, Lee Kuan Yew, first and former prime minister of Singapore who led the city-state for thirty-one years, said, "Without order and stability, nothing can be achieved". Lee was responsible for turning Singapore from a fishing village at the end of the Second World War into one of the cleanest and richest countries in the world today.

COMPETITION VERSUS HARMONY

Capitalism thrives on free competition on the market, which is supposed to drive economic growth even though such growth may be achieved at a social cost. Competition presupposes freedom and equality, but competition spawns conflicts as well-disputes between management and labour, hostile business takeovers, smearing political campaigns, fights in sports arenas, and even the constant race to be the most popular teen in high school.

As a result of competition, people are labeled as winners and losers. And the rule of competition decides that there are often more losers than winners, resulting in many unhappy people.

In some Asian societies such as China and Singapore, and even in some European countries such as Germany, comparative advertising is banned. In Japan and South Korea, state-guided capitalism softens real competition. "Harmony is at the core of the Chinese culture". Preferred methods of resolving conflicts are building consensus and making compromise rather than many voices competing.

"A pertinent contrast can be developed between the western liberal commitment to many voices and the traditional Chinese concern for a communitarian consensus as a social good". One values pluralism; the other harmony. The "promotion of harmony and goodwill among individuals and their families and community in the context of the five constants: ran, yi, li, zhi, and xin (humanity, righteousness, decorum, wisdom, and trust) is a social responsibility from the Confucian point of view". However, the ancient Chinese sage would be flabbergasted to witness the transformations China is going through today. Since China ushered in the market economy and private enterprise, competition is becoming a new way of life, bringing relentless assault on traditional values and leaving the conservatives lamenting the decline in moral standards.

ADVERSARIAL WATCHDOG

Press in the West takes pride in being a watchdog of the government. The uncovering of the Watergate scandal has inspired young journalists to follow the footsteps of Bob Woodward and Carl Bernstein. Dan Rather's dogged pursuit of the truth in Bush's service in the National Guard cost his career. To deal with an inquiring press, government officials hide behind press secretaries.

In traditional societies, people tend to be in deference to their governments. In Confucian societies, the government is supposed to take care of the people, and the people are expected to respect the government. "Confucianism holds that man is born for uprightness, and that people's goodwill is essential for good government in the context of an intellectual democracy headed by a benevolent ruler".

Chinese "benevolent despotism" fascinated Western thinkers. In Confucian societies, the press becomes a tool for nation building. Even in Japan and South Korea, both democratic societies, press tends to keep cozy relationships with the government and is, thus, reduced to a lapdog.

The dichotomy of dominant Western and Eastern values does not imply that there are no overlapping areas between Western and Eastern cultures. There are Western philosophers such as Plato and Rousseau who put emphasis on the state and the collective rather than the individual and preferred rule by the elite, which is very close to the Confucian ideal of government.

In The Social Contract, Rousseau promotes public good and common interest instead of interests of individuals. In the East, there are also philosophical schools such as Taoism that focuses on individuality and extols the virtue of being free, free from the constraints of governments and institutions for the full and free development of the potential of each individual.

But these philosophical schools in the East or the West have not become the dominant influence in their respective cultures. By and large, contemporary Western societies extol freedom and individuality, while Asian societies emphasize interests of the collective and the concept of responsibility regardless of political systems.

Some critics may contend that few Asian societies today including China can be described as Confucian societies because of the influence from the West. Indeed, modernization has inevitably had an impact on Asian societies, especially the young, who are much more accepting of what is Western.

Tu Wei-ming said: "The Westernization of Confucian Asia, including Japan, the two Koreas, mainland China, Hong Kong, Taiwan, Singapore, and Vietnam, may have forever altered its spiritual landscape. But its indigenous resources, including Mahayana Buddhism, Daoism, Shintoism, Shamanism, and other folk traditions, have the resiliency to resurface and make their presence known in the new syntheses."

Confucianism is neither a political system nor a religion; it is a way of thinking and a way of life. It is deep-rooted in the cultures of Confucian societies, and it is reflected in the decisions people make in their everyday lives, including the value of family ties, education, and hard work. A recent media farce in China provides a glimpse of the undisputable respect Confucius still enjoys in China today.

A Peking University professor was quoted in the media as saying that Zhang Ziyi, an internationally known Chinese actress, who was featured on the cover of an issue of Newsweek in 2005 and at the Oscar award ceremony in 2006, was greater than Confucius.

The statement, perceived as an insult to the Chinese culture, sparked a public outcry on the Internet condemning the professor. Bombarded with interview requests from the media, the professor had to post an article on his blog, claiming that he was misquoted by the media for sensationalism.

He explained that Confucius represented China's elite culture, while Zhang Ziyi represented its pop culture. The professor hoped that with the actress's international appeal, she could attract more worldwide interest in Confucianism.

An examination of dominant Eastern and Western values helps provide a more balanced foundation for building a new press model. A New Model: The Two-Dimensional Freedom Responsibility Coordinate System

THE SYSTEM

Based on earlier press models and on an analysis of the salient values of the Western and Eastern cultures, a new press model is proposed here, which is a two-dimensional coordinate grid with the horizontal axis denoting the degree of freedom in a press system and the vertical axis indicating how responsible a press system is. The system illustrates that a free press can be responsible or irresponsible, and that a press that is not free can also be responsible or irresponsible. Merrill also believes in the possible existence of responsible authoritarian systems and responsible libertarian systems.

THE TWO-DIMENSIONAL MODEL

The major difference between what is proposed here and most of the theories and models before it is that this proposed model has departed from the traditional one-dimensional models, which focus mainly on the degree of freedom in a press system, reflecting Western philosophical emphasis on the concept of freedom.

The proposed two-dimensional model, instead, has broadened the foundation of theory building to include a key Asian cultural emphasis on the concept of responsibility. The Asian emphasis on the concept of responsibility is not only a result of Confucian moral influence, but also a result of the socio-economic realities of Asia, where development journalism originated and is still being pursued and where guerrilla warfare or religious and ethnic rivalries can flare up as a result of provocative news articles.

And even in Hong Kong, where dominant discussions tend to focus on the survival of press freedom, Chief Executive Donald Tsang encouraged journalists to think about what was important to society rather than what was popular to readers at the 2005 News Awards ceremony.

Confucius's teachings mesh well with the aspirations of development journalists in Asia, who see the role of the press as agents for social change. Through their work, they want to improve the quality of life of their people. Pakistani media researcher Owais Aslam Ali (undated) analysed the major differences between Western news values and Asian news values, which he summarized as elitist press versus press for national development.

He pointed out the futility of Western news values in "the monumental uphill struggle" of the Third World toward economic progress. Given the diverse economic and social realities of the countries of the world, it is not difficult to see why different philosophies of journalism and news values exist around the world. Some Western libertarian thinkers also addressed the issue of responsibility, rationality, or limits in exercising freedom. Locke gave impetus to the concept of "responsible individualism," predicated on a love of reason and the importance of natural law. According to Locke, individuals live in a social context and need order, not anarchy, for their own well-being.

"Therefore, reason serves as an automatic limitation on freedom. In order to guide themselves in living an orderly and moral life, which is the essence of humanity, rational people voluntarily give up much freedom". Even though well known for his libertarian ideas in his pamphlet On Liberty, Mill held an elitist view on entitlement to freedom. "Mill felt that his freedom principle was appropriate only in societies of relatively high educational standards in which people could rationally exercise freedom".

In the field of journalism, debates on press responsibility and accountability have never stopped, such as the work of the Hutchins' Commission, which gave rise to the social responsibility press theory, and the ongoing experimentation with civic or public journalism in the United States. If there is public concern over press responsibility, the concern should be addressed in building a new theoretical model.

The newly added dimension of press responsibility adds balance to existing press models by bringing in cultural values important not only to the West but also to the East, presents a fuller description of a press system, and helps address an important public concern over press responsibility and accountability.

DEFINING AND MEASURING PRESS RESPONSIBILITY

The immediate question that arises is the definition of responsibility as what is considered responsible in one culture may be viewed as irresponsible in another culture. The notion of responsibility is always culture-specific. Similar to the argument that all concepts of responsibility are relative, the concept of "a free press" is also relative, as there is no absolute freedom of the press in this world, not even in the United States. Addressing press freedom worldwide, Merrill said, "... in fact, there are no free-press nations".

Because of the challenges in setting the standards of a responsible press that can be universally accepted and in deciding who should have the authority in setting the standards, and because of media's aversion to the concept of "a responsible press" imposed from the outside as illustrated by the fate of the Hutchins' report and by the "survey methodology" section of the 2005 Freedom House report that practically equates press responsibility with government control, discussions about press responsibility often hit a dead end.

They do not have to be. Ali (undated) emphasized the watchdog role of the media in development journalism, warned against the discussions on Asian values in journalism being hijacked by government officials as justification for the control of the media, and urged Asian journalists, "who have been struggling to reduce government involvement in the media," to create a form of journalism relevant to the needs of their societies. Only then will the concept of Asian values have credibility, Ali wrote.

UNIVERSAL VALUES IN JOURNALISM

A starting point in exploring the standards of a responsible press can be the search for universal values in journalism, and the Hutchins' report can serve as a helpful reference, such as being accurate and providing balance and diversity of opinion in news coverage, acting as a watchdog of the government, businesses and all other powerful social institutions, addressing issues of public concern, covering all sectors of the society instead of just the prominent, and avoiding invasion of privacy and sensationalism.

If the list continues to include the elimination of hate speech, which is banned in Germany, and pornography, which is banned in the Muslim world, most of the Asian countries, and perhaps some African and South American countries as well, the exploration for universal standards of a responsible press will soon become controversial. And questions such as what is balanced to one may not seem to be balanced to another remain.

CURRENT COMMUNITY STANDARDS

To deal with such tricky issues in setting the standards of a responsible press, the standards used for deciding what is obscene can be borrowed-current community standards. If the majority of readers believe their press is responsible, then they have a responsible press. Vice versa, if the majority of readers believe their press is irresponsible, then they have an irresponsible press. As the concept of responsibility is highly cultural-specific, the best solution is to let the local population decide instead of imposing standards from the outside.

INDEX OF PRESS RESPONSIBILITY-A COMBINATION OF UNIVERSAL VALUES AND LOCAL STANDARDS

Based on accepted universal values in journalism, which may include truth, accuracy, and balance, and results of public opinion surveys on press responsibility, an index of press responsibility can be compiled for each country to help media researchers and students better analyse the characteristics of a particular press system. If survey results distort reality such as in a controlled society, where a survey of honest public opinion is not feasible, universal values in journalism can serve as primary checkpoints.

In the meantime, despite the fact that they sometimes serve as a helpful reference, the criteria of the Freedom House in determining the ratings of press freedom in each country should be revised to add balance to the current standards, which do not take into account media content. The current methodology examines the legal, political, and economic environment of the media, but not the results of those environments-media content.

The survey questions are predominantly negative. Data are not collected through systematic or scientific method but through arbitrary answers by a small group of hand-picked interviewees, including "correspondents overseas, staff and consultant travel, international visitors," and "specialists in geographic and geopolitical areas." Such data collection methods raise serious questions about both the reliability and validity of the results.

THE FOUR CORNERS AND FOUR QUADRANTS

If a pair of dotted diagonal lines are superimposed on the coordinate grid, four corners of the grid will appear, representing four extreme types of press systems-free and responsible, free but not responsible, not free but responsible, and not free and not responsible. As the four corners indicate maximum or minimum degrees of freedom and responsibility, very few press systems fall exactly on those four corners; most of the press systems will fall somewhere within the four quadrants.

FREE AND RESPONSIBLE

While it may be hard to find a perfect example of a free and socially responsible press, some media endeavors are definitely directed toward that goal, such as public broadcasting in Britain and the United States, the civic and public journalism in the United States, and community and development journalism in India and Pakistan. Even though these types of journalism do not represent the mainstream media in their respective societies, they are the free press's attempts to be responsible and relevant to its readers.

The press in this group is mostly free and chooses to avoid sensationalism and play a positive role in society on its own. With or without public funding, it provides mostly quality information and often a public servicefighting crime in neighborhoods, boosting voter turnout, and educating and empowering the poor rural population.

Depending on events of the day, its content can be a mixture of negative and positive stories. In well-developed and free media markets, the press can afford to choose to be responsible because such a press would be assured of market support if there is public demand for a free and responsible press. Even in underdeveloped societies such as those in South Asia, press responsibility in the form of development journalism can exist because of support from the vast rural audience. For the press to be free and responsible, the market has to demand it and has to be well developed enough to finance it.

FREE AND NOT RESPONSIBLE

It is not very difficult to find free but irresponsible press around the world, press that chases profits or power under the name of press freedom.

Under such press systems, the press is free to pursue whatever story sells on the market with little concern for the consequences of such reporting. In the race to be the first on the market, accuracy in reporting and ethical standards are often compromised.

If criticized for their low professional standards and lack of accountability, journalists in such media environment often invoke the defence of freedom of the press. Such press systems tend to exist in intensely competitive media markets, such as new democracies in Taiwan, Indonesia, the Philippines, and some East European countries, where media outlets mushroom and bring immense pressure on the media market and where new regulations are still taking shape.

Even in China where the press is becoming increasingly commercialized, tabloids, sensationalized news, or even made-up news stories are not hard to find. Such press systems may also exist in well-developed, saturated and consolidated media markets where it is very challenging to expand market share such as Hong Kong and Thailand. Because of the profit-oriented nature of such press systems, media companies are regarded as moneymakers, regulated by market demand only. Circulations and ratings become the only measure of success.

Whatever sells is repeated in the media, resulting in over-coverage of some topics and events, such as celebrity journalism and press conferences, and the undercoverage of other less glamorous topics and events, such as poverty. Under such systems, the media spend far too much time covering and far too little time uncovering.

As they become pure businesses, such media are financed mostly with advertising dollars and subscriptions. Another form of press irresponsibility is the partisan press or political patronage of the press, in which case some press allows itself to be used as political tools especially when the democratic system is still young.

With a political power vacuum as a result of the dismantling of control mechanisms, political families, parties, or organizations often rush to take control of the media and use the media to advance their particular agendas, often employing such tactics as personal attacks or smear campaigns. Such a press tends to exist in free but less developed media markets as political patronage provides much needed financial support for the media.

Under such press systems, media content is often negative, full of political attacks in partisan press, or sex and violence in tabloids instead of stories about progress, which is often a long and less dramatic process. Tabloids and partisan press are typical products of such a press system.

RESPONSIBLE BUT NOT FREE

The very term seems to be an oxymoron. Critics may ask how a press can be classified as responsible if it is not free. The answer can depend on the definition of responsibility according to local community standards.

Such press systems tend to exist in more traditional societies where the emphasis is on the group rather than the individual and where cultural traditions or religions have a major impact on public life. Press in this group tends to stress the importance and interests of the country, society, community, and families rather than freedom and rights of individuals.

It tends to follow moral or religious principles and societal goals in news coverage rather than follow market demand because to publish what is perceived to be responsible is more important than to publish what sells.

The emphasis is on publishing what is right versus the right to publish, which is the difference between what is ethical and what is legal.

The goals of such a press may vary from country to country, including social order and stability, economic development, or reinforcement of religious values. The press in this category tends to support these societal goals under government or public pressure, or both.

For example, in Saudi Arabia and much of the Islamic world, newspapers devote sections to the teachings or discussions of Islam while criticism of Islam is forbidden. And in most of the Islamic press, the content is very clean, free of pornography.

Elsewhere in the world, many of the developing countries in Asia, Africa, and South America see national development as the top priority and expect the media to serve as a tool for nation building.

In Singapore, because of the fear of ethnic and religious riots and the importance of its relations with its neighbors, the press cannot report on issues concerning race, religion, or its neighbors to maintain order and stability.

If the majority of the people in these societies support those goals, then the press is responsible. However, in some cases, especially when a country is involved in a war, current community standards may prove unreliable when the public is caught up in a patriotic frenzy. When that happens, it would depart from the universal values in journalism, such as accuracy and balance.

Because it has special roles to play in society, press in this group may obtain financial support from the government, public or social institutions, or the church even though a major part of its income may still come from the market.

NOT FREE AND NOT RESPONSIBLE

The press in this group does not enjoy much freedom of operation, and the controls applied unilaterally by the government are most likely not supported by the people. The most typical examples are perhaps the press in North Korea and Turkmenistan, where there is very little information but plenty of glorifications of the state leaders in the press. Hardships endured by the people can hardly be found in the news media.

The press in this group is also prohibited from criticizing the government or exposing corruption. The press in this group does not have the freedom to make its own editorial decisions, and public opinion is suppressed. After a review of the different types of press systems, where should the Japanese press be plotted on the coordinate grid?

It should perhaps be placed somewhere close to the origin of the coordinate grid as being partly free and partly responsible. It is free from government control but not free from industry control. And if the press refrains from uncovering high-level scandals in the government or big corporations, it cannot be described as socially responsible.

But until the Japanese people start to reject their press, which is opposite to the fact that Japanese newspapers enjoy the highest circulations in the world, the press in Japan cannot be described as irresponsible either. A responsibility index as discussed earlier plus a more accurate press freedom rating can help determine the position of the Japanese press on the grid and the positions of the press in other countries.

A Dynamic Model

The proposed two-dimensional Freedom-Responsibility coordinate system attempts to provide a more balanced press model in explaining press systems around the world, measuring not only the degree of press freedom but also the level of press responsibility. The validity of the new model will be determined by how many press systems in the world it can satisfactorily describe and explain. But societies are constantly changing, and so are their press systems. One of the advantages of the new model is that it can accommodate such changes in the system.

For example, the American press seems to be trying to be more responsible and relevant to its readers while having some of its freedom curtailed because of the War on Terror.

Comparing with the press elsewhere in the world, the American press is best known for being free but not necessarily for being responsible.

The low credibility of the news media in repeated public opinion polls shows public dissatisfaction with media performance. Civic and public journalism seems to be pushing the American press toward more press responsibility when the press tries to be more relevant to its readers and more conscious of the role it can play in society, such as helping crime-fighting and boosting voter turnout.

And in the age of war on terror, the Bush administration is tightening up press access to information, citing national security concerns. It also launched an investigation into the leaking of the National security Agency's domestic spying programme to discourage such disclosure of information.

During the war in Iraq, the government controlled reporters' access on the battlefield with a system of embedded reporters. And the concentration of ownership also reduces the independence and freedom the press once had.

The press in China seems to be moving slowly in the opposite direction-freer but messier even though sometimes more relevant to its readers. The press in China used to follow only Party lines. Now it also has to follow market demand by addressing public concerns.

Some local papers target rural poverty by providing tips on how to grow better crops or how to generate cash by engaging in non-farming businesses. Competition, unheard of before the economic reforms, has given rise to diversity in the media. The Internet has provided a channel for news stories turned down by the traditional media. These changes are clearly pushing the Chinese press toward more freedom and responsibility.

However, competition also drives down the quality of news coverage and the ethical standards of journalists as sensationalism and bribery are prevalent. The Chinese press is in a state of flux as different factors are pulling it in different directions with deepening economic reforms. The most important factor, however, is still government policies. The press in Russia presents perhaps the most intriguing case for study as the degree of press freedom and responsibility shifted dramatically with the changing political climate of the country. Described as the prototype communist media, the press in the former Soviet Union was a political tool, following Lenin's ideal of press's functioning as collective agitator, propagandist, and organizer.

After the fall of communism, the press in Russia changed overnight from not free to completely free. Then under the presidency of Putin, press freedom in Russia was once again being curtailed. With a new president coming into the Kremlin, the status of press freedom in Russia is yet to be determined.

The proposed new Freedom-Responsibility model is dynamic not only because it can accommodate the changes within particular press systems, but also because it can reflect changes in the structure of the model. In the debate on press freedom and press responsibility in the West, the concept of press freedom often trumps the concept of press responsibility.

The same is true on the global scene as free news media in the West dominate the global information flow. The call for the New World Information and Communication Order from developing countries was drowned out in the West's battle cry for the free flow of information.

And the Freedom House measures press freedom, not press responsibility. Given the dominant position of press freedom in the coordinate system, the press freedom axis represents the yang arm of the coordinate system while the press responsibility axis stands for the yin arm of the system. The yang and yin axes complement each other, forming a balanced system.

However, the pendulum of history never stops swinging. Laozi, an ancient Chinese philosopher, sees reversal as the way the natural order operates: "everything that has gone far in one direction will move in the opposite direction, and to be in a low or weak position is to be in a state in which one will thrive".

That is the law of the dialectics. If the abuse of press freedom becomes a global issue and the world's press is forced to be more responsible because of public pressure, there can be a paradigm change within the coordinate system with the concept of press responsibility becoming the dominant feature of the model and thus, the yang axis of the system, and the concept of press freedom becoming the yin axis of the system.

But that may take a long time to occur even though such changes will never stop. Confucius advocated the "middle path" and Aristotle promoted the "golden mean," each avoiding the extremes at either end. The same principle applies to press performance-there is neither absolute press freedom nor absolute press responsibility. The desirable middle path would be the optimal combination of press freedom with press responsibility, a blend of the West and the East.

The two-dimensional system proposed in this chapter is an attempt at exploring a more balanced model in studying press systems around the world. The major challenge in the application of the model would be the measurement of press responsibility in a press system. So far no effort is ever made in that regard, given the expected controversies it is bound to draw.

If media observers and researchers can agree that development journalism and press responsibility do not automatically translate into government control of the press, measuring press responsibility does not have to be a forbidden task. The compilation of a global press responsibility index can provide a helpful guide in studying the characteristics of a press system.

A good starting point can be the identification of universal values in journalism as discussed earlier. The more universal values societies can agree upon, the more reliable the index can be. "Current community standards" in the form of public opinion surveys offer a way of accommodating values specific to local culture.

Debates on universal values in journalism can be messy, but the results can be crystallizing and enlightening. With more research, media researchers from the East and the West may find more common ground than they expect. One weakness of the model is perhaps that Western and Confucian philosophies and values tend to dominate the discussions even though there are so many other religious and philosophical influences in the world. Therefore, this study is only exploratory in nature. It can be enriched and improved with perspectives from more cultures or serve as a starting point for future research.

In future research, alternative concepts or dichotomies can be explored in building new models, such as an observer-interventionist/activist dichotomy, or commercial-ideological dichotomy. The point of departure will depend on the angle of analysis and on the perspectives and approaches of researchers.

Chapter 10

Interaction of Reader and Reporter

The hypothesis that public journalism designs would visually convey interactivity between readers and the media more than non-public journalism (H2) was also significant. Seventy-five per cent of the public journalism issues in this sample used visual elements to encourage readers to contact the media, while 46 per cent of non-public journalism issues sampled did so.

In addition, the number of different ways public journalism provided for readers to contact them (address, phone, e-mail, web site, fax) was highly significant. Small circulation mean = 2.1, large circulation mean =.5). There were no significant differences between small and large circulation issues on this variable, as would be expected if all size papers were practicing public journalism the same way.

PHOTO OPS AND PHOTOS OF 'REAL PEOPLE'

The two public journalism characteristics that were not significant when public and non-public journalism issues were compared but whose means were in the direction hypothesized both dealt with photographs; whether public journalism relied on managed photo opportunities less often than non-public journalism (H3), and whether public journalism photos featured citizens and real people more often than candidates or experts (H4). The non-significant findings may be due to the low number of cases sampled (N = 41), but it is important that for both hypotheses the mean ratios of non-managed photos and photos of real people to total photos showed that the public journalism issues sampled used fewer photographs from managed photo opportunities and also used more photos of citizens and real people than candidates or experts.

Comparisons within public journalism showed no significant differences between small and large papers' photos in this sample regarding photo opportunities or the use of citizens and real people in photos versus candidates or experts.

Textual analysis revealed both small public journalism papers, Binghamton and Wisconsin, used all photos of real people from non-managed photo sources. In the large public journalism category, San Francisco used all non-managed photos featuring citizens in its series on transportation. Since Binghamton's series was on the local economy and primarily covered the citizen's forums, and San Francisco's series was on commuter woes, it is perhaps not surprising that they were able to find photo subjects that did not involve officials and experts.

It is more unusual for election coverage to avoid photos of candidates, yet that is just what the Wisconsin paper did. It achieved this goal mainly by running only one photo (citizens at a forum) over all seven issues; six issues had no photos at all. In the large non-public journalism genre, Omaha used all photos of candidates, as would be expected for traditional journalism.

The variation is mainly explained by the non-public journalism Philadelphia paper's use of all non-managed photos of real people, and the public journalism Charlotte paper's heavy use of managed photo ops of candidates — findings that are counter to what would be expected in ideal public journalism. The story subjects provide partial explanation.

In its series on a typical suburban neighborhood, Philadelphia used five to eight pictures every day in its non-public journalism series, all were of real people and none were from photo opportunities. In its election coverage, the public journalism Charlotte paper used mug shots or photo collages of candidates on nearly every cover, plus cutout photos of candidates in its full-page graphic of candidates' answers to voters' questions. In addition, Charlotte used four conventional campaign trail photos over the course of the series, in traditional political photojournalism style.

The only real-people photos Charlotte used were approximately three to five photos daily of the citizens who asked questions of the candidates or whose opinions were quoted. The Charlotte design director indicated in a telephone interview that the amount of campaign-trail photographs shot were "not nearly as many as five years ago... An effort was made to take photos of real people, but that makes things harder." The convention of candidate photographs for election coverage apparently remains strong, even at papers that have embraced public journalism principles.

The design director's acknowledgment that finding photos of real people is harder than attending photo opportunities is a candid admission that goes to the root of the difficulty of altering established conventions.

Comments by designers at the public journalism papers in Binghamton, Madison, and San Francisco, all indicated their photographers tried to avoid photo opportunities in favour of real people; however, photo ops could not be entirely eliminated. The former graphics editor at the Madison paper provided some background on the thinking:

The photo staff hates dull pictures, first of all. There is nothing worse than a talking head (politician) or a grip-and-grin. They do try and look for action or images from the issue they are addressing. It is a combination of public journalism and aesthetics.

He also attributed the lack of photos (one photo over seven issues) to aesthetics: With 'We the People,' the premiere events are these town meetings. They don't make particularly good photos. They are often held in the capitol, which has miserable lighting, and it's a sea of people sitting around.

The marching orders are we will shoot that, but we would probably try to limit that to one. Otherwise, we would have photos and stories about journalists from different media getting together to organize 'We the People'."

The idea of using photos of real people that are not the

result of photo ops orchestrated by people seeking to manipulate publicity goes to the heart of public journalism philosophy and reflects a conscious effort to avoid agenda-setting effects. The use of this type of photo would be a sign that public journalism's goals are beginning to be translated into practice. Helping citizens participate in civic life

Of the two remaining hypotheses, neither showed any significant differences between public and non-public journalism. One was the hypothesis that public journalism would visually convey more mobilizing information to help citizens participate in their communities than non-public journalism (H1). There were no significant differences between the sampled public and non-public journalism issues' use of mobilizing information.

However, when comparisons were made within public journalism between large and small papers' issues, there was a highly significant difference in the visual communication of mobilizing information, with small papers scoring better. Only 14 per cent of large papers' stories used visual elements to convey mobilizing information, whereas 71 per cent of small papers' stories used one visual element, and 7 per cent used two. In the public journalism genre, issues from both large papers sampled (Charlotte, San Francisco) used no mobilizing information in visual format. However, both small public journalism papers sampled visually conveyed mobilizing information. The topics—the Charlotte Observer's election coverage — cannot be the reason, however, since the two other papers which carried election coverage, including one non-public journalism paper (Omaha), listed mobilizing information.

The other large public journalism paper, San Francisco, gave almost no mobilizing information on its transportation series. Both small public journalism papers listed mobilizing information frequently; Wisconsin had the most and most regular mobilizing information with its boxes for forum broadcasts, call-in lines and registration information for upcoming town meetings. Wisconsin even developed regular graphic devices its designers called democracy boxes.

Perhaps the convention of having these boxes to fill kept mobilizing information in the forefront for Wisconsin designers. Binghamton usually publicized an upcoming priority setting conference or results of the economic teams' reports.

One reason for these results could be that mobilizing information is not new or unique to public journalism the way other variables can be.

For this study, mobilizing information consisted of news citizens could use to participate in community life. However, the importance of information which allows people to take action has been discussed in scholarly and trade publications since at least the 1970s.

Well before the advent of public journalism, traditional journalism has offered dates of neighborhood watch meetings, names and addresses of redevelopment agencies that offer grant money, etc.

Because of the length of time over which journalists have been aware of the importance of mobilizing information, and the ubiquitous nature of such information, it may not be surprising that there are no significant differences in the amount of mobilizing information conveyed visually in public and non-public journalism.

The greater resources at larger papers cannot help explain why small papers used more visual devices for mobilizing information than large papers. Mobilizing information should be quite familiar and top-of-mind to designers at both small and large papers, public journalism and non-public journalism.

Perhaps another explanation for the highly significant difference between small circulation and large circulation public journalism designs that visually convey mobilizing information can be found in James Lemert and colleague's findings. Because small papers may better reflect their small communities, there is more awareness of readers' desire for visual display of mobilizing information.

If large public journalism papers are not providing mobilizing information, this supports Lemert's theory that mobilizing information is regularly missing when issues are located outside of town, where audiences ordinarily can't look up addresses and phone numbers. This may be the case for large newspapers that cover many different communities.

VIEWS OF REAL PEOPLE

The other hypothesis that was not significant was that public journalism would use more visual devices to convey views of real people (H5).

This non-significant finding between the public and non-public journalism issues sampled is interesting because views of real people rather than experts or politicians are one of the central tenets of public journalism.

Although all designers interviewed said they tried to include views of real people, two said it was a copy desk decision and would be done mainly through pullquotes. However, textual analysis revealed that not all public journalism papers visually displayed views of real people. Both Wisconsin and San Francisco used no graphics or design elements for views of real people, although these views were carried within the text.

A lack of significant difference between public and non-public journalism's use of views of real people may signify that visual journalists do not fully understand or embrace this idea. If a significant difference were found to exist in the written communication of views of real people, but not in the visual communication, this would have implications for the integration of the designers and copy editors with the reporters and editors.

It may indicate that designers have not been included in sessions devoted to explaining the philosophies of public journalism and do not understand its principles fully, or, they are aware of the importance of views of real people but are leaving it to reporters to include in stories rather than employing content-driven design to convey this visually. There was also no difference in the sampled issues between small and large public journalism's use of visual devices to convey views of real people, but this would be expected if all papers practiced public journalism the same way.

THE IMPORTANCE OF UNDERSTANDING

Two final points of interest were revealed in the interviews when designers were asked whether they designed differently for public journalism than for non-public journalism.

Designers at two papers said yes, public journalism design was different from non-public journalism design, and designers at the other two papers replied no, there was no difference.

Interestingly, the no difference responses came from designers whose papers did not have training sessions on the concepts and techniques of public journalism, or who did not include visual journalists in those sessions.

Both affirmative responses came from newspapers whose designers did participate in public journalism education sessions. Understanding of public journalism principles was one of the explanations offered for some of the findings in this study, and the perception of designers regarding the difference in designing for public journalism reinforces such an explanation.

Visual journalists who did not attend sessions aimed at explaining public journalism's goal and principles may not understand it as well as those who did and, therefore, may not consider ways to visually communicate those goals and principles.

Also, one of the designers interviewed complained that too many journalists at the paper felt like they had been ordered to do public journalism with no opportunity for discussion or input.

This chapter did not offer training sessions in public journalism. "If they're really going to get people on board to do this and do this well, there has to be that discussion," said the designer, who asked to remain anonymous.

"There are numerous ethical challenges in doing this, and they need to at least be explored, as do the possible pitfalls." Both these insights have implications for managing editors contemplating introducing public journalism into their newsrooms.

Table. Large Public Vs. Large Non-Public Journalism: Percentages and Fisher's Exact Test of Public Journalism Characteristics by Size of Paper

Variables (per cent with yes values)	Large PJ stories	Small PJ stories	Exact Probabilities
Common ground and solutions	36%	0%	.025
Interactivity with media	71%	46%	.13
Mobilizing information	25%	63%	.42
Views of real people	50%	39%	.25
N=27			

This study has used the emerging theory of public journalism, which claims a significantly different content than non-public journalism, and the theory of content-driven design, which says that visual meaning must reflect the written content, to examine the question prompted by these theories: If the content of stories generated through public journalism methods is different, and design is driven by content, shouldn't design for public journalism be different than design for non-public journalism?

The results from this study are mixed. Of six hypotheses that speak to the question of whether public journalism is visually different from non-public journalism, two showed significant differences among the newspaper issues sampled. Public journalism stories in this study used more visual devices to convey common ground and solutions, and ways to contact the media than did non-public journalism stories.. Four hypotheses showed no significant differences between public journalism and non-public journalism, but two had means in the direction hypothesized.

The public journalism issues sampled were more likely than non-public journalism to use fewer managed photo opportunities and more photos of real people than candidates or experts, but the differences were not significant

These are signs that some of public journalism's goals may be beginning to be translated into practice by visual journalists, but that there are other goals that are not being addressed visually, at least in these newspapers. The fact that the public journalism issues sampled were not significantly different from the non-public journalism issues in how they visually conveyed views of real people — one of the central tenets of public journalism — should be of concern. That the public journalism issues sampled visually communicated no more mobilizing information than the non-public journalism issues is less cause for worry because mobilizing information is not unique to public journalism the way the other characteristics can be.

This study has also found that, in some cases, public journalism papers that have established new conventions in place of the old have found it easier to adhere consistently to public journalism principles; for instance, the development of standing graphics such as democracy boxes for mobilizing information.

One problem in the consistent communication of public journalism characteristics seems to be with journalists' fundamental understanding of public journalism. Confusion over and even unawareness of public journalism principles seems to be a basic, underlying reason why the practice of public journalism is not significantly different from non-public journalism in terms of visual communication.

In addition, it appears that not all designers are practicing content-driven design. For instance, this research found stories which included views of real people in the text but not in the design.

In conclusion, there appear to be some significant differences in this sample in the way public journalism is visually communicated compared with non-public journalism. However, there is not enough significance to say that it represents a radical departure from non-public journalism, at least in the issues studied here. It appears another researcher's conclusion regarding the content of public journalism may be correct for the visual display as well: "there is no overriding, core philosophy of public journalism at some of the papers practicing it; instead it has become a label used to name a variety of special projects."

The news industry has been undergoing a fundamental paradigm shift since the end of last century. An increasing number of media companies around the United States, such as the Washington Post in Washington, DC, Media General in Virginia, the Tribune Company in Chicago, and New England Cable News, have taken solid steps to merge different media such as newspapers, television stations, radio stations, and online journalism companies to disseminate news content on multiple media platforms.

As a result, in a metropolitan area, one company would own print, TV, and online venues. Media call this industrial trend "media convergence," though the concept means much more than media mergers. Media convergence muddies the lines among broadcast journalism, print journalism, and online journalism, leaving college journalism educators to wonder whether traditional journalism programs have become dinosaurs.

After surveying 200 newspaper publishers worldwide, the World Association of Newspapers (WAN) found, "Despite a somewhat gloomy outlook for wholesale convergence in media companies worldwide in the near term, convergence is already being implemented with varying degrees of enthusiasm and speed among the world's media companies". The Innovation International Media Consulting Group estimates that at least 100 of the world's multiple media companies are planning and implementing integration strategies. South and Nicholson (2002) drew a sketch of a converged media company: Daily journalists need to embrace the 24-hour news cycle, with continuous deadlines. And the story needs to be reported and produced for a multi-platform audience. That may mean delivering content first to the Web and cell phones, a streaming video broadcast later in the day, a TV talk-back interview still later, and a "second day" interpretive story for the next morning's newspaper.

Dominic Gates pointed out, "Convergence with broadcast and online media is the shape of things to come for newspapers." The trend remains controversial. Critics complain that such cross-ownership of both a television station and a newspaper in the same market is a threat to democracy because it limits the number of voices.

Delegates of the Communication Workers of America, a 60,000-member guild, passed a resolution in June of 2002 at the group's annual convention in Las Vegas, pledging to increase public awareness about the risks of ongoing media convergence. The delegates complained that shrinking media markets are a threat to editorial diversity and job security. In 1975, the Federal Communications Commission (FCC) ruled that no new broadcast licenses would be granted to companies that own a major daily newspaper and a local television station in the same city. Fairness & Accuracy In Reporting (FAIR) calls on the FCC to roll back limits on media consolidation.

The Newspaper Association of America (NAA), on the other hand, has asked the FCC to appeal the rule. On June 2, 2003, the FCC voted 3 to 2 to relax or eliminate some ownership restrictions, such as a rule barring media companies from owning television stations in markets where they publish daily newspapers. Although some lawmakers and advocacy groups are still fighting in the courts and on Capitol Hill to overturn the FCC's new media ownership rules, these rules will be likely to encourage cross-media ownership in the years to come.

The mergers have raised questions about whether they are good for the craft of journalism itself. Critics complain that by requiring journalists to be jacks of both trades, print and broadcast, the journalists will be masters of none. Robert J. Haiman, president emeritus of The Poynter Institute, compared the media convergence trend to an Amphicar, a cross between a boat and a car.

The Amphicar, hawked in Florida during the 1950s, flopped. "It flopped because people quickly discovered that while it really was an ingenious combination of a car and a boat, it was a lousy car (because it also had to be a boat), and it was a lousy boat (because it also had to be a car)".

Willingly or unwillingly, many news practitioners' functions are gradually changing or are expected to change as media convergence rolls on. For a reporter in a converged media environment, knowing how to write is probably no longer enough. S/he could be expected to write the same story for different media in a timely manner. Ideally, s/he can readily talk in front of a video camera. As a photographer, knowing how to tell a story both in video and in still images is more and more in demand.

A designer should know how to prepare still graphics for print, moving graphics for television and dynamic graphics for the Web. At the online version of the Chicago Tribune, for instance, staffers are supposed to cover stories, take pictures, operate video cameras, and create digital pages. The editors, too, need a wider variety of skills than the traditional paper editors. Along with infrastructure changes and the attempt to create synergy among the various media outlets, a new breed of journalists-digital or multimedia journalists-is expected.

As media jobs become more demanding, some news practitioners are beginning to team up to complete projects. At the same time, fear, confusion, and frustration from news practitioners are creeping into newsrooms. Carr wrote: "Convergence frightens many people who wonder whether their current skill sets have prepared them for-or will even be needed in-that great undiscovered country, the future.

This is probably the primary reason why I still find such great hostility to convergence among certain journalists." Killebrew, a mass communications professor from the University of South Florida, suggested that "journalists must be prepared to either crosstrain themselves or seek training from other sources while management must be prepared to give them the opportunities and time to do so." The 1999-2000 president of the Association for Schools of Journalism and Mass Communication (ASJMC), Shirley Staples Carter, questioned whether, in the midst of the "Internet revolution," programs are prepared to educate journalists of the future. When specifically talking about writing, Keith Hartenberger, manager of news and programming for Tribune Regional Programming, said that journalism schools should make their students aware of the many ways to present the news. "It's a multimedia world out there," he said. "If you're just being prepared to write newspaper stories, you won't be prepared".

"At some point, this [cross-media training] is something we're going to expect from everyone".

Media convergence, as a trend that is gradually shaping the landscape of the media industry in the new century, has called into question the conventional journalism school practice of having separate tracks-print, broadcast, etc.

Journalism educators around the country also are trying to figure out what they should do, if anything, to better prepare students for the converged media. For instance, should journalism educators consider merging different sequences such as magazine, newspaper, broadcast, and photojournalism, or still teach all such courses as if they were unrelated media? "Traditionally defined segments of the communications industry are less and less distinguishable for technological and market convergence," observed Moon. Are college journalism educators themselves both theoretically equipped and technologically prepared to teach their students for converged media? What do media companies expect from future news practitioners? What do current news practitioners in converged media feel is lacking? For both news practitioners and professors, the two most urgent questions cry for answers: Should journalism schools train specialists or fit for-all generalists?

And how should college journalism education balance the teaching of critical thinking and technical skills? Apart from all these education-related questions, we are also interested in finding out what are the driving forces behind the media mergers, who are regarded as the beneficiaries of this trend, and how people's political beliefs are related to their attitude toward teaching media convergence in colleges? These questions pertain closely to college journalism education, which has been the subject of debate and criticism for two decades.

A national survey was conducted among colleges, daily newspapers, and commercial television stations to explore the issue of how journalism schools should prepare students for the trend of media convergence from the perspectives of news editors, news professionals, and journalism professors. The study measured the level of general support for convergence education and determined if a new model of journalism education was called for.

If so, it examined whether consensus existed among the three groups on the direction educators should take when revisiting programme designs. Where consensus was not apparent, divisions among the sample of educators, editors, and reporters were defined. The goal of the study is to provide evidence that will help journalism educators make informed decisions about how to respond to media convergence in their curricula and courses and lay an empirical foundation for further discussions and conversations about media convergence.

The search results show that media convergence is a comparatively new topic in media research, though articles about it have inundated the Internet, magazines, and newspapers. Most research writings appeared no earlier than 1998. Articles about the relationship between media convergence and higher education are rare and have shown up more recently in trade magazines such as Presstime, Quill, and Journalism Education Today and in Web sites. A few research writings were found in academic conference (i.e., AEJMC) proceedings.

Many writings have addressed one of the toughest questions: What is media convergence? How to define "media convergence" had a direct bearing on how we conducted this study. Out of these writings, we identified four categories of media convergence that directly affect how journalism will be taught in colleges.

CONTENT CONVERGENCE

As Tremayne noted, decades ago, the term media convergence referred to the content convergence between competing newspapers and even among newspapers, magazines, and television.

Today, pure content convergence continues on the Internet. For instance, the St. Petersburg Times has incorporated local Channel 10's TV news into its online newspaper though they are independent business entities. In other words, media convergence may not necessarily be tied to media merger.

Form convergence (or technological convergence). Around the mid-1990s, as Tremayne and Wurtz noted, computer technology and Internet technology made possible the convergence of all forms of mediated communications including video, audio, data, text, still photo, and graphic art for "on-demand" audiences.

Using these different forms to tell news stories on the World Wide Web has been widely regarded as the future of mass communication regardless of the fact that most online news sites have had a hard time making ends meet, let alone making a profit. Form convergence, often called technological convergence, has been a fundamental force to guide and lead convergence in the market, industry, and regulation.

CORPORATE CONVERGENCE

Since the late 1990s, media convergence has been escalated to the level of media mergers. The News Centre located in Tampa, Florida, owned by Media General, and the Tribune Interactive, owned by the Tribune Company, for instance, are the products of media mergers.

In The News Centre, WFLA-TV, The Tampa Tribune, and Tampa Bay Online operate out of the same building. They share daily tips and information, spot news, photography, enterprise reporting, franchises, events, and public service. Each of the three entities in The News Centre has its own independent newsroom, but they issued a joint statement of coverage principles, titled "News Centre Pledge".

The Tribune Interactive has brought together the interactive functions of the company's four newspapers and more than a score of television stations including WGN-TV and CLTV. The individual media outlets have their own newsgathering staff, but their coverage is enhanced by their multimedia desks in the Chicago Tribune newsroom and the Tribune Media Centre in Washington.

"A synergy-team of print editors and TV news veterans

at the Chicago Tribune work together to manage resource sharing and the relationship". Media merger has made both content convergence and form convergence handy.

Corporate convergence via vertical and horizontal integration, mergers, alliances, and acquisitions will make traditionally defined segments of the communications industry less and less distinguishable.

Chapter 11

Role convergence of Press and Media

Russial identified several examples of role convergence in newsrooms. For instance, the roles of reporter and librarian, the roles of copyeditor and compositor, the roles of graphic artist and Web designer, and the roles of photo editor, darkroom technician, and photographer are all converging in different media. In more recent years, content convergence, form convergence, and especially corporate convergence have sparked more in-depth role convergence among news practitioners.

For instance, Victoria Lim from The News Centre in Tampa revealed at a February 2002 conference on media convergence at the University of Florida that she primarily works as a television reporter for WFLA-TV, but she also has to write for the company's newspaper, The Tampa Tribune, as a senior consumer investigative reporter and for the Web company TBO.com on a daily basis; at the time of the conference, she was working on 31 stories.

A newspaper reporter may also produce a newspaper in QuarkXPress or serve as a TV news anchor, while a newspaper photographer may shoot video stories or produce interactive online stories in Flash. Role convergence requires that both reporters and editors re-equip themselves both journalistically and technologically.

Of the four types of convergence, role convergence has the most direct effect on future journalism education. Within the media industry, there are serious doubts about whether training cross-media journalists are possible or desirable. When asked whether reporters of the future must be equally skilled in print, TV, and online, Forrest Carr, news director of WFLA-TV at The News Centre in Tampa, said no.

He said he believed that there would always be areas of specialization and students may still choose specialties, but said that it no longer makes any sense to pretend print journalists and electronic journalists are in different professions.

On the other hand, he said that journalists who have skills in TV, print, and online media certainly will be more valuable to their employers; and he emphasized that prospective employees must be willing to work in an environment where reporters cooperate across platforms. In most cases currently, he said, cooperating across platforms simply comes down to the sharing of tips and information.

Charles Kravetz, the vice president for news and station manager of New England Cable News (NECN), the largest regional news network in America, concurs with Forrest Carr. When asked "Do you see a time when all journalists will have to be able to file stories on all platforms (print, TV, radio, online)?" Kravetz said: "I am not sure that is the way it is going to work out.

This notion we had that one-journalist-fits-all-media is perhaps not that realistic.... There are very few people we will talk about in the future that are TV/newspaper/internet reporters". Gates agreed, "The 'backpack journalist'-a superhack master of multimedia who can do it all and who routinely packs a laptop and a video camera along with the tape recorder and steno notebook-may be the subject of avant-garde j-school courses, but it's not likely to become the norm."

Some other media executives have tried to define the extent to which role convergence is expected. Gil Thelen, executive editor and senior vice president of The Tampa Tribune, for instance, gave suggestions to journalism educators based on his two years of experience in The News Centre.

"The fully formed, all-purpose, multiplatform, gadget-laden journalism grad is NOT what we're looking to hire....

Journalism schools must continue to produce graduates who are competent in one craft area: reporting, design, producing, directing, editing." However, Thelen encouraged journalism schools to train writers to write for print, online, and broadcast and train print photographers to learn how to shoot and produce TV packages. Thelen said that cultural resistance is the biggest hurdle for converging newsrooms, and that employees or current journalism students need to learn to cooperate and collaborate across newsrooms.

What is unclear is whether these media administrators' predictions are limited by the status quo of the current generation of news practitioners who might not be very well prepared for convergence or who might even resist the notion of media convergence. At Brigham Young University, students with multiple skills are more valued and feel more comfortable in the converged media environment.

In addition, sharing tips and information does not entail convergence. Reporters have been doing this for decades. It seems that keeping convergence only on the level of sharing tips and information can hardly justify the high cost of rebuilding infrastructures like The News Centre. We are interested in finding out what expectations media companies have for future journalists. From news professionals' self-evaluations of their preparedness for media convergence, we should also be able to infer what is most desirable in the media industry nowadays.

In the face of increasing demand for technically skilled journalists-conversant with QuarkXPress, Photoshop, Avid, and Dreamweaver and able to crunch statistics using spreadsheets and other statistical methods in order to uncover the hidden story-should longstanding staples such as ethics, law, and theory remain at the heart of journalism curricula?

Or should such materials, commonly grouped together as "critical thinking", share equal hilling with technology or "skills" training? In other words, how should journalism schools balance the teaching of professional skills and that of critical thinking in an era when technology penetrates every facet of news gathering, preparation, editing, production, and delivery? Convergence further complicates this age-old battle in journalism education. Abraham noticed that the goal of most restructuring in journalism institutions is to provide an integrated skills environment where students would get the chance to practice the skills of multimedia production. Abraham argued: "The role of journalism academy should be very different from that of the industry. Its role should not simply be to inculcate skills that will help students to flag down jobs. They should aim to provide a scholarly background for a deeper intellectual understanding of our lives, media forms and of communication in general".

The dean of the University of Nevada at Reno thinks the ability to use multiple media skills is essential. Brigham Young University, which has built a working converged newsroom into its curriculum, expects students to graduate with multiple skills. University News Director, Dean Paynter, said, "We expect our students to more than anchor, more than report, and more than produce. The best ones can do it all, including write for the newspaper".

Mitchell Stephens, professor of journalism and mass communications at New York University, holds up the other end. "In a world where corporate pressures on 'content providers' seem to be increasing and civic affairs decreasing, the argument for emphasizing the basics does have much to recommend it."

Thomas Kunkel, dean of the Philip Merrill College of Journalism at the University of Maryland, sums it up: "Today's journalists, first and foremost, must be strong critical thinkers who know enough about geography, history and the human condition to understand why events play out as they do. They must be intellectually curious.

They should speak a second language. They should read something other than Jim Romenesko's MediaNews site. They ought to have a world view."

A controversy in late 2002 at Columbia University demonstrates how volatile the argument is currently. The debate arose when the graduate school of journalism at Columbia University halted its search for a dean. The new university president, Lee Bollinger, wanted to re-evaluate the school's mix of craft versus theory, and the move created a flurry of opinion about the journalism school's existing curriculum.

This critical curriculum question is often reflected in the questions of whether and how new technology classes should be included in the existing curriculum and how they should be taught. Some journalism schools are preparing to embrace the wave of media convergence in their new curricula by converging print and electronic media sequences to adapt to the industrial trends and the new technological environment. Blanchard and Christ warn that universities with limited resources will no longer tolerate duplicating specializations with separate courses such as writing for television, writing for newspapers, writing for public relations, and writing for advertising. Blanchard and Christ add that the communi-cations revolution (the media's convergence and related trends) is making journalism and mass communi-cation's traditional sequences obsolete.

Actually, Blanchard and Christ's opinion is not something new. Early in 1972, the University of Iowa School of Journalism already eliminated its sequences but at the expense of being denied reaccreditation by ACEJMC. About thirty years later, their decision seemed to be finding more sympathy.

Many schools are still exploring where to go. In October 2001, seventeen professors and leaders of new media from thirteen journalism programs across the country gathered in Berkeley, California, and had a discussion about new media in journalism education. The University of Nevada, Reno, offered several different elective courses in new media, but it did not have a special sequence.

It was struggling with how to incorporate them in other classes. The University of Florida had a concentration in online media, which was equivalent to other concen-trations such as reporting and editing and photojournalism.

Students who were not in that concentration couldn't always squeeze in the online media courses because they did not have any leftover électives they could take in the school.

American University had three divisions, journalism, public communication, and visual media, but they did not work together very well most of the time.

The University of South Carolina was restructuring its graduate masters programme in newspaper leadership and was focusing it on convergence. The University of Maryland had an online curriculum, but it was not formally structured as such. Northwestern University had an introductory New Media course at the undergraduate and graduate level, which was offered as an elective.

It was packed with everything from new skills training to wrestling with the business issues of new media to actual production. After three admission cycles, enrollment declined. The University of Minnesota established the Institute for New Media Studies, which merged broadcast journalism and print journalism programs to make them a concentration with the idea that future journalists would work in a multi-channel environment and should know how to operate within all those channels.

Although editors and academics sometimes agree on the qualifications a journalism student needs, an ideal curriculum doesn't always include convergence preparedness courses. In a 2000 poll, editors and educators agreed "on the same five of 14 types of knowledge considered most necessary for journalism graduates and listed them in the same order of importance". Technical skills were not mentioned in the top five, surpassed instead by "understanding of a journalist's responsibility to the public, understanding of the ethics of journalism, knowledge of current events, broad general knowledge, and knowledge of government".

With so much variance across universities, we are interested in finding out how many journalism schools have revamped their curricula to prepare students for the trend of media convergence, what professors' attitudes are toward teaching critical thinking vs. teaching technical skills and training generalists vs. training specialists, and what editors' and news professionals' attitudes are toward the same issues. In this regard, several scholars and news practitioners have tried to give advice to journalism professors and students in the context of media convergence.

In 2002, David Bulla from the University of Florida presented his "Media convergence: Industry practices and implications for education" to the AEJMC annual conference in Miami. This is the first research writing of its kind. The theme of the paper is the closest to that of this study. Bulla's study looked at the changing nature of contemporary mass communications practices, focusing on multimedia or converged journalism.

It described what scholastic journalism scholars are doing to prepare their students for these changes and provided recommendations to educators about how to update curricula to account for convergence.

The research questions for that study were:

- What are journalism educators currently doing to incorporate convergence into their curricula;
- What abilities, skills, and attitudes do professional journalists expect from their newest employees?

Media convergence in Bulla's study was defined as multimedia journalism, which means reporting, writing, and disseminating content in two or more media platforms.

Because of the controversy about media mergers, Bulla tried to find answers to some hot issues concerning democracy including: Does corporate media merging reduce public discourse and hinder democracy? Will it ultimately mean the need for fewer and fewer reporters, as the development of other technology has meant a decline in the number of employees in other areas of the production process? All these questions pertain to our study.

Bulla obtained a sample of 114 news practitioners working at newspapers, television stations, wire services, magazines, radio stations, and online publications in the United States. The sample was randomly selected from Editor & Publisher and Yahoo lists of media companies in the U.S. Media Web sites. With a response rate of 36 per cent, Bulla interviewed 41 news practitioners. Bulla also interviewed college educators, but he did not state how he sampled them.

What is unclear is the extent to which the Yahoo list and Editor & Publisher list overlap each other and if a sample from two potentially overlapping lists is any longer a random sample. In addition, since Bulla's questions were almost all unstructured, that is, he conducted interviews, he did not really need a random sample. Researchers strive for depth rather than breadth and don't mean to claim external validity in the statistical sense by conducting interviews. Finally, if he did need a random sample, a sample of 114 people with a 36 per cent response rate could be statistically defective because of big statistical errors. Bulla needed a better research design to make his study valid and reliable.

Some scholars doubt whether journalism school professors are theoretically and especially technologically prepared to teach media convergence. In an article written for Journalism Education magazine, John Irby, a professor from Washington State University and a veteran newspaper editor and publisher, for instance, was concerned about the disconnection between the newsroom and the classroom. Irby asked: Are universities and educators effectively preparing students for the work force? Do educators understand what newspapers are looking for in future reporters and editors? Does the newspaper industry have a responsibility in the division between educators and professionals? Are journalism educators "discounted" by professionals who believe those who teach couldn't succeed in newspapers?

Irby said older generations of newspaper reporters also appeared on radio and television periodically though they had no training; they never even felt like it was part of their job and thus did not take it very seriously.

But now, he continued, print journalists do need to take it seriously; journalism educators need to re-evaluate, and probably modify, the separatetrack approach in training print and broadcast journalists. Irby believed that there is still a need for specialization, but he told students to take both broadcast and print courses and told them that computer literacy is as crucial as the old-fashioned kind.

A study about the impact of media convergence on

journalism education without consulting Robert J. Haiman's article "Can convergence float?" should be considered incomplete.

Haiman's fervent talk against media convergence raised some challenging questions that educators must face. Haiman, president emeritus of The Poynter Institute, argued that the converged media world is one from which good journalism, and good journalists, are going to be in great need of defence.

He stuck to his notion of the mission of good journalism he stated 40 years ago: "To inform the public about the public's business, creating a society that is equipped with the knowledge it needs to make the right civic decisions more often than it makes the wrong civic decisions, and thus helping to perpetuate self-government and democracy."

Expressing his deep concern for journalism, Haiman said: "I think that convergence may end up being good, maybe even very good, for media companies. I fear, however, that it is going to be bad, and maybe even very bad, for journalism." He continued to explain:

I think it is going to be bad for journalism because, even if it goes as well as it possibly can, I believe that it is going to distract journalists, journalism teachers, and journalism students away from that single most important imperative of the craft - to create an informed society capable of intelligently governing itself.

And if it does not go well, I fear it is going to subject journalists to time, resource, craft, and ethical pressures, all of which will be bad for journalists, bad for journalism, and bad for the country. In his talk, Haiman mentioned a top education reporter who had done a" superb job" for more than 18 years. Now, he had to do short reports for the TV station with which that newspaper was converged.

However," he's not exactly ready for prime time." After this reporter retires, Haiman is afraid that that he will be replaced by" someone who may not report like a buzz saw and write like a dream, but who probably will report and write education okay and who will also look good and sound good on television." " When that happens," he continued," the journalism quality of all of the education reporting coming out of that converged news operation is going to go down." We believe that few people would disagree with Haiman's point that quality content is the king, to use his own words, but Haiman's above comment could be limited, again, by the performance of the current generation of reporters who are not prepared for media convergence.

Haiman was suggesting that a future reporter who has been trained to work for different media platforms and who has learned more about reporting would produce reporting of less quality.

In our study, we would like to find out to what extent Haiman's concern is shared by editors, news professionals, and professors. While convergence is still in its infancy, Haiman suggested that journalists, journalism students, and journalism teachers do three" terribly important things":

- For journalists who want to keep good journalism alive in the converged world to take a blood oath to fight, scrap, kick and scream whenever any attempt is made to dilute good journalism values.
- For journalism schools and journalism teachers to offer students the right curriculum to function best in that converged world, and this does not mean offering new courses in convergence.
- For journalism students to emphasize the right areas of study and take the right courses so they will be able to defend themselves against the evils of convergence, prosper in that new world, and contribute to the effort to sustain informed self-government.

Haiman said," If we decide to teach anything about convergence at Poynter, that is the lesson I hope we'll teach."

To students, Haiman said that the journalists who will be the most successful in the converged world are the same ones who are the most successful today, and they are the ones who are best trained in six areas: reporting, writing, editing, ethics, and media law, research techniques and specialized knowledge such as business, finance, law, science, health, aging, and the environment. Since the top reporter in education Haiman mentioned can hardly survive the converged media world, our question is whether gaining knowledge in these six areas is sufficient and what else, if any, students need to learn. Do students need to learn any new skills? What new skills do news practitioners need?

Also, we would like to see how the attitudes of the respondents from these three groups toward media merger affect their views of how to train future journalists. As South and Nicholson commented," If the industry doesn't agree on what new skills journalists need, it will be hard for journalism schools to know what to teach."

LARGER CONTEXT OF THE STUDY

The questions concerning teaching skills vs. critical thinking and training specialists vs. generalists are not new. They have been contextualized in ongoing conversations across disciplines over decades on many campuses in the United States. But such conversations take on new meanings in journalism schools when many reporting jobs today are becoming high-tech-oriented and many news companies are demanding high-tech skills from new hires upon their graduation.

The impact of such industrial demands on universities brings us back to the core issue-the role of the university in the shaping of the young souls in its charge. In other words, how should a university achieve the desired product-a truly educated human being for newsrooms.

The question of teaching skills vs. critical thinking winds down to a perennial competition between acquiescing pervasive vocationalism with its emphasis on skills training in an attempt to enable college students to survive outside academic institutions and establishing the relevance of the broad spectrum of knowledge to the career goals and lives of individuals. E. D. Hirsch argues: "Narrow vocational education, adjusted to the needs of the moment, is made ever more obsolete by changing technology... What is required is education for change, not for static job competencies".

Probably no one has better expressed than Joanne G. Kurfiss the importance of imparting critical thinking as skills of analyzing and constructing arguments, as construction of meaning, and as the manifestation of a contextual theory of knowledge. "Critical thinking can result in a new way of approaching significant issues in one's life or a deeper understanding of the basis for one's actions. Or it might result in political activity".

Along the similar line as Kurfiss's critical thinking theory and unlike Allan Bloom,. who condemns the introduction of non-Western materials into the university curricula so as to protect the curriculum from the contamination of ideological conflict, Jerry Herron also highly promotes the teaching of critical thinking by calling on faculty to bring their conflicting ideologies into open engagement so that students can discover what is at stake in different ideas and can see their representational meaning.

The questions are whether universities should totally give up the teaching of skills today and how the needs of the job market and the goal of college education can be in harmony. In other words, can the teaching of common traditional content and the teaching of higher order skills join forces? Patracia Graham, ex-dean of the Harvard Graduate School of Education, argues that we need both commonality and flexibility in American education and there is no reason we cannot have both at once.

The question of training specialists vs. generalists is an extension of a larger conversation about reforming the fragmented curricula in higher education. Often classified as "cultural right," Ernest Boyer, Allan Bloom, and E. D. Hirsch share similar views about the problems in higher education. They point out that the university now is anarchistic. There is no vision of what an educated human being is. The curriculum is disjointed and disciplines are fragmented into smaller pieces.

Undergraduates find it hard to see patterns in their courses and relate what they learn to life. Careerism conflicts with the liberal arts. And finally, schools have failed to thoroughly carry out the educational goal of promoting mature literacy for all our citizens. They all agree that an educational reform is needed to teach more common traditional content apart from the higher-order skills that are commonly emphasized.

Boyer calls for a balance between individual interests and shared concerns while the actual priority is given to the latter. To promote a liberal education, Boyer advocates the "integrated core" or "enriched major"-a programme of general education that introduces students not only to essential knowledge, but also to connections across the disciplines, and, in the end, to the application of knowledge to life beyond the campus.

Boyer points out, knowledge becomes important only when we use it and apply it to humane ends; therefore, the undergraduate experience should not only generate new knowledge, but channel that knowledge to the service of the society. It is a matter of invigorating "the claims of community while protecting with full vigour the dignity and origins of each individual," to use Boyer and Kaplan's words.

In a similar vein, Bloom calls on teachers to look toward the goal of human completeness and to provide students a liberal education, in which learning is both synoptic and precise. To Bloom, liberal education feeds the student's love of truth and passion to live a good life. It also requires that a student's whole life be radically changed by it.

Bloom offers an ivory tower vision of the university-"the good old Great Book approach"-undergraduate students spend four years reading certain generally recognized classic texts for answers to philosophical questions of personal and human identity and aspirations. Bloom thinks that man may live more truly and fully in reading Plato and Shakespeare than at any other time because then they are participating in essential being and are forgetting their accidental lives.

In accordance with Boyer's and Bloom's points of view, Hirsch argues that "the greatest human individuality is developed in response to a tradition, not in response to disorderly, uncertain, and fragmented education" and "only by accumulating shared symbols, and the shared information the symbols represent can we learn to communicate effectively with one another in our national community".

However, Hirsch places emphasis more on the content of education, ensuring that students acquire all the "right" elements of knowledge that will enable them to get along in the Real World.

He believes that neither the content-neutral curriculum of Rousseau and Dewey nor the narrowly specified curriculum of Plato is adequate to the needs of a modern nation. Hirsch calls for a curriculum, including extensive curriculum and intensive curriculum with an emphasis on the former, which is traditional in content and provides students with a common core of cultural information. "The conception of a two-part curriculum avoids the idea that all children should study identical materials" Hirsch says.

Based on our literature review, media convergence in our study is defined as the assimilation of media content for multiple media platforms. Media convergence may involve any combination of the convergences of media contents, media forms, media companies, and roles of news practitioners. Our general research question is how college professors should prepare students to cope with media convergence. To be specific, should college professors prepare generalists who can competently work in multiple media platforms or prepare specialists who know inside out how to work for one particular medium platform? And how should journalism schools balance the teaching of critical thinking and technical skills?

Corresponding to these two questions, we also would like to find out if college journalism educators themselves are both theoretically equipped and technologically prepared to teach their students about media convergence. The study serves both as an attitude finder and a fact finder.

We believe that professors, editors, and news professionals are the best candidates to answer these questions. Editors represent the media companies to hire news staffers with news reporting abilities desired by the company. News professionals work in the forefront of news reporting and know best about what news reporting abilities they need.

The attitudes of the editors and the current generation of news professionals toward media convergence will have a great implication on future journalism education. Professors run journalism schools, and they have the final say about where their schools are going. Their attitudes toward journalism education in terms of media convergence will have the most direct influence on the kind of education journalism students will receive and how the students will perform in tomorrow's media.

Editors include daily newspaper editors in charge of newsroom operations or online news operations and news directors in charge of newsroom operations in a commercial TV station with news content, both in the United States.

News professionals refer to non-management news staff, such as reporters, anchors, photographers, designers, producers, Web staff, etc., working in American media companies. Journalism professors are defined as full-time instructors with any academic rankings who teach journalism courses in a U.S. journalism school, department, programme, or division, which could be administratively affiliated with an institution with a name like College of Communications or Department of Communications Studies.

To obtain opinions about media convergence, we could have targeted our survey only at those editors and news professionals in a converged media environment. The opinions obtained from those editors and news professionals, however, could be biased. Those media companies that have not gone through convergence must have a reason for not doing so. We also wanted to find out what they are doing about convergence. Balanced views both from the converged and un-converged media companies will better assist colleges in their strategic planning.

We conducted a national survey among editors, news professionals, and journalism professors with three different versions of online survey questionnaires posted on a school Web site. Respondents were asked to fill out the questionnaire online and submit answers online as well. The answers went through a commercial form handler and reached the primary investigator's email address. By doing so, the primary investigator had no way to detect who answered the questionnaire unless the respondent voluntarily revealed his/ her email address to request the findings from the study.

There were twenty-two questions in each of these three questionnaires. Almost all questions were close-ended. About half of the questions used a 5-point Likert Scale from "Strongly Agree" to "Strongly Disagree." Some questions across the three questionnaires shared similarity, so that comparisons could be made when analyzing data. A text field was created for respondents to provide feedback to the survey freely.

The textual answers in the text field will be reported along with the statistics to illustrate and explain the quantitative findings. All questionnaires went through pilot tests. The unit of analysis was each participant.

In order to conduct a systematic random sampling of editors and news professionals, we needed a list of newspaper editors and TV news directors in the United States and a list of newspaper and TV news staffers. We found that such lists did not exist, though lists of newspapers and lists of TV stations did exist in multiple places online like Editor & Publisher Yearbook and Broadcasting Sr Cable Yearbook. Therefore, we decided to construct our own.

To do so, we went through two steps. First, we constructed a combined list of daily newspapers and TV stations so that we could sample these news institutions. Second, we visited the Web sites of all sampled news institutions to find the email of the editor/news director and the email of one news professional randomly chosen.

After further research, we decided that newslink.org's daily newspaper list was the most comprehensive and workable list for sampling daily newspapers. In total, 1,190 U.S. daily newspapers with a valid URL were listed alphabetically by state. We sampled one out of every four dailies. Then, we visited each of those Web sites to find the email address of the managing editor, chief editor, online editor, or equivalent in each of those dailies and sent out a survey invitation email to him/her. If an individual email address was not available, we replaced it with a generic email address listed on their Web site and specified that the email was for the editor.

In total, there were 1,093 companies ordered alphabetically by state. From the list, we removed PBS network companies, which mostly did not provide staff information, companies that did not generate news content such as WB network companies and UPN network companies, religious TV stations, and foreign language stations. In total, we extracted 674 TV stations with a valid URL. Since this population is smaller than that of the newspapers, we over-sampled it. Instead of sampling every other four, we sampled every other station.

Then, we visited each of those Web sites to find the email address of the news director or equivalent in each of those TV stations and sent out a survey invitation email to him/her. If an individual email address was not available, we replaced it with a generic email address and specified that the email was for the news director. In total, we successfully sent out invitation emails to 523 newspaper editors and TV news directors as our sample.

We also sampled one news professional out of each of the sampled U.S. dailies and TV stations for the survey. Since there was always more than one professional in a company, we simply randomly clicked on one name and picked him/her and made sure that s/he was on the news staff.

Then, we sent him/her a survey invitation email. If an individual email address was not available, we replaced it with a generic email address and specified whom the email was for. S/he was asked to fill out a questionnaire that was worded in a slightly different manner. In total, we successfully sent out invitation emails to 398 news professionals.

We also needed to conduct a systematic random sampling of college journalism professors, but we were disappointed that all lists we found had many J-schools, even major ones, missing. Therefore, a new list was built upon the existing lists and upon the findings from a more careful search in the Yahoo U.S. Colleges and Universities site. In total, the new list contains 205 alphabetically ordered U.S. J-schools that contain 2,194 journalism professors.

We sampled one out of every four professors from the virtually running list of all journalism professors across the schools. For instance, if a school had six journalism professors, we picked the fourth one; then, the second journalism professor from next school was picked. We sent an invitation email to every professor in the sample. In total, we successfully sent out 500 emails.

The three samples of editors, news professionals, and professors included 1,421 cases.

We understood that nonresponse had been a serious problem with online surveys in recent years. In order to counter possible low response rates in our survey, we created three samples for editors, news professionals, and professors containing roughly 500 people for each group, which were much larger than the sample sizes for populations recommended by Mildred Patten in her book Understanding Research Methods: An Overview of the Essentials so that, if low response rates occurred, we could base our confidence limits on the actual number of responses themselves. We also sent out one reminder email to the samples, which drastically boosted the response rates, especially for professors and news professionals.

After two weeks of online data collecting in November 2002, we received 223 responses from professors (a 44% response rate), 151 responses from editors (a 29% response rate), and 142 responses from news professionals (a 35% response rate). The overall response rate is 36%. As Singletary notes, returns of 30% to 40% are common in mail surveys. The response rates of this online survey seem typical. However, the response rates are still comparatively low. A response bias is potentially present. Many respondents (41%) left textual answers to explain and illustrate their answers to the close-ended questions and/or made comments on the topic.

- What is the status quo of media convergence in the industry?

By the end of 2002, 19% of the newspapers and commercial television stations with news content in the United States had gone through media mergers. Being merged or not has to do with the size of a company. Larger companies tend to have been merged while smaller ones have not. Roughly half of the news professionals surveyed (48%) reported that they produced news content for multiple media platforms on a routine basis; that was true both in merged media (50%) and non-merged media (48%). In other words, media merger is not the precondition for practicing news for multiple media platforms. The pressure on news professionals to learn to produce multimedia content is also felt in many non-merged media companies. This finding confirms that media convergence is not necessarily related to media merger.

A typical editor or news director was a man (71%) between 36-45 years old (42%) with a bachelor's degree (76%) who had worked for at least two media (57%) for more than 20 years (53%). A typical news professional was either a man (52%) or woman (48%) between 26-35 years old (43%) with a bachelor's degree (84%) who had worked for at least two media (60%) less than ten years (62%).

Editors had generally worked for more years than news professionals, but they did not have more multiplatform experience than news professionals. As more news companies are practicing cross-media reporting with or without their companies being merged, it is important that editors with multiplatforrn experiences are chosen to direct newsroom businesses. Many editors need cross-media training more urgently than news professionals do if the news company they work for produces news contents for multiple media platforms on a daily basis.

- Should J-schools train specialists or generalists?

Gil Thelen said that writers should learn how to write for multimedia and still photographers should learn how to shoot videos, but he was not interested in hiring people with multiple sets of skills. We designed four questions to test how popular Thelen's opinion was.

The majority of the respondents (84%) agreed or strongly agreed with Thelen that journalism students should learn how to write for multiple media platforms. One-way ANOVA shows significant difference among the means for professors (4.35), professionals (4.05), and editors. Tukey HSD post hoc tests show that professors were more positive on this statement than editors and professionals, while no significant difference existed between editors and professionals.

A similar number of respondents (85%) agreed or strongly agreed with Thelen that journalism students with a visual emphasis should learn how to produce and edit photos, videos, and online interactive images. One-way ANOVA shows significant difference among the means for professors (4.55), professionals (4.22), and editors. Tukey HSD post hoc tests show that professors were more positive on this statement than professionals, while professionals were more positive than editors.

Most respondents (78%) agreed or strongly agreed that all journalism majors should learn multiple sets of skills, such as writing, editing, TV production, digital photography, newspaper design, and Web publishing.

Oneway ANOVA shows significant differences among the means for professionals (4.28), editors (3.99), and professors (3.86). Tukey HSD post hoc tests show that news professionals who worked in the forefront of news production felt this need more deeply than other respondents. Editors also had such an expectation for them.

There is no significant difference between editors and professors. These findings support the growing evidence that news professionals are being asked to wear multiple hats. The findings also indicate that Thelen's view has its market at this moment when news professionals with multiple sets of skills are highly desirable but not easy to find. Such a view may change as more journalism graduates equipped with multiple sets of skills enter the job market.

The professors' textual answers show that some of the difficulties J-schools have come across include the lack of a friendly curriculum, lack of credit hours to include the components of convergence content, lack of willing cooperation among faculty from different sequences, and lack of expertise, interest, or even time for some professors to develop new courses on convergence.

When asked whether journalism students should still have a specialization, such as writing, photojournalism, broadcasting, and new media, over half (63%) of the respondents agreed or strongly agreed. Over a quarter of the respondents (28%) were negative and 9% were not sure. One-way ANOVA mean comparisons show no significant difference of attitude among professionals (3.42), editors (3.51), and professors (3.72).

Comparing the support rate for this question to those for the first three questions, it is fair to argue that editors, news professionals, and professors emphasized the importance of cross-media training more than that of specialization, though they believed that specialization should not be neglected either. Currently, students in many J-schools specialize in one area by subscribing to a sequence such as news-editorial, magazine, photojournalism, and broadcast. When asked whether sequences should be reorganized considering the trend of media-platforms merging in the industry, 56% of the professors agreed or strongly agreed, 22% were not sure, and another 22% disagreed or strongly disagreed.

The concept of sequences is being shaken among professors though it is still being accepted as a legitimate means of training students in various specialization areas in some J-schools. Speaking on behalf of herself and her colleagues, Professor offered some special insight on this issue: We can't teach for the" now." We have to prepare students for when they graduate...which in most instances is now five years out. And, we feel a commitment to expose them to all types of writing in all platforms so they can be flexible about their career choice at the front end of their academics. Then, they can apply the skills to a specialty area where they are totally proficient.

"Flexible" is a key term repeatedly seen in editors' and news professionals' textual answers as a suggestion for future journalists. Editor's statement is typical:

Our job descriptions are open ended and new hires

understand that they are being hired for their skills. They may be hired today to cover the city beat. In six months or in two weeks, if necessary, a person with Quark skills may be asked to fill in or shift duties to include pagination of a particular section. It is important that hires stay flexible.

The new hires, wrote Editor, "need to understand that the information they gather and process can have many different uses, audiences and shelf lives. They need to understand the complexities of the audience mix and be able to respond." "Those unwilling to be flexible may find themselves in a difficult scenario later in their careers".

From a different perspective, Professional concurred: "Students must be flexible, have a vigorous skill set and be prepared to get laid off and move around in the changing media arena." In short, "young journalists must be prepared to fill a variety of roles if they hope to succeed". "The most successful journalists are those that take on assignments willingly, can learn and want to learn".

Specialization in journalistic jobs is still honored, but is losing its favour to cross-media capability in converged media. Today, professionals with different specializations team together to work on multiple media projects. Tomorrow, it is likely that one-man bands will be more and more desired in newsrooms.

- How should J-schools balance the teaching of critical thinking and that of technical skills?

Most respondents (93%), especially professors, agreed or strongly agreed that journalism students should both learn technical skills, such as online information search and Web design, while learning critical thinking skills in media law, ethics, etc.

One-way ANOVA shows significant difference among the means for professionals (4.35), editors (4.38), and professors (4.76). Tukey HSD post hoc tests show that professors were more positive on this point than editors and professionals, while no significant difference existed between editors and professionals.

But, should journalism students spend more time on

learning critical thinking skills than on technical skills? Opinions were divided.

More than half of the respondents (62%) believed that should be the case, but 19% of the respondents were not sure and another 19% of them did not agree. Oneway ANOVA shows significant difference among the means for professors (3.21), professionals (3.87), and editors (4.3). Tukey HSD post hoc tests show that editors were more positive on this point than professionals, and professionals were more positive than professors.

Throughout all the answers from the three groups of respondents, critical thinking was highly regarded as being more important than technical skills.

Editors, news professionals, and professors all liked to see good stories, and good stories come from good thinking ability. An editor said: "Journalism graduates need to have a broad, well-rounded education; be critical thinkers; have the ability to write clearly; have a serious work ethic; and know computer basics - in that order". "You can teach a monkey to type," echoes a writer. Therefore, he strongly suggested that J-schools "get more critical thinking skills pounded into the skulls of the students". While highly emphasizing the importance of critical thinking ability, editors did not mean to neglect the importance of teaching technical skills in schools.

We will develop this point when we discuss the next question. Comparing the professors' highest mean for the first question and their lowest mean for the second question, it is clear that professors saw critical thinking as highly important, but preferred a comparatively balanced approach for the teaching of the two sets of knowledge. One professor's comment illustrated this observation:

Knowing technical skill alone will not make you a "good" journalist. Critical thinking is vital not just to a career but to life itself. Without developing your ability to discern and evaluate, you will become "the prey" of society. Next, a technical skill is critical to a career in journalism today. Even print Journalism is very high tech these days and all electronic media require extensive computer knowledge as well as other technical skills. I would place critical thinking skills first on your list of things to do because a developed mind will make it that much easier to develop a creative and technically sound understanding of the technical side of the business.

From a holistic view, there was no substantial disagreement between classrooms and newsrooms when we examine the issue of teaching critical thinking vs. teaching technical skills.

Compared to Terry's 2000 poll, this study shows that professors gave a higher status to technical skills in journalism curricula in 2002 than they did in 2000.

This is a period during which media convergence garnered its momentum. In short, all respondents generally agreed that J-schools should place emphasis on teaching critical thinking, but at the same time, should not neglect teaching technical skills.

- Should technical skills be learned at work or in school?

News professionals were asked, "If you wish to possess the technical skills you don't have now, do you prefer to learn them at work or wish you had learned in school?" Editors were given the same question with a slightly different wording.

Chi-Square test shows that the difference between editors and news professionals is significant. This finding well supplements the findings from the preceding questions. It suggests that editors not only looked at future journalists' critical thinking ability, but also hoped that future journalists would already possess the skills needed in a converged newsroom when they are hired.

On the other hand, most professionals preferred that they spend most of their school time on gaining critical thinking ability and learn skills largely at work. The professionals' general preference, to some extent, also reflected their need for technological update at their current positions, so that they can better qualify for multimedia productions.

Many editors and reporters said that school is the best place for journalism students to explore every facet of the media and acquire basic technical skills, though some advanced skills can only be learned on the job. Learning skills while in school, they said, can build confidence and an expansive and broad understanding of the entire field and help with damage control and communication in newsrooms.

"If editing and the technical skills were more prevalent in college courses," wrote a multi-tasking editor, "I think I could stave off a lot of headaches when the students become professionals."

An internship was the news professionals' and editors' most recommended venue for enhancing and learning more technical skills and gaining other practical experience. Reporter said: "While I value my college education, my internship and first job provided me with the most valuable skills today." Another reporter said: "While education is great, students who work in media while in school fare much better in the real world." Some editors had complaints about graduates with a 3.5 GPA but no practical experience and no published news work. An anchor/reporter said that it is important even "for a freshman or sophomore in college to visit a newsroom and shadow someone. So many students wait until they are juniors and seniors to do this and then they realise they made a mistake in selecting their major. You will learn more by watching and doing". One reporter said, "To remain competitive, education must continue throughout a career".

The implication of the discrepancy from this finding suggests that Jschools should place emphasis on teaching critical thinking, expose students to new technology, and design a comprehensive internship programme for students to gain real-world knowledge and further develop their crossmedia technical skills.

- What skills do news professionals need to learn most at their current positions?

Both editors and news professionals were given this unstructured question with slightly different wordings. We read through all the answers, and categorized them into the following nine facets in random order:

Multimedia production: producing and editing news stories on video, for the Web, and for print; re-purposing the same story for different media. New technology: knowledge of software for producing video, Web sites, graphics, newspapers, and magazines; knowledge of how to operate a computer and use the Internet.

Good writing: knowing how to write to make people remember and/or take action, write about the beats with an expert's view.

Good editing is also expected:

- *Critical thinking:* Having good news judgment, understanding what is legal and ethical, knowing how to report with insight, knowing how to crunch statistics.
- *Computer-assisted reporting*: Expert's knowledge of conducting online information search, database knowledge.
- *On-camera exposure*: How to report like a TV news anchor before a camera for a newspaper reporter.
- *Visual production*: A newspaper writer must know how to take photos, or a TV reporter must know how to shoot video.
- *Second language*: Knowing how to fluently speak and read a foreign language.
- *Time management*: Well organizing time to work for multiple media platforms; the ability and willingness to work as a team to produce multimedia news stories.

Then we ranked these facets according to the percentage scores each facet got separately from the editors and the news professionals: This ranking shows more agreement than disagreement between editors and news professionals. No matter how technology changes and whether media are converged, editors and news professionals believed that learning how to write good stories is still the top priority and writing is the very basic skill all news professionals should learn. One editor pushed the importance of good writing to the extreme:" I've worked in markets 170 to 20, and having training in multiple media will not help you get a job, but being a good writer will".

Most editors and news professionals, however, did believe that learning multimedia production, new technology, and computer-assisted reporting are also among the top priorities." I would strongly urge students to prepare themselves to the best of their ability to be able to report/edit the news in a variety of platforms and to learn how to truly engage readers/ listeners/viewers in what they are writing about," said Editor.

Editors and news professionals both believed that it is not very important for a newspaper reporter to learn how to talk like an anchor in front of a video camera. This skill was even regarded as being less important than knowing how to speak a second language. Some editors and news professionals also mentioned learning how to manage time for producing multimedia news stories. Editor hoped that journalists in a converged environment would learn to avoid" extra" work by working" smarter" and with greater awareness of the requirements of the different publishing media. This finding, again, shows that editors valued critical thinking ability more than news professionals did. Editors wanted news professionals to be good thinkers first, and the latter wanted most to learn how to express their thinking in different media.

- If news professionals have to re-purpose their work for multiple media platforms, will the quality of their work suffer?

Since some authors such as Haiman expressed the concern about the possible decline of work quality if news professionals have to "re-purpose" stories for multiple media platforms, we tried to find out to what extent this concern was shared by editors and news professionals. Opinions split.

Thirty-eight per cent of the editors and professionals agreed or strongly agreed that the quality would deteriorate, 40% disagreed or strongly disagreed, and the other 22% were not sure. Editors and professionals showed no significant difference on this attitude T-test. Such a concern was not prevalent in the news industry.

In response to such concerns, the news director from a converged media company wrote: "When reporters do cross platforms we give them the time to finish the project for all three platforms. Quality does not suffer. If we were to try to force reporters to cross platforms while operating under daily deadlines then quality could suffer depending on the nature of the story and the extra time consumed".

Another editor summed up this issue: "Some employees can capably handle multiple media and tell stories effectively. Others cannot.

Certainly strong technical skills and training can help, but it's not just dependent on that; it depends more on the attitude and aptitude of the journalist". Quality multimedia work also involves a solid understanding of different cultures in different media. Editors both for and against media convergence noted the difficulty of merging different media with different cultures, and editors in those merged media called for flexibility in aptitude and willingness to cooperate across platforms.

For instance, Editor wrote: Clarity of what convergence means to the news organization is vital and often lacking. This causes unneeded anxiety. Managers have to realise that each medium has its own culture, language, skill set and timetable and is naturally skeptical of anything unfamiliar. It is also true that these same journalists' stock in trade is learning a new culture, language, skill set and timetable-on a daily basis. Therein lies the hope for an efficient news operation running on all cylinders and an effective -maybe even happy-staff.

If most editors and news professionals are not concerned about the quality of the work prepared for multiple media platforms and if news professionals are given enough time to complete their cross-media work, there is little reason to worry that future journalists, if well trained both theoretically and technologically for multiple media platforms, will produce work of poorer quality.

Training students to practice news in multiple media platforms will help bridge newsroom cultures from different media and eventually erase such differences.

We have noticed that no significant statistical differences existed between the editors and news professionals from the converged media companies and their counterparts from the not-yet-converged media companies when they answered the questions reported above.

- How are J-schools coping with media convergence?

From 1998 to 2002, about 60% of the J-schools in the United States redesigned their curricula or developed new courses to prepare students for practicing news in multiple media platforms.

A typical journalism professor was a man (71%) between 46-55 years old (42%) with a doctoral degree (63%) who worked in news media for one to ten years (48%), may still be practicing news (45%) in one way or another, and conducted academic research (66%).

More professors claimed that they were theoretically equipped (81%) than technologically prepared (53%) to teach students how to report news in multiple media platforms.

More than half of the professors (57%) had not taught any journalism courses in the last five years where skill sets were beyond their own expertise; 25% of the professors taught one such course and 11% taught two.

Nevertheless, the majority of the professors (84%) added content about media convergence either to their existing courses or to new courses or participated in cross-media team-teaching in the last five years.

Worries, concerns, and, sometimes, misconceptions about media convergence appeared in professors' textual answers. For instance, a professor from Montana said: "convergence is not happening". A professor who no longer practiced news said, "In my judgment, the writing portion of preparing news for print and for the Web is exactly the same".

Another professor maintained that it was not necessary to teach cross-media news practicing because "few 'want ads' for newspaper reporter and editor positions specifically listed multimedia platform skills as required or preferred experience for new hires". Many professors worried that media mergers would restrict the number of voices in a community. They regarded media mergers as a grand experiment in the profession and waited for the FCC's ruling on the cross-ownership of different media in the same market.

Wait-and-see-that was the strategy some universities took for teaching media convergence. One professor said that he needed to see the substantive contribution media convergence could make before he would be more serious about this phenomenon. He said that J-schools should be cautious about embracing convergence. Some other universities didn't have the time and resources to teach convergence courses or make major curriculum changes.

Most professors, however, did believe that media convergence was a reality; and "anybody serious about practicing media needs at minimal an acquaintance with various media and at best multiple competencies," as Professor said. Many professors (and editors and news professionals as well) had a clear opinion as to which comes first, teaching critical thinking or teaching technical skills.

While acknowledging the need for incorporating media convergence content in curricula, especially the technological components, professors cautioned against sacrificing conceptual and theoretical courses such as law, ethics, history, cultural studies, critical perspectives, etc. Professor analogized critical thinking as meat and potatoes and technical skills as dessert and side dishes and argued that "the meat and potatoes need to come before one begins to worry about the dessert and side dishes (or side shows)." This viewpoint was popular. Professor wrote:

It's the message, not the medium, that is of paramount importance. If students cannot understand and appreciate the underlying concepts, principles and ethics of journalism, then they cannot produce the type of content that will be of value to a free society. A thorough grounding in journalism must come before any training in tools. The tools are means to an end, not the end in and of themselves.

Incidentally, a reporter had similar thoughts: The medium isn't the message, the message is the message. In short, the fundamental analytic and synthetic skills of the news writer are paramount to the message.

The medium does not alter the reporter's craft of interpreting news events in the context of the society in a way that will make sense for the receiver of the information.... Additional skills may be desirable, but for the most part they can be learned on the job.

Obviously, the more skills one can offer, the better the employment opportunity. Those ancillary skills should not come at the expense of thorough proficiency as a news writer.

We fully understand why these respondents emphasize the teaching of critical thinking and the fundamentals of good reporting over the teaching of technical skills, and we strongly agree with their opinions. But, we also see the danger of over-stretching the point by treating the two sets of knowledge as two opposing poles.

Those arguments are based on the presumptions that message and medium can be easily separated, content and form can be detached, and readers for different media are from the same population. But, is that right? It is true that content is the king. It is true that "the medium does not alter the reporter's craft of interpreting news events."

News practice, however, is not only about news-gathering and writing. It also includes production, editing, and delivery. Without a solid grasp of grammar and style, how can a writer effectively express his/her good analytical thinking? Without knowing the available features and limitations of online news delivery, how can messages be constructed to their fullest potential?

Without understanding the technical difference between video news and print news, how can messages be constructed appropriately? In the digital era when almost all steps of news transmission involves technology, if professors don't teach students technical skills, will the computer majors, who know little about news practices, be expected to produce newspapers, TV news, and online news?

Writers, for instance, do not necessarily have to be conversant in constructing news reporting with Flash for online presentation or know how to operate a video camera to shoot video stories.

But knowing the principles and rules of news video-taping and what Flash or other software can offer will surely help writers more effectively convey their messages and better cooperate with visual reporters. Creativity distinguishes artists and artisans. Critical thinking ability distinguishes master journalists and technical writers. But artists must first know what artisans know and a master journalist must possess all that a technical writer knows for a living. Skills are intrinsic instead of extrinsic to ideas.

Teaching critical thinking and teaching technical skills are not mutually exclusive. Teaching journalism students how to express their critical thinking with conversant technical skills in different media seems to be a big challenge for J-school professors in the years to come.

From the professors' textual answers, we have observed different philosophical approaches to teaching convergence. Unlike some professors who took the wait-and-see approach, a professor from the University of Texas at Austin claimed that "convergence is already happening, and journalism schools should be leading the parade and not following it".

A popular viewpoint was that "skills across platforms must be taught, but more importantly storytelling, ethics, and critical thinking skills should be even more important in the journalism school curriculum".

One professor from Texas Christian University said that it maintained the existing sequences but required broadcast students to take print courses and vice versa.

Team-teaching was an often-used approach in some J-schools such as Indiana University for courses involving multiple sets of skills while professors learned from each other. Another professor, from the University of Colorado at Boulder, said convergence meant that "students work together to produce multimedia content for the Web-not that each individual should attempt to become proficient in all media".

To overcome the hurdle of the ratio limited by the ACEJMC accreditation standards between journalism courses and liberal arts courses, a professor from Bowling Green State University suggested that journalism undergraduate students stay for five years and devote the fifth year entirely to practice. Some professors said that journalism students only need to know a little about the practices in media other than their own while some other professors firmly maintained that students should "be the master of many arts and the explorer of all".

- Who benefits from media convergence?

All respondents were asked, "Do you think that merging media companies such as television station, newspaper, radio station, and online news from a local area will benefit any of the parties listed on the left? Check all entries that apply."

The entries included "The general public," "News professionals," "Media companies," "Nobody," and "Not sure." We designed this question about the legitimacy of media merger as a barometer for testing the respondents' political view on media convergence. We presumed that a respondent's answer to this question could be related to his/her way of answering other questions regarding teaching media convergence or requirement for new hires.

Most respondents (66%) from all three groups pointed to media companies as the beneficiary of media mergers. In comparison, only 37% of the respondents said that media mergers also benefit the general public, and even fewer (27%) said that media mergers benefit the news professionals.

By reading the percentage numbers horizontally, we can find that consistently fewer respondents believed that media mergers benefit the general public or news professionals; also consistently more respondents believed that media mergers benefit media companies.

It is also noticeable that 47% of editors believed that media mergers benefit the general public while the other 53% didn't. Editors' opinions on this point were roughly equally split. This finding indicates that media merger is a grand experiment in the media industry. Its benefits to the general public, which can better legitimize media mergers, are to be explored in the years to come.

By reading the percentage numbers both vertically and horizontally, we also find that editors were the most positive about the benefits media mergers could bring to all three parties while professors were least sure of such benefits. It is logical to reason that management personnel, such as editors and news directors and the companies they represent, are the primary forces behind today's media merger movement.

The question is that, since most professors, editors, and even news professionals believed that media mergers do not benefit news professionals and hardly benefit the general public, why do most news professionals still want to be trained to be cross-media practitioners and why are so many Jschool professors enthusiastic about training such graduates? Considering the editors' most positive attitude toward media convergence, we wonder if news professionals are under the pressure to do so, and J-school professors are under the pressure to follow the industrial trend. Our surmise is partially corroborated by some textual answers. A news anchor from a merged media company agreed that new hires should have received cross-media training in writing and visuals and should possess multiple sets of skills. She showed her understanding for media mergers:

The merging of media companies is almost a daily occurrence. The pool of entities providing news services is shrinking. I think there is a danger that the public will lose in this race for media giants to accumulate wealth. At the same time, with the amount of competition in the industry from cable networks, the Internet, DVD's etc., I see the financial need for companies to merge to survive.

A newspaper reporter also from a merged media company expressed a similar feeling: "I am not all for the media convergence... At the same time I find it quite beneficial to be savvy in all branches of the industry. It helps the journalist become more knowledgeable about her or his job". News professionals were not alone in having such feelings. Here are two excerpts from two professors who have expressed similar feelings:

It's a harsh reality that I checked the box saying that news companies are the ones that are sure to benefit from media convergence. It may not be great for the public or even for news professionals who are going to be asked to bring more and more skills to the table and to have more and more responsibility on the job. Even so, convergence in one way or another is gonna happen and we need to prepare our students. Finally, my answer on merging media companies... reflects my disdain for the corporatization and concentration of control in the media. I think we ought to train mass communicators for a converged world, but as professors we ought to fight like hell against media mergers.

Very few respondents (19%) believed that media mergers benefit all three parties, the general public, news professionals, and media companies, but about one third of the respondents (35%) believed that media companies are the only beneficiaries to such a practice. These 35% respondents, who were almost equally proportionally found in editors, news professionals, and professors groups, could be regarded as the most critical toward media mergers.

We compared these 35% respondents with the rest of the sample and found no significant difference in their answers concerning the necessity of teaching journalism students cross-media writing and visuals and teaching multiple sets of skills. Always, more respondents believed that professors should teach all those things. In short, the respondents' political view was not directly tied to their views of teaching students cross-media practices.

Chapter 12

Social Responsibility of Media

An important consideration in doing ethnographic research in the study of new electronic media is the social presence attributes of the technology itself.

Short, Williams, and Christie were apparently the first researchers to conceptualize the construct they called social presence, which they defined as being a quality of the communications medium itself.

As they elaborated, social presence "varies between different media... affects the nature of the interaction... and interacts with the purpose of the interaction to influence the medium chosen by the individual who wishes to communicate".

Media perceived as high in social presence are generally judged (on Semantic Differential Scales) by users as warm, personal, sensitive, and, sociable; those low in social presence as cold, impersonal, insensitive, and unsociable.

Chief among the reasons for differentiating media in their degree of social presence is the medium's ability to restrict stimulus-conveying information. More specifically, media that are less able to convey nonverbal elements are more likely to be judged as being low in social presence.

In another sense, social presence is the degree to which a medium is perceived as conveying the "presence" of the communicating participants; it is dependent not only on the words involved in the communication but on the full range of verbal and nonverbal cues, and the communication context.

Thus CMC technologies typically would be judged lower in social presence than face-to-face communication (FTF) because of the lower bandwidth of information conveyed by the former (vis-a-vis verbal and nonverbal messages).

This notion of the bandwidth of the medium is closely related to media richness, a construct developed by Daft and Lengel. Rice describes the term as the:

Extent to which media are able to bridge different frames of reference, make issues less ambiguous, or provide opportunities for learning in a given time interval, based on the medium's capacity for immediate feedback, the number of cues and senses involved, personalization, and language variety. The essential underlying element in both of these notions is that a good match between the medium's characteristics (high in social presence or media richness) and the intent of the communication activity (getting to know someone, strategic decision making) should lead to higher performance and satisfaction.

The importance of all of this to ethnographic research is, how can one adequately do participatory research with media that are judged low in social presence or media richness?

Stated another way, how will the ethnographic researcher be able to make adequate sense out of communication that restricts important cues such as nonverbal behaviours? in their study of e-mail in organizations, Garton and Wellman have discussed the consequences of e-mail's exclusion of nonverbal cues: E-mail does not supply nonverbal interactional cues to group members, such as eye contact, gestures, nodding approval, frowning, or hesitating before replying.

There are no contextual cues, either: Participants cannot use seating arrangements to identify coalitions and cleavages, or choose meeting sites to identify the importance of sponsorship of meetings. Because e-mail users typically are identified by name only, people are not constantly reminded of the social roles cues others have beyond the narrow confines of the task group.

Users may not be aware of another group member's gender, race, expertise, or organizational position. One approach to this dilemma is to take account of the ways participants do compensate at times for the restricted bandwidth of the medium by providing clarifying cues in their messages.

Social role cues can be transmitted in e-mail (either implicitly or explicitly) by adding status information to their "signatures," by their writing style, or by forwarding communications to (or from) important persons.

Baym also found the standard components of Usenet posts for a soap opera news group—e.g., "from" line, "subject" line, "organization" line (site of message's origin), and the quotation system, in addition to signatures—to provide subtle contextualizing cues about the sender's interests and status.

Other examples of clarifying cues are:

- Emotions used to pictorialize emotional states (e.g., the computer "smiley face"),
- Meta-messages included to communicate physical states (e.g., using " " to designate jocularity),
- Acronyms used to designate degree of emotion (e.g., "FOTFL" to represent "failing on the floor laughing," or a greater degree of merriment beyond a mere smile or grin).'

As Walther, Anderson, and Park noted in their meta-analysis of computer mediated interaction, the interpersonal effects expected to accrue rapidly in face-to-face interactions can (and do) occur in CIVIC, but these interpersonal cues require extended time interactions.

That is, interactional, contextual, and social cues that provide immediate feedback in FTF communication have to be stated explicitly in CIVIC and require more time to develop. Deep knowledge of an organizational culture may also enhance the participants' hermeneutic ability to embeliish an e-mail with meaning.

Of course, social cues do more than merely clarify or boost informational richness in FTF or CMC encounters; they also mark a person's identity (e.g., gender, age, ethnic, class, sexual, cultural, occupational, etc.) as being of a certain moral or political character. Gender norms, for example, are a powerful means of designating the inappropriate or disvalued behaviours of men and women in specific contexts and vary widely from ideologically dominant expressions to the communication contexts and media of subaltern groups.

Thus, women ethnographers learn very quickly how their bodies—not only skin colour and body shape, but also aspects of clothing, adornment, hair style, and facial, gestural, and speech styles—affect the way they are perceived in the field, and the roles and motives attributed to them.

Embodiment in all of its forms is not a condition that can be controlled independently or somehow neutralized. Rather, it is through the ethnographic body performing with other cultural members that one learns the schemes of cultural valuation. Practical problems of "fitting in" are of a piece with issues of acculturation which are enormously important to understanding the scene being studied.

In CMC environments, where perceptions of identity derive almost totally from what and how one writes, the notion of representational reality collapses and the ambiguity of action becomes foregrounded. Multiple identities are tried on, and specific traits or behaviours may be expressed more boldly in the widespread use of aliases, aptonyms, and role-playing domains in which players build characters for themselves. By detaching self-expression from the politics of the body, CMC liberates its users from certain kinds of discriminatory practice and promotes a low-risk, often playful, exploration of skill sets.

Certainly, the texts one writes may unwittingly leak signs of personal identity which could be attributed by readers to the author's embodied self.

As long as there are other users supervising the actors and the threads of their discourse, standards of plausibility, coherence, and trustworthiness will still apply to the textual contributions. Ultimately, the CMC ethnographer should be prepared to confront the ambiguity of identity performance as a central fact of virtual life, worthy of study on its own terms.

Concerns about testing the informational richness, or the authenticity, of virtual action against criteria of embodied action may be much less important to the project of ethnography than issues of how computing worlds are socially constructed, what recognizably human purposes they serve, and how they relate to a range of other "possibility spaces." Reduced social presence also affects the way in which researchers enter virtual scenes. Interaction management seems to function similarly in FTF and CMC in the opening and closing phases of encounters, but in CMC the choice of names and the use of attention-getting strategies are critical decisions.

The risks of field entry may be lessened by learning the norms of such strategies in advance. Thus the "outsider" designation one usually expects in the first stages of an FTF project may be less of a problem in entering a virtual space once the right level of competence has been gained via observation.

On the other hand, veteran members often do not suffer novices gladly, and the ethnographer may need to ask for the cooperation of the group (or its influential members) in order to be heard, or to engage them in directed queries or tasks. Researchers face subtle differences in the social makeup and interactional preferences of virtual scenes, which may require them to devise different strategies for entry and field positioning than in FTF situations.

SOCIAL STRATEGIES

Matters of self-presentation and scope of action are critical to the relations built among researchers, the virtual "places" populating the Internet, and the cultural membership. Correll, for example, was able to convey the location, look, and meanings of the "furniture" of the Lesbian Cafe mostly from her observations of electronic postings, but also from interviews. Compared to Leal's analysis of the relation of TV sets to the domestic material culture in working-class Brazilian homes, the mise-en-scene of the Cafe is not nearly as dense, tactile, and sensuous.

Despite this possibly unfair comparison, "the sense of a common reality [in the Lesbian Cafe] was used by patrons much like physical settings are used by co-present conversationalists—as a source of mutually relevant topics". Like the dialogue one hears in a radio play, conversationalists in the Lesbian Cafe must include many more references in their ordinary talk to objects, the current status of the objects, and the presence or absence of people in and around those objects in order to maintain orientation and sustain a convincing sense of as-if reality. The lean exposition Correll offers would likely be unacceptable in other forms of ethnographic work, but it turns out to be the one that matters to the women who "drink" and socialize there.

Media ethnographers begin their on-line presence in a variety of ways. One mode used by some is that of the unknown, unobtrusive observer. Over a three-year period, Harrington and Bielby collected and printed messages posted on two soap opera BBS's by subscribers to two commercial on-line computer services. They do not report interactions of any kind between themselves and the posters.

Presumably, the computer services were not notified of the initiation of the research activity, nor were the BBS system operators. Interestingly, while the authors appear unconcerned about their own lurker posture, they note the suspicion held by many of the BBS users that their conversations were being overheard by "industry insiders". Scodari also relies on transcripts of fan BBS discourse in interpreting critical reactions to changes in the soap, Another World, although she aligns her own interests much more closely with the fans she quotes than Harrington and Bielby.

Open participation characterizes the approach of several other studies and more closely resembles normative field practice. Baym started as an unabashed soap fan and news group contributor and found it easy to continue openly as an analyst of the group:

My position in the [rec.arts.arts.soaps, or r.a.t.s., newsgroup] is that of a participant at least as much as a researcher. As a long-time fan of soap operas, I was thrilled to discover this group. It was only after I had been reading daily and participating regularly for a year that I began to write about it. As the work has evolved, I have shared its progress with the group members and found them exceedingly supportive and helpful. They have acted as research participants as well as subjects and have treated me more as an ambassador than a researcher.

The confidence each party had in the other paved the way for Baym to obtain other forms of data besides the news group's messages, especially electronic mail correspondence with several participants and responses to open-ended questions she posted to r.a.t.s. Similarly, Correll's membership in the Lesbian Cafe, and the approval she got from the bar's founder, assisted her in posting queries and interviewing several of the patrons both by e-mail and in person.

Some researchers actually run the facilities that enable computer users to "find" the research project. In an early study, Myers operated a university BBS for two months and set up a number of networked research tools in order to investigate the perceived social context of CMC: on-line surveys, a focus group, and a role-playing game.

More recently, Lindlof et al. launched a Web home page for X-Men fans that offered graphic content (thus participating in the X-Men array of more than 60 Internet locations), links to other X-Men sites, a survey to capture data, and a solicitation for dialogues with on-line X-Men users and page producers.

Like the Baym and Correll studies, the research purpose was stated openly in order to invite cooperation; however, its sudden appearance and the research team's initial contacts with users were sometimes met with suspicion, critique (of their knowledge of X-Men), and humorous skepticism.

It became clear that the World Wide Web page of hypertext URLS's (Uniform Resource Locator) that linked to other pages related to the X-Men topic constituted the study's "gatekeeper" in the traditional sense of enabling an initial contact.

The study also hints at the possibilities of participatory design in which ethnographers may act as the interpreters of diverse voices, usage interests, and aesthetic tastes in the design of networked systems.

A final strategy for consideration moves the researcher physically alongside the user in order to "read" his or her real-time decision making and styles of engagement.

The user's dyadic interplay with a computer forms a focal interest, but included in this arena would be the material context of computing (e.g., its location in a room, the CD-ROM's on hand), the institutional culture (e.g., considering open viewing of sex sites as sexual harassment), interpersonal resources or constraints (e.g., informal rules for sharing URL's), and the specific reality of what it means to "do computing" that these signify for users.

Models for this approach exist in the literature on social television viewing and family computer usage. However, since Internet usage is typically a solitary venture, the more promising route would seem to lie in some version of the "shopping with consumers" protocol from the field of consumer behaviour.

Accompanying users on their way through the kinetic pathways of virtual space and eliciting talk on a wide range of subjects, either retrospectively or on-the-spot, enables the researcher to understand the more embodied dimensions of CMC. In effect, the researcher shadows the user's on-site computing. The advantages of the approach are its close proximity to the user and setting, and the ability to comprehend computing performance as an activity that has a rich, localized back stage—that is, as more than lines of type scrolling down a screen.

In ethnographies of embodied social scenes, the researcher must continually negotiate with the culture membership and convince them of the value of the study and the reasonableness of the person doing the research. It is not unusual for ethnographers to have to adjust their persona somewhat differently as they pass through a scene, or disclose different versions of the project, since the members of a group often relate asymmetrically or even conflictively to each other.

CMC ethnographies, as we have shown, also involve some degree of negotiation when anonymous observation is not the method of access. Virtual spaces offer a limited window in which to explain one's purpose, and electronic text is not the most suitable medium for engaging in a sensitive interaction.

Trust tends to be a heightened concern where entry and

exit and unbridled information disclosure are easily accomplished. Mistakes, once made, can have disastrous results, and be very hard to rectify. Institutional principles for informed consent are now being formulated for research on the World Wide Web, but it will take longer for ethnographers themselves to develop a consensus around protocols for responsible virtual space entry and ways to insure the fair treatment of those they study without compromising very seriously the conduct of inquiry.

TECHNICAL UTILITIES

In this section, we discuss the use of technical utilities for accomplishing research tasks. Some computer systems allow asynchronous communication interactions to be studied either by saving the individual messages, or archiving all postings for later perusal. Most of these have been around for some time. The ones we discuss here are electronic mail, news groups over Usenet, and list servers.

Electronic mail is asynchronous (users generally are not communicating in realtime), quick (in terms of transmission and reply), text-based, and configured for dyadic or multiple connections (can be sent one-to-one, one-to-many, or many-to-many). Moreover, e-mail can be stored and manipulated. As Garton and Wellman noted in a recent review:

E-mail can be stored in external memory for future retrieval, searching, editing, and forwarding to others. People can edit their own or other's messages to change their meaning. The historical record of interaction may be used for surveillance of individual and group interactions, to review past decisions (as Oliver North belatedly learned), and to bring new members up to date.

What makes this modality particularly suitable for ethnographic research are its personal-contact and archival functions.

For example, in his 9-month participant-observation study of "Zytech," a computer systems firm, Workman utilized e-mail in the following ways:

- Being placed on the company's various distribution

lists, which on a daily basis delivered internal documents, minutes of meetings, meeting agendas, and announcements;

- Scheduling interviews;
- Accessing hundreds of BBS's, including Zytech correspondence going back several years;
- Communicating with informants, including follow-ups to FTF interviews.

Though the staggered progress of e-mail interviewing does not promote the same qualities of rapport or spontaneity as personal interviews, it does permit a more elastic time frame for both interviewer and participant to think carefully about the meanings of questions and replies.

In another organizational study, special software was used to automatically save the headers (but not the message content) of all departmental e-mail to a designated file whenever a user read or transmitted a message, yielding a nonreactive means of learning who communicates with whom, when, and about what.

For ethnographic purposes, the value of this procedure lies in its capacity to augment such methods as interviews or on-site observation.

However, the ability to retrieve and store this information without the users' permission (or below their conscious awareness, even when permission is granted) carries the potential for ethical abuse at worst, and suspicion on the part of participants at best. Usenet is a protocol that describes how groups of messages can be stored on and sent between computers, many of which lay outside of the Internet. In actuality, Usenet forms a "virtual forum" for the electronic community that is divided into a plethora of news groups dedicated to varied areas of interest. News group articles are read and written through programs called newsreaders that keep track of articles that have been read, allow users to edit what has been read, and enable readers to reply to previously posted messages in the aforementioned study, Baym reported her participant-observation of a news group made up of soap opera aficionados.

Even though some Usenet sites can archive messages off-line, Baym herself saved the messages posted on the r.a.t.s group while she was an active member. Even working with a medium often described as low in social presence or media richness, she was able to develop a "thick" description of the personalities of this community based on features of their postings:

- Signature files (files automatically attached to postings containing identifying information about the sender),
- Humour in the messages,
- Self-disclosure,
- Comments made about personal lives.

By capitalizing on the features of Usenet news groups, variations of focus group interviewing become possible. During a two-month period of operating a public BBS, Myers set up a computer-mediated focus group "to determine what motivated frequent and active BBS use". As an alternative to a simple discussion, a focus group consisting of a theoretically interesting set of users could work on a virtual task. MacGregor and Morrison describe an editing-group protocol in which groups of people were given the opportunity to re-edit existing news reports (including video footage) in order to produce a more "ideal" version, thereby enabling them to understand viewers' journalistic values more concretely.

It is not difficult to see how this task could be adapted to computer news groups and the multimedia capabilities of high-end work stations, although techniques for training and monitoring the users in their editing-group activities would need to be developed.

Listserv groups (managed by listserver software) are similar to news groups in that they are discussion groups, but they operate in a completely different way by using the Internet e-mail system to exchange messages. Once a person subscribes to a Listserv group (or Listproc group, as they are called on networks other than the early Bitnet), their name is added to a mailing list that receives postings from everyone else subscribed to the list.

Many listservers offer features that allow users to search and retrieve files that are archived, and search the archives using keyword searches. Thus, anyone from a remote site can access archived messages for study from the host computer.

This capability raises interesting ethical issues: How does one receive consent to study the stored communications of users of a particular listserver? Is open access to a person's communications implied in the use of this service? Are the archived files considered the property of the individual subscribers, or are they "owned" in some form of fiduciary relationship by the listserv operator? Because the Internet has developed so rapidly, many such legal and ethical questions have yet to be resolved.

The CMC technologies mentioned above have been in place for a while and are generally well known to most researchers. Most of the communication from these sources is asynchronous, i.e., it is archived for later review and becomes an excellent database.

However some of the newer systems allow for the actual observation of synchronous, or real-time, communication behaviour. It is to these we now turn.

Some of the more recent real-time technologies are:

- Internet Relay Chat (IRC) systems, or" chat lines";
- The entire gamut of multiple-user technologies, e.g., MUDs (Multiple User Domains, formerly known as Multiple User Dungeons), MOOs (MUD Object-Oriented), and MUSHes (Multi-User Shared Hallucination);
- Groupware,
- Desktop videoconferencing over the Internet. All of these systems operate synchronously and as such more approximate face-to-face communication.

Internet Relay Chat (IRC) is a multi-user synchronous communication capability available worldwide to users with Internet accessibility.

These real time" chat lines" provide for mutithreaded conversations from more than two users in something very similar to an" electronic cocktail party". In these" chat rooms" users are able to don bogus" personas" (false identities) and communicate with interactants from all over the globe. These chat lines are very popular on commercial services like America Online and are now available through various web browsers (e.g., students can" chat" with the president of a university via its Web site).

One step up from IRC is a whole family of computer programs that allow more than just written conversation in real time. These are multi-user programs that, in addition to providing text, allow the additional depiction of a physical environment. Multiple User programs are designed to offer a pseudo-physical dimension via its object orientation. In MOOs, for examples, individuals" virtually" move through" rooms," interact with virtual" objects" such as chairs, doors, and the like, and have virtual conversations with others. As Reid has remarked, in MUDs," text replaces gesture and has even become gesture itself".

A third, more recent technology is found in a generation of software called" groupware." Unlike MUDs, MOOs, MUSHes, MUCKs, and the like that are used more for entertainment and amusement, groupware is being developed mainly for business and professional uses.

Most of the newer groupware programs use Web-based technology and allow not only for sharing e-mail but for conducting synchronous multiuser conferencing.

The promise for ethnographers in this technology lies in the" common thread" that runs through all these programs--i.e.," the construction of shared memory" and recording of group discussions.

In essence, groupware allows for observing the" virtual office," i.e., electronic mail, conferencing, scheduling, shared documents, electronic" whiteboards," and so on, and recording these interactions. All of this can function in real time or be archived for later study.

Appearing now on the horizon is the capability to use the desktop computer for real time videoconferencing. Using fairly inexpensive video cameras attached to desktop computers, and software such as CU-SeeMe technology, mediated FTF interactions are now available for study. As soon as compression capabilities for full-motion video are perfected, these dispersed FTF interactions, mediated by the computer, can be recorded and used in data analysis.

When considering all these new technologies, the type of research done may have to be dictated by the characteristics of the medium. That is, for asynchronous media, the type of research conducted would be more akin to that for studying other forms of written communication, while synchronous media enable types of research more equivalent to naturalistic observation--i.e., observing the unfolding of communicative events in real time.

It was inevitable that interpretive analysts would turn their attention to the profusion of common culture now moving through the Internet. Forms of ethnographic inquiry are being applied to many of the events that occur in virtual space, although questions remain about how well these approaches engage CMC phenomena.

One such question is the appropriateness of" community" as a conceptual device. The conventional idea of community as a stable locus for the practice of ritual, custom, and moral obligation applies to cyberspace groups, albeit in the context of a shifting sense of commitment.

When members can easily come and go, when many" members" do not even post, and when identities cannot be verified beyond the current situation, the power of a community ethos may be weakened considerably. The structural properties of the Internet also raise questions about how far a user community extends. For example, can any array of Web sites found by a search term be considered a" community," and if not, what criteria do we use for including a site in the community set?

Finally, what is the relationship of computer-mediated action to local social networks? It has been suggested, for example, that the growing reliance on computer technology for communicating with distant others may undermine the vitality of public life in so-called real communities or play a role in their economic and social fragmentation. Answers to these and other important issues about virtual community await further and more inventive empirical studies.

If there is one theme that runs through the differences between FTF (embodied) and CIVIC (virtual) ethnography, it is the problem of participation. CIVIC ethnography moves us into questions of what it means to engage in and explain" experience" without being co-present with others. Screen-life is a social sphere of its own with vocabularies, motives, and expectations that increasingly re-interpret the meanings of off-screen-life (e.g., mail becoming known as" snail mail").

Objectifications of life in the screen world are also a part of that world. Computer users do act as textual performers and analysts, and knowingly comment on the skills of other text-makers. The use of symbolic codes like" FOTFL" and the real-time deployment of a character in a MUD are operations that create the affect of participation for users, and it would be unusual for ethnographers; not to consider their situated usage.

However, the sites of semiotic action in CMC are not the texts, but the persons who produce them. The text-threads from a Usenet news group or a stack of e-mail messages exnominate the moments in which they were created and read, and the influences of local institutions on their users' action are seldom seen in the messages themselves. In the years ahead, ethnographers will be struggling with basic questions of what it means to" participate" in simulated worlds as well as with developing tactical ways to participate as researchers.

Closely related to the problem of participation are issues of trust and ethical conduct to which we have alluded at various points in this chapter. These issues assume even more importance than usual in research practice due to the greater potential for engaging in covert surveillance of CIVIC social life and the still-unsettled distinctions between" public" and" private" behaviour across the range of cyberspace contexts.

The problem of the stable identifiability of persons who post in Usenet news groups, respond by e-mail, or visit a Web site may also confound the principle of informed consent as a precondition for engaging a human subject's participation.

Generally, there is little debate about the need to provide as much disclosure as possible about research procedures to those who are asked to participate, and to shelter them from the possible harmful consequences of participation and subsequent publication.

However, as King notes, extremely wide ranges of" group accessibility" and" perceived privacy" exist on the Internet. The highest accessibility characterizes those public BBS groups that are unmoderated and unregulated, while the least accessible community is" a private, closed e-mail group where the subscription address is not published and there are enforced requirements to join".

Perceived privacy varies in terms of both the sensitivity of the information (in which, for example, a substance abuse support group would seek a very high level of privacy) and the need to disseminate information to the widest possible client group (the National Communication Association's CRTNET would seek a low measure of privacy).

Yet a great many Internet conversations can in fact be monitored with relative ease, which complicates the understanding of what is permissible to study and whether observation is truly" covert" if no barriers are erected to keep one from observing.

Of course, it probably does matter to many virtual groups whether it is a naive visitor who is stopping briefly at their fora, or a person whose goal is to cast a long-term, analytic eye on their activities and publish the result. The conventional view holds that any research of on-line participants should" strive to obtain some degree of informed consent whenever possible.... Most importantly, researchers should negotiate their entry into electronic communities, beginning with the `owner' of the discussion, if one exists".

Preserving the dignity and empowerment of the persons being studied, even if their" real" identities and locations are unknown, demands that the researcher take steps to explain all of the elements of the study that may bear on tneir decision to participate voluntarily. Taking a different view, Jones argues that the highly elusive, evanescent presence and essentially unknowable identity of most of the subjects in cylberspace obviates the need in most cases for pursuing consent formally:" If the research does not involve identifiable subjects, there is no risk to subjects, and therefore the protection of these rights and interests no longer applies".

Jones goes on to argue that the strict application of conventional human subject protections would be especially detrimental to the study of cyberspace, which exists as an arena in which individuals can enjoy the freedom of withholding, revealing, and even fabricating information about themselves.

Somewhere between these positions is King, who states that" the perceived level of privacy with which most members of cyberspace forums post notes is the level that researchers are obligated to protect".

At the stage of publication, she advocates the removal from messages of all headers, signatures, references to the name and type of the group (e-mail, Usenet news group, etc.), and references to any person's name or pseudo-name. It may be that the evolving use of networked systems will alter the customs and arguments for what constitutes" privacy" and" autonomy," in turn informing the ethical practice of ethnography.

Finally, the implications of computer networks for the construction of the research text are of great importance. One can adapt the same hypermedia programming tools used in other scholarly efforts to the production of ethnographies that would in turn be fully compatible with the World Wide Web's system architecture. An example of such an effort is the Survivors of the Shoah Visual History Foundation, which has set out to videotape oral histories of all living Holocaust survivors and digitize them in hypermedia format along with maps, documents, photos, and written texts of the interviews.

The files, perhaps numbering 150,000 by the end of the decade, will be fully cross-referenced and accessible for on-line searches by key words. Similarly, ethnographies of CMC culture can be envisioned which would provide the discursive threads that underpin an analysis, along with field notes, full-text interviews, generations of Web page design, graphic material, and URL's to the ethnographic sites themselves and related research projects. Presumably the author would also be" available" in a rather immediate sense to readers via the research text's Web site or e-mail.

What distinguishes an archive a reader can navigate at will from a research text is that the latter usually embodies arguments, claims, and evidence in a style conventionalized within the discipline. While readers have always had non-linear access to a text, it is the linear narrative designed by the author that academic communities recognize as the only one subject to critique.

The capabilities of hypermedia threaten this formulation of the research product and the concept of authorial control that stands behind it.

If readings of an ethnography are neither the ones an author intended nor the ones deemed important or legitimate by a discipline, then its use-value becomes as widely distributed among communities of practical interest as the Internet itself. The move to modular, multi-threaded (but not necessarily plotless) research texts not only reduces the researcher's story to the stature of one among a potentially limitless number, it also accelerates the epistemological decentering of inquiry that began with the challenge to objectivist ethnography nearly twenty years ago.

Bibliography

Byrne, D. (2002) Talk to the students of the MA Investigative Journalism course at Nottingham Trent University, 29 April 2002.

Calvert, J. (2004) Interview with Hugo de Burgh, 28 May 2002.

Central TV (2004) The Cook Report: 'Where did the Money Go?' Birmingham: Central TV. Transmitted 5 March 2004, producer Clive Entwhistle, reporter Roger Cook.

Channel 4 (2003) Dispatches: 'An Age Apart'. London: Channel 4 TV. Reporter/producer Hugo de Burgh.

Isaacs Norman. Untended Gates: The Mismanaged Press. New York: Columbia University Press, 2001

Johnstone John W. C., Edward J. Slawski, and William W. Bowman. The News People. Urbana: University of Illinois Press, 2003

Keir Gerry, Maxwell McCombs, and Donald L. Shaw. Advanced Reporting: Beyond News Events. New York: Longman, 2002

Kerlinger Fred N. Foundations of Behavioral Research. New York: Holt, Rinehart and Winston, 2004

Rossiter Clinton, and James Lare(editors). The Essential Lippmann: A Political Philosophy for Liberal Democracy. Cambridge, Mass.: Harvard University Press,2002

Rubin Bernard. Media Politics, and Democracy. New.York: Oxford University Press, 2005

Schmidt Benno C., Jr. Freedom of the Press vs. Public Access. New York: Praeger Publishers, 2003

Index

I

J

L

M

N

O

P

R

S

T